PRAIRIE POLITICS AND SOCIETY: REGIONALISM IN DECLINE

Dr. Roger Gibbins,
Associate Professor,
Department of Political Science,
The University of Calgary

- 9 6 9 3 -

ꓕꓐ (4)

Butterworths
Toronto

© 1980 Butterworth and Company (Canada) Limited
2265 Midland Avenue
Scarborough, Ontario, Canada   M1P 4S1
All Rights Reserved.
Printed and Bound in Canada.

The Butterworth Group of Companies:

Canada: Butterworth & Co. (Canada) Ltd., Toronto, Vancouver
United Kingdom: Butterworth & Co. (Publishers) Ltd.,
London, Borough Green
Australia: Butterworth Pty. Ltd., Sydney, Melbourne, Brisbane
New Zealand: Butterworths of New Zealand, Ltd., Wellington
South Africa: Butterworth & Co. (South Africa) Pty. Ltd., Durban
United States: Butterworth Inc., Boston
Butterworth (Legal) Inc., Seattle

CAMROSE LUTHERAN COLLEGE
LIBRARY

Canadian Cataloguing in Publication Data

Gibbins, Roger, 1947-
Prairie politics and society

Bibliography: p.
Includes index.

ISBN 0-409-83320-7

1. Prairie Provinces – Politics and government –
1905-1945.* 2. Prairie Provinces – Politics and
government – 1945- * 3. Regionalism – Canada.
I. Title.

JL27.G52   320.9712   C80-094286-8

JL
500
.P7
A43

29,974

To my parents,
Frances and George Gibbins

AUGUSTANA UNIVERSITY COLLEGE
LIBRARY

TABLE OF CONTENTS

CHAPTER ONE

INTRODUCTION

In discussing popular impressions of the Canadian prairies, J. E. Rae made the following comment:

> To most Canadians the Prairie provinces are a curious region, peopled with farmers complaining about the weather or wheat prices, and convinced that they have been victimized by "eastern interests" who manipulate a complex tariff structure to exploit the West. On the infrequent occasions when they think of the Prairies, the images that are conjured up are those of vast fields of waving, golden grain and strong taciturn men who braved the wilderness (and the winter wind at Portage and Main).[1]

These images mirror my own perceptions when growing up in the interior of British Columbia, an area physically close to but psychologically remote from the Prairies. Later, when studying political science as an undergraduate at the University of British Columbia, earlier images of wheat, blowing dust, grain elevators, and flat horizons were overlaid with those arising from the radical political history of the Prairie provinces. Thus came images of the agrarian revolt of the Progressives, of the Saskatchewan CCF led by men cast in the unmistakable mold of T. C. Douglas, and of the Alberta Social Crediters pursuing a fundamentalist heaven in a political chariot fueled by prairie oil. And, of course, John Diefenbaker emerging from the Prairies to seize the national government and to see his own eventual repudiation by his party and by his country. And in the background always were the fields of wheat, the combines marching in line across an unbroken prairie horizon.

These images ill-prepared me for the prairie society I encountered upon moving to Calgary in 1973. The reality I came up against was one of sprawling urban growth, highrise apartments, proliferating condominiums, and a white-collar, technocratic economy. The extent of my misconceptions about prairie agriculture was driven home to me when I hoisted my son aboard an immense air-conditioned, quadraphonic "Big Bud" tractor at an agricultural show and was informed by the salesman that the machine, a general purpose tractor and the smallest in its line, retailed for $91,000. Nor did the incumbent prairie politicians fit the preconceptions I had ready for them; Peter Lougheed, Allan Blakeney and Ed Schreyer little resembled the leaders of agrarian radicalism that I had encountered in such graphic form in prairie political history. It is thus out of my own efforts to fit the old Prairies and the new Prairies together, to understand how the latter evolved from the former, and to comprehend the political changes that have occurred along the route that this book springs. Hopefully what lies ahead will enable western Canadian readers to better understand their own political past and present, and will make that past and present more comprehensible and less eccentric to readers outside the Prairies.

The principal objective of this book is to provide an integrated overview of federal and provincial politics on the Prairies from 1905 to the end of the 70s. Fortunately, western Canada has generated a rich historical literature that can be tapped in this regard, one that is particularly impressive in the field of provincial politics. Studies with a more regional, cross-provincial perspective, however, have been less common.[2] A completely satisfactory regional political perspective, one that captures the temporal and spatial scope of prairie politics, has yet to be offered and it is to this gap that the present work is addressed.

In addition this book reaches beyond a regional analysis of political behavior to examine the social and economic prairie soil within which political behavior is rooted. The distinctive character of prairie politics grew out of the region's unique combination of peoples, economic activities and the enveloping geography; in this sense George F. G. Stanley discusses the "molding process of plains geography and plains economy."[3] It is, therefore, an explicit assumption of this analysis that the past character of prairie politics, and in particular of political radicalism on the Prairies, can only be explained through reference to the social and economic order within which it was rooted, and that changes over time in that order have had a profound effect upon the evolution of prairie politics.

The changes that have occurred in the Prairie society have been both multitudinous and dramatic in their effect, and coming to grips with them is a formidable task. There is, however, an underlying pattern to the change and it is upon this pattern that we will focus. In general the economic, demographic and social changes over the past 70 years have been such to erode the regional distinctiveness of the Prairie society. The differences in economic activities, in culture, in entertainment and recreation, in the media, in consumptive activities, and in lifestyle between individuals living in Edmonton and Toronto have been steadily diminishing with the consequence that the regional distinctiveness of the Prairie society is today only a pale shadow of its former self. If, then, political behavior is rooted in the socio-economic order we would expect to find a parallel trend in political behavior—there should be a decline over time in the regional distinctiveness of prairie politics. It is the decline of political regionalism in western Canada that serves as the present work's integrating theme.

The argument that social and economic factors are in a sense determinant of political behavior is not new to the analysis of prairie politics. C. B. Macpherson's classic study of the Alberta Social Credit set the stage,[4] while the differences in social composition and agricultural production between Alberta and Saskatchewan have been examined repeatedly in the attempt to explain the strikingly divergent political histories of the two provinces. More generally, Ira Sharkansky's impressive analysis of political regionalism in the United States links socio-economic characteristics to ". . . regional peculiarities in politics and public policies."[5]

Yet at the same time the degree of socio-economic determinism in the present analysis should not be overstated. It is not suggested that the social composition and economic underpinnings of a region rigidly predetermine the character of political behavior. Rather the argument will be that the emergence of a regionally distinct political style, particularly one marked by political radicalism, is dependent upon certain identifiable social and economic preconditions; that the political behavior of individuals and societies takes place within broad but existent socioeconomic constraints. In the Prairies of 40 to 75 years ago conditions were such to impell the prairie population towards radicalism and a regionally distinct style of political behavior. Today the preconditions for both radicalism and regionalized political behavior have largely disintegrated. To paraphrase Emile Durkheim, territorial divisions lose their significance as they become "less and less grounded in the nature of things."[6] Significant differences between the nature of things on the Prairies and the nature of things elsewhere in English-speaking Canada are becoming harder to detect.

In discussing the relationship between socioeconomic conditions and political behavior, or between changes in the former and changes in the latter, it must be kept in mind that the relationship is not uni-directional. While to a large degree political behavior and the evolution of political institutions may be dependent upon the social order, at times it is the political system that molds the surrounding social and economic environments. As Black and Cairns point out in a keynote article on the evolution of Canadian federalism, "political integration is not an inevitable consequence of urbanization, industrialization, and rising standards of living."[7] In Canada, they argue, political institutions and leaders have played a key role in shaping, giving expression to, and perpetuating distinctive regional outlooks. Here the argument will be made that the near absence of regional political institutions in western Canada, coupled with the growth of strong provincial governments, has fragmented the prairie region along the lines of provincial boundaries and that the effect of this fragmentation has been to reduce the regionalization of politics in the Canadian west.

REGIONALISM AND WESTERN CANADA

It is commonplace for academics, journalists and politicians to emphasize the regional nature of Canadian politics. In the words of Richard Simeon and David Elkins, "Canadian politics is regional politics; regionalism is one of the pre-eminent facts of Canadian life. . . ."[8] Historian J. M. S. Careless notes that ". . . the experience of regionalism remains prominent and distinctive in Canadian history—and time has tended less to erode it than to develop it."[9] As Simeon has cautioned, though, there may be an element of self-fulfilling prophecy in the concentration on regionalism—"to some extent we usually find what we are looking for: thinking regionalism to be important, that's what we study, and lo, that is what we find."[10]

While Simeon's cautionary note is to be taken seriously, at the same time there is no denying the centrality of regionalism in the study of Canadian politics.

The region that has undoubtedly received the most attention is the Prairies where the roots of a distinctive regional politics have been traced back to the Riel rebellions of 1869 and 1885.[11] Although the rebellions had little lasting impact on the evolution of western Canada and the Métis have since been pushed to the margins of the prairie society, the Métis led by Louis Riel have assumed an important symbolic role in characterizations of prairie politics. As Carl Berger has written, ". . . the Métis became the archetypical westerners—misunderstood by an uncaring and ill-informed government in distant Ottawa, provoked into protest by policies which adversely affected their vital interests and about which they had not been consulted."[12] The pre-eminent historian of the Canadian west, W. L. Morton, marks the Riel rebellions as the beginning of a distinctive regional bias to prairie politics, a bias built around regional agrarian protest to the policies and at times the institutions of the federal government.[13] As Morton concludes, "that there has been, and is, some significant difference between the politics of the three Prairie provinces and those of other regions of Canada is a matter of both common observation and of academic study."[14]

That the three Prairie provinces constitute a region, political or otherwise, has also been readily acknowledged by other observers of the prairie scene.[15] David Smith, one of the most astute political commentators on the Canadian prairies, wrote that:

> the region's geography, economy, and people set it apart from the rest of the country . . . [The] ethnic mix, the one-crop economy, and the vast terrain have helped mold provincial and federal politics in the region. In turn, economic, social, and political institutions, policies, and traditions of remarkable distinctiveness have developed at both levels of government.[16]

Black and Cairns made the interesting observation that only on the Prairies are provincial boundaries not meaningful geographically.[17] Finally, even politicians from central Canada have been quick to pay homage to the distinctive regional character of the Prairies. Speaking in 1973, Prime Minister Trudeau remarked that "there is a different culture in the West than there is in central Canada . . . it's not a different civilization but certainly it's a different form of culture than exists elsewhere."[18]

Others have been more hesitant to cast the three Prairie provinces into a single region. In the words of Rodney Sykes, former Mayor of Calgary, "such phrases as 'The West', 'Western Unity', and the 'Prairies' are in actuality meaningless, dreamed up by people who find all that space west of Bay Street a little hard to define."[19] One more example comes from James Gray, among the most prolific of prairie historians:

> In most discussions of the regions of Canada, Manitoba, Saskatchewan, and Alberta are usually lumped together into three Prairie provinces. The curious truth is that they have very little in common, and even the use of the word 'prairie' is a misnomer. The dictionary defines 'prairie' as 'a meadow destitute of trees and covered with long grass.' Very little of western Canada fits that definition, for what is not bush, forest, foothills, and lakes is more likely to be arid short-grass country. Nor is there much in the way of common bonds of tradition, ethnic grouping, or commercial enterprise. The region was riven with economic and geographic divisions, and the people themselves were most mismatched.[20]

Reservations of this type need not weigh too heavily in the analysis of prairie politics during the early part of this century, although even then they cannot be entirely dismissed. However, the social and economic changes that have occurred in recent decades have served to increase the heterogeneity within and among the Prairie provinces and in so doing have undermined the analytical utility of regionalism.

The writings of W. L. Morton have been important not only for their own richness but also for their imprint which is to be found on the works of other scholars who have tilled the historical prairie soil. Morton stressed a sense of 'western separateness'[21] and, in his political analyses, featured the "interplay of a distinctive region in a federal state."[22] Morton, however, also went to considerable effort to point out that although regional differences have persisted over time the West has nevertheless been rather successfully integrated into the national society. Thus in 1955 he concluded: "It may be said, in short, that old Canada was extraordinarily successful in making the Prairies Canadian."[23] The seemingly paradoxical theme in Morton's work, that a distinctive prairie political style has persisted while at the same time the Prairies have been successfully integrated into the national political fabric, constitutes a point of departure for this book. Here we will examine the integration of the prairie society into the Canadian mainstream, the political integration and thus decline in political regionalism that followed in its wake, and finally the extent to which political institutions and patterns in the West have resisted integration into the national political system.

CONCEPTUALIZATION AND MEASUREMENT

It must be recognized that 'region' and 'regionalism' are analytical concepts not inherent in the physical environment. According to the American Association of Geographers,

> A region is not an object either self-determined or nature-given. It is *an intellectual concept, an entity for the purposes of thought*, created by the selection of certain features that are relevant to a real interest or problem, and by the disregard of all features that are considered to be irrelevant. (emphasis added).[24]

In general the delineation of a region implies some spatial organization of values or behavior.[25] Individuals within the designated region are assumed to be similar in the way they behave and the values they hold while living within an institutional environment that is in some significant way conditioned by their place of residence. Geography, then, becomes a significant organizer of social values and behaviors; the product is regionalism, ". . . the dynamic social action that takes place within a region."[26] However it must be stressed that geography per se cannot affect behavior, or at least can do so only in marginal, uninteresting ways. Political behavior is more directly shaped by social class, occupation, the institutional environment, cultural patterns, and political history, although factors such as distance from central places cannot be ignored. Thus to the extent that regional differences in political behavior exist we should expect some underlying regional differences in social class, ethnicity, occupation, language, religion, or other politically-relevant characteristics. In this sense Mildred Schwartz approaches regionalism from the perspective of "special combinations of population and resources . . . interacting in a given place."[27] It will be argued here that in the early part of this century the Prairie provinces did form a distinctive region in terms of social and economic composition, and that a distinctive form of political behavior flowed forth as a consequence. However, social change has sharply eroded the earlier distinctiveness and has left in its wake a relatively enfeebled shell of the earlier regional politics.

It should also be noted that people may face or perceive themselves to face political discrimination solely on the basis of their physical location within the political system. A segment of the electorate may share a set of

regional grievances that are largely independent of any underlying concentration of social and economic characteristics. A sense of
powerlessness, a sense of exclusion from the corridors of power or
distance from the centre of power may coalesce a regional electorate even
when significant social and economic differences between the region and
the broader society are difficult to detect. This approach to regionalism,
while largely irrelevant for an historical analysis of the Canadian
prairies, sheds some light upon the altered character of political
regionalism in western Canada today and upon the nature of contemporary western alienation.

Perhaps the best definition of a region is that provided by Rupert
Vance:

> A region is a homogeneous area with physical and cultural characteristics
> distinct from those of neighboring areas. As a part of a national domain a
> region is sufficiently unified to have a consciousness of its customs and ideals
> and thus possess a sense of identity distinct from the rest of the country.[28]

Regionalism, then, becomes the expression of this sense of identity
through folklore, language, religion, the arts, or political behavior. It
must be kept in mind, however, that to demonstrate the existence of
regionally distinctive patterns of political behavior stops short of an explanation for their existence. As Simeon and Elkins point out:

> . . . we use the term regionalism simply as a descriptive statement about the
> way provinces or other areas differ. It is not an explanation. Regions are
> containers, and other factors are necessary to account for variations in their
> contents.[29]

There are some evident similarities between the conceptualization of
region employed here and what anthropologists call a *culture area*, ". . .
a term which signifies clusters of geographically contiguous, yet distinct,
cultures which are highly similar in content and, secondarily, exploit a
broadly common geographic environment."[30] Harold Barclay's discussion of the impact of technological change on culture areas is of particular relevance to the present work:

> . . . if we are concerned with technologically simple ways of life . . . there
> may be less cultural cushioning between the individual and the physical en-
> vironment so that culture and environment have a better 'fit'. But the more
> cushioning that is introduced, that is, the more technological elaboration,
> the easier it becomes to transplant and spread the same cultural system from
> one geographical area to another. . . .[31]

In the past the geographic isolation of the prairie society facilitated the
evolution of regionally distinctive patterns. In the contemporary society
social change, much of it technological in character, has eroded the

previous isolation and has fostered the spread of a more homogeneous national culture largely oblivious to regional distinctions.

Common practice in Canadian political science tends to equate regions with provinces. The equation is understandable given the importance of provinces as political actors and given the fact that three of the major "regions" of Canada are also provinces. For Ontario, Quebec and British Columbia, which together contain almost three-quarters of the Canadian population, the designation "region" seems redundant and imprecise. In the case of the Prairie and Atlantic provinces, however, the appropriate conceptual path is unclear. At times the individual provinces within these two areas are treated as regional units while at other times they are aggregated into the prairie and Atlantic regions. Not infrequently the same piece of analysis will apply the term "region" to both individual provinces and aggregations of provinces. For example Mildred Schwartz states in *Politics and Territory* that ". . . for our purposes, "region" and "province" are often synonymous."[32] Yet elsewhere in the same book Schwartz groups the Prairie and Atlantic provinces into two regions, stating that ". . . relative to the rest of the country, the makeup and problems of the constituent provinces are sufficiently alike to make it meaningful to speak of each of them as distinct units."[33]

In dealing with the Prairies, then, there is considerable room for confusion as to what constitutes a region; are regions and provinces synonymous, or does the term "region" more properly refer to some larger physical unit encompassing all three Prairie provinces or parts thereof, such as the plain stretching across the southern portion of the three provinces? Here the term "region" will be used only to refer to the three Prairie provinces as a single unit; it will not be used in reference to individual Prairie provinces. Thus the argument that political regionalism is in decline in western Canada does not preclude an emerging provincialism within the prairie region. There are critical differences between regions that are provinces and thus have an institutional, governmental and bureaucratic structure, and pan-provincial regions such as "The Prairies" that lack the same.

The measurement or demonstration of political regionalism follows from the definition of region set forth by Rupert Vance. If now or in the past the three Prairie provinces are to be considered as a political region then the pattern of political behavior on the Prairies must be *distinctive*. The character of prairie politics must be clearly distinguishable from that of the nation as a whole or from that of other regions in Canada. Secondly, common patterns of political behavior that transcend provincial boundaries on the Prairies must be evident. In other words, there must be some *homogeneity* of political behavior across the three Prairie provinces. Thus in examining the regional character of prairie politics attention will be fixed on these two principal indicators of regionalism: distinctiveness and cross-provincial homogeneity.[34]

In practice, the assessment of distinctiveness and homogeneity faces some rather trying obstacles. The major difficulty in the use of the homogeneity criterion is deciding just what conditions will be used, for it can be safely assumed that no regions are homogeneous across all potential dimensions of analysis.[35] The principal problem with the assessment of distinctiveness lies in the selection of an appropriate comparison; distinctive compared to whom or what? As Sharkansky explains:

> When an author fails to make a systematic comparison between his region and others, it is not possible to accept any claim that his region is peculiar . . . the specific nature of regional differences cannot appear in the examination of one region alone. Only by looking more broadly at the nation is it possible to identify the regions that show uniform and distinctive traits, and to determine the analytical utility of the region as an ordering concept in political science.[36]

Comparing the political behavior or the socio-economic composition of the Prairies to Canada as a whole seems questionable because of the heterogeneity within the comparison group. For example, the political history of Quebec has been sufficiently divergent from English Canada's that any amalgamation of Quebec and English Canadian political histories would yield a dubious comparative base. One might exclude Quebec and simply compare the Prairies to the amalgam of British Columbia, Ontario and the Atlantic provinces but here the comparison group would be an ungainly artifact lacking any significant analogue in the political history of Canada.

The comparison that will be employed in this instance is that between the Prairie provinces and Ontario, a comparison that gains historical significance from the fact that Ontario tried, and largely failed, to shape the settlement of the Prairies in its own image.[37] Ontario, which contains approximately two-thirds of the Canadian population living outside the Prairies and Quebec, will serve as the English-Canadian norm against which the movement of the prairie society and polity can be assessed.

The assessment of regional homogeneity runs up against some more difficult problems. The first relates to the regional aggregation of electoral statistics. The difficulty can best be illustrated by reference to Figure 1:1 which displays the percentage of the 1908-1979 federal vote won by the Liberal party in each of the Prairie provinces, along with the percentage of the total prairie popular vote won by the Liberals in each election. It is clear from Figure 1:1 that, with respect to the Liberal vote, the three Prairie provinces oscillate to essentially the same electoral rhythm even though the rhythm may be more exaggerated in some provinces than in others. At times there has been little difference in the Liberal share of the popular vote across the three Prairie provinces. For example in 1979 the spread was only 1.7%; across the region the Liberals won 22.4% of the vote while their provincial variability means that the prairie average accurately describes a regional result, a result that was relatively uniform across the three provincial units comprising the prairie region. However, in the federal election of 1926 the Liberal share of the popular vote ranged from 24.5% in Alberta to 56.8% in Saskatchewan, a spread of 32.3%. In this instance the meaning one can ascribe to the Liberal's share of the regional prairie vote (42.1%) is much more questionable.

The problem, then, is that the presentation of regional electoral data, or socio-economic data, without breaking such data into their provincial components conceals inter-provincial variations that in some cases may reach substantial proportions. Thus one might argue that electoral data should always be presented province-by-province. However, to systematically disaggregate regional patterns into their provincial components is to admit at the outset that a regional analysis of prairie political behavior is inappropriate. The approach that will be taken here is to first present regional patterns that will enable us to assess the distinctiveness of such patterns relative to the Ontario comparison. Once regional patterns and trends have been scrutinized intra-regional variability among the three provincial units can be considered.

The existence of intra-regional variability raises another problem the resolution of which must wait for the analysis to unfold. The problem arises from changes over time in the degree of inter-regional and intra-regional variability. To continue the illustration provided by Figure 1:1, the *range* in the percentage of the popular vote won by the Liberal party across the three Prairie provinces appears to decrease over time, suggesting *increased* regional homogeneity. Yet the interpretation of this change is problematic. On the one hand the decreased intra-regional variability may be indicative of an increased regionalization in political behavior. On the other hand variability may also be declining outside the region as well as within. Thus political behavior across the Prairies may be becoming more regionally homogeneous while at the same time it comes to increasingly resemble political behavior in Ontario and elsewhere in the country. An apparent regionalizing trend of decreased intra-regional variability may be offset by decreased distinctiveness between the Prairie provinces and Ontario. Sharkansky encountered this problem in his American study when he concluded that ". . . it is true that regions resemble each other more than in the past . . . but it is also true that regions themselves are becoming more uniform. . . ."[38]

To bring this methodological discussion to a close a couple of final points should be brought to the reader's attention. The first is that in the pages to follow terms such as "the West", "western Canada", and "western Canadian politics" should always be read to exclude British Columbia. Politics on the west coast have evolved in a manner largely, though not entirely, independent from political events on the Prairies. British Columbia also has an entirely different economic base than the

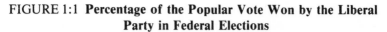

FIGURE 1:1 **Percentage of the Popular Vote Won by the Liberal
Party in Federal Elections**

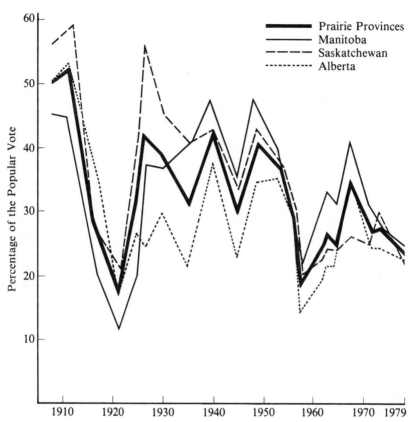

Prairie provinces, apart from a shared reliance on resource exploitation, and has experienced a considerably different social history.

The second point relates to the type of data that will be utilized. Discussions of prairie regionalism, and particularly of western alienation, have too frequently relied upon evidence that is both quizzical to nonwesterners and evasive of empirical documentation. For example, David Smith writes as follows:

> . . . it is at the level of public consciousness that the region has achieved its lasting identity. Visually, to anyone travelling between the rim of the Shield and the foothills of the Rockies across a thousand miles of "black soil sliding into open sky", the Prairies merge as one vast land. For those who have never seen the Canadian plains but know their history and literature, the region is myth, of the mind. . . .[39]

The sentiment of Smith's statement is not contended. Nor is it my intention to ignore the attitudinal and mythological aspects of prairie regionalism. However, attitudinal data, whether impressionistic or empirically garnered, provides an inadequate base for the examination of regional patterns in political behavior, particularly when such an examination is concerned with the character of change over time. Hence the principal focus here will be upon federal and provincial election data spanning the period 1905 to 1979. Popular vote figures will be used primarily as the distribution of seats tends both to mask patterns of electoral behavior among individuals and to exaggerate regional differences.[40] The complementary socio-demographic data will rely largely upon census publications. As both sets of data are part of the public record only the interpretations drawn from them are unique to this analysis. Thus it is hoped that some of the mythology and even romance that clouds discussions of western Canadian politics in general, and of western alienation in particular, can be stripped away through the use of simple empirical data.

For the most part the provincial election results used will date from 1905 when Alberta and Saskatchewan were created from the Northwest Territories by the Autonomy Acts and held their first provincial elections. The analysis of federal election data will start with the subsequent federal election held in 1908. Prior federal elections will be excluded from the analysis, the assumption being that the Prairies did not fully emerge as a political region until the provincial creation of Alberta and Saskatchewan and until the massive immigration into the West that began around the turn of the century. This is not to deny that many elements of prairie politics have roots extending back into the 19th century; it is simply to assert that the study of political behavior as envisioned here is difficult prior to the turn of the 20th century. The census data employed will date from the 1901 national census. Prior to that year the census made no distinction between Alberta and Saskatchewan and indeed lumped these areas together with the far north and parts of northern Manitoba, Ontario and Quebec. Thus the census of 1901 provides the most convenient benchmark for the analysis of socio-economic change across the Canadian prairies.

NOTES

1. J. E. Rae, "The Roots of Prairie Society," in David P. Gagan, ed., *Prairie Perspectives*, Toronto, Holt, Rinehart and Winston, 1970, p. 46.

2. The intellectual debt owed to the regional analyses of W. L. Morton and David E. Smith is heavy indeed, and their works will figure prominently in the present work.

3. George F. G. Stanley, "The Western Canadian Mystique," in Gagan, ed., *Prairie Perspectives*, p. 14.

4. C. B. Macpherson, *Democracy in Alberta: Social Credit and The Party System*, Toronto, University of Toronto Press, 1953. Macpherson's characterization of Alberta society, it should be noted, has not been without its critics. For example, see Thomas Flanagan, "Political Geography and the United Farmers of Alberta," in S. M. Trofimenkoff, Ed., *The Twenties in Western Canada*, Papers of the Western Canadian Studies Conference, March 1972. Ottawa, National Museum of Man, History Division, 1972, pp. 130-169.

5. Ira Sharkansky, *Regionalism in American Politics*, Indianapolis, Bobbs-Merrill, 1970, p. 3.

6. Emile Durkheim, *The Divisions of Labour in Society*, New York, The Free Press, 1964, p. 187.

7. Edwin R. Black and Alan C. Cairns, "A Different Perspective on Canadian Federalism," *Canadian Public Administration*, IX, 1 (March 1966), pp. 27-44.

8. Richard Simeon and David J. Elkins, "Regional Political Cultures in Canada," *CJPS*, VII, 3 (September 1974), p. 397.

9. J. H. S. Careless, "Limited Identities in Canada," *Canadian Historical Review*, March 1969, p. 1.

10. Richard Simeon, "Regionalism and Canadian Political Institutions," in J. Peter Meekison, ed., *Canadian Federalism: Myth or Reality*, Third Edition, Toronto, Methuen, 1977, p. 292.

11. George F. G. Stanley, *The Birth of Western Canada: A History of the Riel Rebellions*, Toronto, University of Toronto Press, 1936.

12. Carl Berger, "William Morton: The Delicate Balance of Region and Nation," in Carl Berger and Ramsay Cook, eds., *The West and the Nation: Essays in Honour of W. L. Morton*, Toronto, McClelland and Stewart, 1976, p. 17.

13. W. L. Morton, "The Bias of Prairie Politics," in Donald Swainson, ed., *Historical Essays on the Prairie Provinces*, Toronto, McClelland and Stewart, 1970, p. 293.

14. *Ibid.*, p. 289.

15. B. Y. Card, *The Canadian Prairie Provinces from 1870 to 1950: A Sociological Introduction*, Toronto, J. M. Dent and Sons, 1960, p. ix.

16. David E. Smith, "The Prairie Provinces", in David J. Bellamy, Jon H. Pammett, and Donald C. Rowat, eds., *The Provincial Political Systems: Comparative Essays*, Toronto, Methuen, 1976, p. 47.

17. Black and Cairns, "A Different Perspective", p. 39.

18. Cited in David E. Smith, "Western Politics and National Unity", in David Jay Bercuson, ed., *Canada and the Burden of Unity*, Toronto, Macmillan, 1977, p. 166.

19. J. R. W. Sykes, "One Prairie Province—Or One Canada", in David K. Elton, ed., *One Prairie Province?*, Lethbridge, Lethbridge Herald, 1970, p. 205.

20. James H. Gray, *The Winter Years: The Depression on the Prairies*, Toronto, Macmillan, 1966, pp. 195-6.

21. Berger, "William Morton," p. 11.

22. *Ibid.*, p. 14.

23. Morton, "The Bias of Prairie Politics," p. 290.

24. Regional Economic Planning, Paris, Organization for European Economic Co-operation, 1961, p. 379. Cited in T. N. Brewis, *Regional Economic Policies in Canada*, Toronto, Macmillan, 1969, p. 45.

25. Richard Rose and Derek W. Urwin, *Regional Differentiation and Political Unity in Western Nations*, London, Sage Publications, 1975, pp. 4-5.

26. Carl Frederick Kraenzel, *The Great Plains in Transition*, Norman, University of Oklahoma Press, 1955, p. 348.

27. Mildred A. Schwartz, *Politics and Territory: The Sociology of Regional Persistance in Canada*, Montreal, McGill-Queen's University Press, 1974, p. xi.

28. Rupert B. Vance, "Region," in David L. Sills, ed., *International Encyclopedia of the Social Sciences*, 13 (1968), pp. 377-78.

29. Simeon and Elkins, "Regional Political Cultures," p. 399.

30. Harold B. Barclay, "On Culture Areas and Regions in Anthropology," in B. Y. Card, ed., *Perspectives on Regions and Regionalism*, Edmonton, University of Alberta Printing Service, 1969, p. 5.

31. *Ibid.*, p. 6.

32. Schwartz, *Politics and Territory,* p. 5.

33. *Ibid.*, p. 6.

34. For similar treatment see K. R. Cox, "On the Utility and Definition of Regions in Comparative Political Sociology," *Comparative Political Studies*, 2, April 1969, p. 70.

35. For a discussion see Robert E. Dickinson, *City, Region and Regionalism: A Geographical Contribution to Human Ecology*, London, Routledge & Kegan Paul, Ltd., 1947, pp. 1-2.

36. Sharkansky, *Regionalism in American Politics*, p. 24.

37. W. L. Morton, "A Century of Plain and Parkland," in Richard Allen, ed., *A Region of the Mind*, Regina, Canadian Plains Studies Centre, the University of Saskatchewan, 1973, pp. 165-180.

38. Sharkansky, *Regionalism in American Politics*, pp. 97-98.

39. Smith, "The Prairie Provinces," p. 46.

40. Alan C. Cairns, "The Electoral System and the Party System in Canada, 1921-1965," *CJPS* (March 1968), pp. 55-80.

CHAPTER TWO

THE ASCENT OF REGIONALISM: 1905-1939

INTRODUCTION

In the first four decades of the twentieth century tumultuous events in western Canada transformed the character of Canadian politics. Settlement of the West advanced to the point where nearly one Canadian in four lived in the Prairie provinces, and western Canadians flexed their newfound electoral muscles in a series of radical political innovations. The earlier simplicity of two-party politics in Canada was shattered by the eruption of the Progressive Party of Canada, the United Farmers of Alberta and Manitoba, the Co-operative Commonwealth Federation and the Social Credit. Outside the creation of new political parties western radicalism manifested itself in the trade union movement, culminating in the Winnipeg General Strike of 1919, and in a barrage of social reform movements spanning prohibition, female suffrage, and the Social Gospel. It was a time when the political evolution of western Canada struck out on a new path, when the Prairies emerged as a full-fledged and regionally distinct actor on the Canadian political stage.

In the discussion that follows it should be kept in mind that the isolation of the first four decades of this century from those that preceded and followed does some violence to an appreciation of the evolution of prairie politics. That evolution has been marked by some relatively smooth patterns of change that were bent perhaps but not broken by the Second World War. The decade of depression preceding the outbreak of the war marked a transitionary stage as the economic expansion of the West wrenched to a halt and the political radicalism of the Progressive era burst forth again in new radical movements. In any event the pre-war period stands apart in many significant ways—social, economic and political—from the years that follow.

The political focus of this chapter will be primarily on national politics on the Prairies. However, the separation of national and provincial politics cannot be completely accomplished for in many ways the two form a seamless web. It is difficult, for example, to discuss the Progressive Party of Canada without at the same time discussing the United Farmers of Alberta, or to discuss the national Social Credit and CCF parties without at the same time referring to their provincial counterparts in Alberta and Saskatchewan respectively.

PILLARS OF REGIONALISM

A) Population Change

At the dawn of the twentieth century the Canadian prairies west of Manitoba lay largely unsettled; the national dream of a rich and populous agrarian heartland had temporarily run aground on the shoals of a world-wide economic slump and the availability of open land further to the south in the United States. The 1901 census recorded only 419,512 people living on the Canadian prairies, less than 8% of the national population. Over 60% of these lived in Manitoba; only 91,000 lived in what was soon to become the province of Saskatchewan and only 73,000 lived in the future province of Alberta. Thirty-four years after confederation the Prairies still lay open, fed by the umbilical cord of the Canadian Pacific Railway but yet to blossom.

However, several factors were coming together to fashion a population explosion in the Canadian west. World economic conditions had started to ease in the mid-1890's and European immigrants were again flowing towards the New World. Yet by this time free land south of the Canadian border was all but filled and the new population surged northward in search of open land. Earlier settlement had demonstrated that the intemperate Canadian prairies could be successfully farmed and new agricultural techniques were steadily improving the prospects of northern agriculture. From 1900 to 1913, 2,500,000 immigrants poured into Canada compared to only 1,500,000 in the previous 33 years.[1] Thus the assertion in 1904 by Sir Wilfred Laurier that the 20th century belonged to Canada reflected in no small way the sense of optimism that gripped the "last, best west" as it entered an explosive period of population growth.[2]

In the decade from 1901 to 1911 the prairie population rose from 419,000 to over 1,328,000, an increase of over 316% in only 10 years. In both Saskatchewan and Alberta the population increased by more than five-fold in this period, and Saskatchewan became the third most populous province in the country, a position it was to hold for 40 years. The region's share of the national population shot up from 7.8% in 1901 to 18.4% in 1911. Over the next two decades the prairie population continued to surge ahead both in absolute and relative terms. By 1931 well over two million people, comprising 22.7% of the national population, lived on the Prairies. The population of Saskatchewan was close to a million and, along with the population of Alberta, was over 10 times that of the 1901 provincial population.

During this period prairie voters found themselves under-represented in the House of Commons as the redistribution of seats could not keep pace with the rate of population growth. The redistribution of seats was dependent upon the 10-year census and even given optimal co-operation from the national government the shift of parliamentary seats into the prairie region could not have kept up with the population growth. However by 1930 the fit between seats and population had been pretty well brought into line; the Prairie provinces then contained 22.0% of the seats in the House of Commons compared to 22.7% of the 1931 national population. This compares to a gap between 12.2% (seats) and 18.4% (population) in 1911, and a smaller gap between 18.3% (seats) and 22.2% (population) in 1921. Understandable as this earlier under-representation was, it should be noted that it was one of the grievances that fueled western Canadian political discontent, contributing to the impression that the West lacked appropriate political power in the national government.

B) Rural Population

One of the most distinctive features of the prairie region was its rural population, a feature that reflected agriculture's dominance of the region. At the turn of the century 75.4% of the prairie population was rural; by 1911 that proportion dropped to 64.7% but then stabilized, falling only to 61.9% by 1941. During the same period Ontario was experiencing substantial urbanization as the industrialization of the province's economy steadily advanced. While in 1901 over 57% of Ontario's population was rural, that proportion shrank to only 38.3% in 1941. Thus throughout the period under examination here the prairie society was decidedly more rural than that of Ontario.

The rural character of the Prairies was related to political radicalism in ways quite apart from agrarian grievances springing from the wheat economy. In the past political protest in western Canada carried a strong anti-metropolitan sentiment as part of its creed.[3] For example, the Farmers' Platform of 1910 stated that "the greatest misfortune that can befall any country is to have its people huddled together in great centres of population."[4] Political protest was thus shaped by the rural lifestyle and values of the prairie population, features that were sharply contrasted to the values and lifestyle emerging in the rapidly urbanizing and industrializing Ontario society. Interestingly, the farm community in Ontario was also reacting strongly to the new directions of the Ontario society, and the threat of rural de-population served as the lynchpin between agrarian protest in Ontario and the Prairies, and helped make the Progressive Party more than an expression of western regional discontent.

C) Ethnic Composition

While the British and French charter groups may form the ethnic bedrock of Canada, immigration since confederation has steadily eroded the predominance of the British ethnic group and of late has threatened the social and political position of the French Canadian community. In 1901, 57.0% of the Canadian population was of British ethnic origin and 30.7% was French. By the 1971 census those proportions had slipped to 44.6% and 28.7% respectively. The major source of change is to be found in two great waves of immigration into Canada, the first occurring between 1901 and 1930 and the second commencing with the end of the Second World War. The first wave had a profound impact on the prairie society for it not only provided the bulk of prairie settlers but also gave the region a distinctive ethnic stamp that set it apart from the central Canadian society. The second wave of immigration largely bypassed the Prairies and undercut the earlier-established ethnic distinctiveness.

By the mid-1870's the immigration of Mennonites and Icelanders had begun to crack the ethnic duality of Manitoba and set the pattern for western Canada that was to follow; the Canadian duality of English and French was not to be replicated on the Prairies.[5] In order to attract settlers to the Canadian west the government set aside blocks of land reserved for incoming ethnic communities, such as the 6,000 German-speaking Mennonites from Russia who had settled in 60 villages in the Red River Valley by 1879.[6] Subsequent blocks were reserved for groups from England, Scotland, Germany, Russia, the Ukraine, Belgium, Scandinavia, and Iceland. The outcome of this policy was that the settlement pattern on the Prairies resembled an ethnic mosaic, a mosaic that was to have a long-standing impact on the character of the prairie society.

By 1891 the first Ukrainian settlers came to Manitoba and significant immigration from the United States, much of it comprised of former residents of eastern Canada, also began.[7] When the immigration floodgates to western Canada were opened at the turn of the century, the flood of immigrants differed considerably in ethnic composition from the Canadian population of 1901. Although large numbers of immigrants came to the Canadian west from Britain and the United States, and many settlers came from eastern Canada, large numbers also arrived from continental Europe, both west and east. Ukrainians, Russians, Poles, Germans and Scandinavians arrived by the tens of thousands. The net effect was to reduce the French ethnic community on the Prairies to the verge of insignificance,[8] to threaten the pre-eminence of British institutions, cultural patterns and political hegemony, and to give the prairie region a distinctive ethnic stamp that was to set it apart from central Canada for decades to come.

Table 2:1 presents the ethnic composition of the Prairies, Ontario and Canada in 1931, the year that effectively terminated any sizeable immigration into Canada until the end of the Second World War. In an important sense, then, the 1931 census marks the point of ethnic crystalization or congealment for the prairie society. By that year the immigration of large blocs of ethnic settlers into the Prairies had ended; when large-scale immigration into Canada resumed in 1945 the prairie region was largely bypassed. Thus the post-war prairie society evolved from the ethnic building blocks that had been set in place prior to the onslaught of the Great Depression. As Morton has commented in a more general sense, by the end of the twenties ". . . the prairie civilization in temper and institutions had been established, if not tested."[9]

As Table 2:1 reveals, the prairie region in 1931 was much more ethnically diverse and complex than was either Canada as a whole or Ontario. In Canada and Ontario the British and French charter groups together constituted 80.1% and 82.7% of the population respectively. On the Prairies their proportion was only 56.5% within which the British were clearly predominant as they were in Ontario. The prairie population contained a much bigger percentage of German, Scandinavian, Ukrainian, Dutch, Polish and Russian settlers than did Ontario.[10] In many cases the differences were extreme. Proportionately, for example, the prairie region contained almost 12 times as many Ukrainians and Scandinavians as did Ontario. In absolute terms 85.7% of all Ukrainians and 71.7% of all Scandinavians in Canada lived in the Prairie provinces. Apart from the two ethnic charter groups Ontario contained a higher proportion of only three ethnic groups—Jews, Italians, and Finns—than did the three Prairie provinces, groups which together made up less than 3% of the national population. Thus in 1931 the Prairies emerged as an ethnically distinct region in Canada, the distinctiveness coming both from the ethnic complexity of the region and from the heavy regional concentration of non-British and non-French ethnic groups.

Before leaving Table 2:1 some note should be taken of inter-provincial variations in the 1931 ethnic composition of the prairie region. For some ethnic groups the variations were substantial. To mention the two most noticeable cases, the proportion of Jews in Manitoba was almost six times that found in Alberta while in Saskatchewan settlers of German ethnic descent made up 14.0% of the provincial population compared to only 5.4% in Manitoba. Generally, however, the ethnic compositions of the three Prairie provinces did not vary greatly. In all three the British component was clearly dominant, the size of this group varying by only 5% across the three provinces. In all three, moreover, settlers of French

TABLE 2:1

Ethnic Composition of Canada, The Prairies, and Ontario
1931 Census

Percentage of the National, Regional and Provincial Populations Comprised of Each Ethnic Group

	British Isles	French	German	Scandin-avian	Ukrainian*	Hebrew	Dutch	Polish
Canada	51.9	28.2	4.6	2.2	2.2	1.5	1.4	1.4
Ontario	74.0	8.7	5.1	0.6	0.7	1.8	1.8	1.2
Prairies	50.8	5.8	10.3	6.9	8.2	1.2	2.7	3.7
—Manitoba	52.6	6.7	5.4	4.5	10.5	2.8	3.6	5.7
—Saskatchewan	47.5	5.5	14.0	7.9	6.9	0.6	2.7	2.8
—Alberta	53.2	5.2	10.2	8.1	7.6	0.5	1.9	2.9

	Indian Eskimo	Italian	Russian	Asiatic	Austrian	Finnish	Other European	Other Unclassified
Canada	1.2	0.9	0.8	0.8	0.5	0.4	1.6	0.3
Ontario	0.9	1.5	0.3	0.4	0.3	0.8	1.6	0.3
Prairies	2.0	0.3	2.7	0.5	1.4	0.3	3.1	0.2
—Manitoba	2.2	0.3	1.7	0.3	1.3	0.1	2.1	0.2
—Saskatchewan	1.7	0.1	3.8	0.5	1.9	0.3	3.9	0.1
—Alberta	2.1	0.7	2.2	0.7	0.9	0.5	3.1	0.2

* Many ethnically-Ukrainian settlers immigrated to Canada from Austria and Poland, and therefore were at times enumerated as Austrians or Poles. Thus the 1931 Census figures may somewhat understate the proportion of Ukrainians in the population.

descent, while a sizeable contingent, were surpassed in number by at least one, and more commonly by several, non-British ethnic groups. Finally the populations of all three provinces were ethnically diverse, with non-charter group ethnics making up over 40% of the population.

The limited provincial variations in ethnic composition are important to note for some effort has been made to link differences in ethnic composition to the divergent political histories of the three Prairie provinces. For example it has been suggested that the emergence of the Social Credit party in Alberta was facilitated by the large number of American immigrants in the province while the success of the CCF in Saskatchewan can be traced to the more British character of the Saskatchewan population.[11] However the differences in ethnic composition seem far too minor to account for such divergent political histories.[12] In 1931, on the eve of both the Social Credit and CCF movements, American immigrants comprised 7.9% of the Saskatchewan population and 10.8% of the population in Alberta.[13] This difference is of questionable magnitude when one is trying to account for the very divergent political histories of the two provinces.

The above discussion of American settlers brings to light an important immigrant group that is concealed in the ethnicity data of Table 2:1. Two centuries ago the United Empire Loyalists, coming north from the United States in the wake of the American Revolution, formed the central pillar of the English Canadian community in Upper Canada. After the turn of the 20th century when the supply of open land in the American west was all but exhausted, when American land prices were escalating, and when the Canadian prairies were just being opened to extensive settlement, American settlers again flowed north. The flow was substantial indeed, surpassing 100,000 a year in 1910, 1911 and 1912.[14] Between 1891 and 1916 over one million Americans arrived in Canada, although for many the stay was short.[15] Unfortunately for the present analysis the Canadian census does not recognize the United States as a point of ethnic origin and thus the isolation of Americans within census data is difficult at some times and impossible at others. Nor do the census data isolate Canadian immigrants to the United States who subsequently returned to Canada—many of the Early American immigrants to Manitoba fell into this category. By any measure, however, the Americans were not a small group. By the 1931 census there were 344,574 American immigrants in Canada, almost half of whom resided on the Prairies; 18,000 in Manitoba, 73,000 in Saskatchewan, and 79,000 in Alberta.[16]

The Americans were an important group in the Canadian west for reasons quite apart from their size. Immigrants from the American grain states were the carriers of diverse forms of agrarian radicalism that were to have a significant impact on agrarian political activity in Canada. The advocacy of direct democracy, and its components of nonpartisanship, referendums, voter initiatives, and voter recalls, found its roots in the American agrarian movements of the late 19th century and in the tenets of Jeffersonian democracy. The American experience served as a model, both positive and negative, for Canadian farmers as they examined their own political predicament in the years surrounding the First World War. In a more direct sense many American settlers were to play an important organizational and ideological role in the mobilization of Canadian farmers. Perhaps the most outstanding example is Henry Wise Wood whose family had been active in Missouri agrarian radicalism. In Alberta, Wood became the central figure in the United Farmers of Alberta and made a major and divisive ideological contribution to the Progressive Party of Canada.

The political contributions of American immigrants raise a more general point about the immigrant character of the prairie population and the political implications thereof. The rich and open prairie land attracted immigrants from around the world and as a consequence the genesis of western Canadian political radicalism took place within a population that was to a large extent foreign-born. In 1911 only 51.3% of the prairie population was Canadian-born compared to national and Ontario proportions of 78.0% and 79.9% respectively. As one moved westward across the Prairies the Canadian-born proportion shrank even more; whereas 58.6% of the 1911 Manitoba population had been born in Canada, the proportions for Saskatchewan and Alberta fell to 50.5% and 43.2% respectively. Twenty years later the gap between Ontario and the West, although closing, was still substantial; 76.6% of the 1931 Ontario population was Canadian-born compared to 66.2% in Manitoba, 65.4% in Saskatchewan and 58.2% in Alberta. In assessing these figures it should be kept in mind that they apply to the entire provincial populations; if only the adult population was considered the Canadian-born proportion of the population would be considerably lower.

The Prairies, then, and particularly the far west, was occupied by people with only a limited exposure to the Canadian political system. It is apparent, moreover, that the juxtaposition of a relatively small indigenous Canadian population and the outbreak of political radicalism was not coincidental; the immigrant character of the Prairies in no small way facilitated the emergence of a radical regional politics. New immigrants, having missed any familial or substantial personal socialization into the Canadian political system, could not be expected to have well-engrained attachments and loyalties to Canadian political institutions and actors. It is true that the Liberal party, through holding office during much of the pre-war immigration boom, was able to attract stronger support from the new population, particularly the non-British population, than was the Conservative party of the time. Yet attachments to either major party were tenuous at best. For immigrants to western Canada the Liberal and Conservative parties were every bit as new and thus every bit as open to acceptance or rejection as were the more indigenous western Canadian political parties that emerged such as the Progressives and the United Farmers of Alberta. As sociologist Harry Hiller points out with reference to Alberta provincial politics ". . . the rejection of the mainline parties was not simply because they were nationally or eastern-oriented, but that they had no strong ties with this recently migrated population."[17]

The eastern base of the Liberal and Conservative parties, however, was not irrelevant to their rejection by the immigrant population. Eastern Canada, its political parties and its political institutions, were geographically remote from the West and remoter still to the personal experience of immigrants settling in the West. The indigenous western parties were more relevant as they arose from those aspects of the Canadian experience and geography with which the new immigrant was most familiar. As W. M. Martin, Saskatchewan's Liberal premier at the end of World War One stated, "the people of this section of the country are principally settlers from the British Isles and the United States, [who] have never known Eastern Canada, and . . . stubbornly hold to the view that the West is Canada."[18] Not only, then, were mainline partisan allegiances relatively weak among the new population but so too was any commitment to the existing party system and the political institutions of the Canadian state.

The impact of immigration on radicalism has been most thoroughly documented in connection with the western Canadian labour movement.[19] As McCormack observes, the fires of union radicalism, which frequently spread to the political arena, were fueled in a variety of ways by the ethnic mix that settled western Canada:

> Radicalism was part of the immigrant workers' cultural baggage, and their prior experience formed their response to the new environment. Ukrainians, Finns, and Germans had been exposed to socialist propaganda in Europe. Many Italians had been indoctrinated with syndicalism. And some Jews were anarchists.[20]

American immigrants were also an important source of radical union ideas, and although the American influence was particularly strong on the west coast the radical philosophy of the Industrial Workers of the World was also to find expression in the Calgary formation of the One Big Union in the spring of 1919. In Winnipeg the north-end eastern European population provided the numerical strength behind the city's socialist movement.[21] In Saskatchewan the importance of the union background of British and European immigrants to later political radicalism in the province has been noted by S. M. Lipset.[22]

Of all the immigrant groups the British had the greatest impact on trade union radicalism. As McCormack explains, "British immigrants, whose skills were essential to industrialization, brought with them a strong tradition of organization; they became the basis of the trade union movement and the dynamic in its growth."[23] In part the British gained importance in the movement through the exclusion of other groups; western Canadian unionists were opposed to most forms of non-British immigration, an opposition based on the belief that non-British immigrants would drive down wages that were already precariously low and would provide a pool of strikebreakers for the opponents of unionism.[24] In this sense the union movement found itself pitted against the development strategy of the national government and the immigration policies entailed in that strategy. The centrality of British immigrants to the trade union movement, however, was also a reflection of the general centrality of British immigrants, and of British norms and values, in the settlement of western Canada:

> Some of us take pride today in the description of our region and country as a cultural mosaic. It is a comforting illusion, at least historically. What really happened in western Canada in the early decades of this century was a "melting pot". And it was the English majority who wrote the recipe and stoked the fire.[25]

Parenthetically it is interesting to note here a comment by Major C. H. Douglas, founder of Social Credit, on the nature of the Alberta population: "the character of the population, chiefly agricultural in interest and more than one-third of it drawn from German and Ukrainian farming and peasant stocks, renders it specially vulnerable to mass agitation and more inclined to accept the printed word and the radio speech at their face value without submitting them to the more cynical criticism of Anglo Saxon civilization."[26] Given the role played by mass agitation and radio speeches in the 1935 victory of Social Credit in Alberta there is a certain irony in Douglas' comment. It is worth speculating what effect additional "cynical criticism" would have had on the acceptance of Social Credit doctrine in Alberta.

Underlying the labour movement in western Canada was a current of regional alienation similar to that galvanizing agrarian discontent during the same period.[27] The radicalism of the labour movement, however, peaked before the agrarian movement was fully politicized. The formation of the One Big Union and the Winnipeg General Strike, both in 1919 and a year before the creation of the Progressive Party, were radical highwater marks in the western labour movement. A sharp decline in radicalism and political activity followed in their wake. The electoral stage was abandoned to the emerging agrarian movements—the Progressives and the United Farmers. Where the radical labour movement had failed in the West, in large part because of the small size of the industrial work force, perhaps the numerically superior agrarian movement would succeed in achieving fundamental economic and political change. When labour returned to electoral activism with the formation of the CCF in 1932 the effect of its return was to broaden the agrarian movement, to lead it beyond the regional sectionalism of the past. Both having failed individually, the labour and agrarian movements would join forces for yet another political assault on the citadels of eastern Canada. This time, however, sectional concerns would be secondary to the demand for fundamental change in the Canadian economy at large.

The ethnic heterogeneity of western Canada was not only a source of new and often radical ideas for the labour movement; it was also the source of a great deal of internal dissention and fragmentation. The existence of union locals formed along ethnic and linguistic lines, the hostility of British unionists to east European and Asiatic immigration, and plain old-fashioned racism all served to divide and thus weaken the small industrial work force in western Canada.[28] There was a parallel fragmentation of the western Canadian socialist movement along ethnic lines. The Socialist Party of Canada, for example, failed to integrate non-English speaking immigrants who then proceeded to go their own way; "the exodus of the eastern and most non-English-speaking socialists shattered the party's organization outside of British Columbia, and even there the party was severely weakened."[29]

These internal problems of the union and socialist movements bring up a more general point. In the early decades of settlement western Canada faced very serious internal problems quite apart from those arising from the National Policy or with the national government. Writing in 1909, J. S. Woodsworth explained the situation as follows:

Within the past decade, a nation has been born. English and Russians, French and Germans, Austrians and Italians, Japanese and Hindus—a mixed multitude, they are being dumped into Canada by a kind of endless chain. They sort themselves out after a fashion, and each seeks to find a corner somewhere. But how shall we weld this heterogeneous mass into one people? That is our problem.[30]

The West was filled with a new polyglot population holding to a multitude of different religious creeds. It was a population, moreover, with shallow social roots, supplied with only the makeshift social institutions of early settlement, and facing an uncertain and frequently precarious economy. The problems of social integration were immense. To the extent that a distinctive regional society existed in western Canada it was perhaps born as much from the struggle with internal problems of integration and assimilation as it was from the struggle with the national government and eastern Canada.

To conclude, the argument is not being made that the ethnic heterogeneity, and in this sense the regional distinctiveness of the West, led directly to new forms of political organization and behavior. Rather the argument is that radical forms of political behavior were facilitated by the existence of an immigrant population poorly socialized into pre-existing Canadian political patterns and bringing with it political ideas alien to the established political practices of central Canada. Commitment to existing political institutions was qualified and difficult to secure in the face of the regional inequities arising from the National Policy. Attachments to the two eastern-rooted national parties, the Liberals and Conservatives, were less intense and more easily put aside than was the case elsewhere in Canada.

D) Religious Composition

Religious controversy played an important role in the early evolution of prairie politics as it did in the more general evolution of Canadian politics. Even before the formation of Alberta and Saskatchewan the religious reverberations of the Riel rebellions and the execution of Louis Riel, coupled with the bitter controversy over language and educational rights that was known as the Manitoba School Question, had charged western politics with religious conflict.[31] In the first three decades of the 20th century the Social Gospel movement, which sought to transform Protestant Christianity into a social religion centered upon man's plight on earth, became entwined with a variety of political protest movements in western Canada.[32] The years of the First World War in particular saw the fusion of the Social Gospel movement with political movements ranging from the suffragettes and the prohibitionists to the proponents of agrarian radicalism.[33] As late as 1929 religious cleavages played a critical role in the defeat of the Liberal government in Saskatchewan.[34] Finally, and perhaps of greatest importance, the number of western Canadian political leaders who were to emerge from the ranks of the clergy was legion including such notables as J. S. Woodsworth, William Aberhart, Ernest Manning, and T. C. Douglas. Although the onset of the Depression in the 1930s reduced the electoral salience of religious cleavages it served to energize political leaders drawn from the religious realm.

In movements like the Social Gospel, and in the prominent roles played by religious factors in the initial success, longevity, and social philosophy of the Alberta Social Credit party, the religious composition of the prairie population has been linked to the emergence of a regionally distinctive political style. However, before granting that the religious composition of the Prairies served as a major underpinning for this regional style a number of questions must be addressed. To what extent did the prairie population differ in religious composition from that of Ontario or Canada as a whole? Have any such differences been sustained or eroded over time? Finally, if the religious character of the prairie population contributed to political regionalism in the past, does the same potential exist today given the generally attenuated impact of religious cleavages on Canadian political life?

Table 2:2 compares the 1931 religious composition of the prairie region with that of Canada and Ontario, and illustrates the degree of religious diversity within the prairie region. The principal comparison to note is that between the prairie region and Ontario. In 1931 the prairie population contained a higher proportion of Lutherans and, to a lesser extent, Roman Catholics, than did Ontario. The mainstream Canadian Protestant faiths—Anglican, United, Presbyterian, Methodist and Congregationalist—were somewhat under-represented on the Prairies, the difference being accounted for by the greater concentration of smaller religious sects. Nevertheless, while the prairie proportion of "other" religious affiliations was over twice that for Ontario in 1931, the dominant religions of Ontario and of Canada were also dominant on the Prairies. Anglicanism, Roman Catholicism and the various mainstream Protestant affiliations (United Church, Presbyterian, Methodist and Congregationalist) represented over 74% of the 1931 prairie population, compared to over 85% for both Ontario and Canada. While the prairie population was somewhat distinctive in its religious composition that distinctiveness was curtailed by the affiliation of the great bulk of prairie residents with the major denominational orders of the land. Religiously the Prairies played only minor regional variations on a national theme, and the religious differences between the Prairies and Ontario paled next to those between Ontario and Quebec.

The religious composition of the Prairies reflected the region's ethnic diversity as immigrants by and large brought their religious faiths with them. By way of illustration, American immigration served as a vehicle through which many smaller religious sects established themselves in western Canada. Although immigration was only one method of transmission, its contribution was important as Christian Science, Mormon and Evangelical faiths spread northward. In terms of the total number of adherents these sects were not large in 1931 but they have nevertheless been credited with a considerable impact on the social and political evolution of the prairie society.[35] Many of the smaller sects, however, practised a self-imposed isolation from the political system. The Doukhobours, Hutterites and Adventists, to name only the most prominent, withdrew from political activity as a matter of religious conviction. Their voluntary withdrawal from politics rendered them irrelevant to the forces molding the political evolution of the prairie society.

It should also be noted that although for the most part the same religious denominations held sway on the Prairies as in eastern Canada, we cannot imply from census data that the religious and social content of those denominations were necessarily the same. Richard Allen has shown that the Social Gospel was a more virulent force within western Protestant churches than it was among those in central Canada.[36] Facing both a different socio-economic environment and energetic competition from

TABLE 2:2

Religious Affiliations
1931 Census

Religious Affiliation	Percentage of Census Population						
	Canada	Ontario	Prairies	Manitoba	Saskatchewan	Alberta
Anglican	15.8	22.3	15.7	18.4	13.8	15.5
Baptist	4.3	5.0	3.0	1.9	2.9	4.2
Jewish	1.5	1.8	1.2	2.7	0.5	0.5
Lutheran	3.8	2.8	10.3	6.7	12.3	11.
Roman Catholic	41.3	21.7	25.2	27.1	25.4	23.1
United, Presbyterian, Methodist, Congregational	28.0	41.8	33.8	33.2	33.9	34.1
Other*	5.2	4.5	10.9	10.0	11.1	11.4
TOTAL	100.0%	100.0%	100.0%	100.0%	100.0%	100.0%
Population	10,376,786	3,431,683	2,353,529	700,139	921,785	731,605

* The major religions included here are as follows, with the number of adherents across Canada given in parentheses: Mennonite-including Hutterites (88,736); Salvation Army (30,716); Pentecostal (26,301); Confucian (24,087); Evangelical Association (22,213); Mormon (22,005); Christian Science (18,436); Adventists (16,026); Church of Christ, Disciples (15,811); Buddist (15,784).

Source: 1931 Census Canada, Vol. 1, pp. 239-42.

fundamentalist evangelicalism, the Protestant churches on the Prairies responded in a manner that was not at all in keeping with clerical patterns in central Canada. The long list of radical prairie politicians with strong clerical roots demonstrates the interpenetration of religious and political concerns, an interpenetration that had become markedly less characteristic of Ontario politics. While in Quebec the interpenetration of religious and political concerns was evident until the onset of the Quiet Revolution, the Catholic church contributed few leaders from its own ranks. The Quebec case is thus not fully analogous to that in western Canada where many Protestant clergymen moved directly into electoral politics.

Perhaps the most notable example of the impact of religion upon prairie politics comes from the role attributed to religious fundamentalism in the success of the Alberta Social Credit movement. As Mann explains, there were strong parallels between evangelistic fundamentalism and the Social Credit movement: "both were lay rather than professional movements, non-conformist in temper, hostile to the respectable well-to-do and to eastern interests, and both made their strongest appeal to the economically hard-hit sections of the population."[37] Both drew inspiration from holy texts and both held out the promise of salvation, be it from worldly sin or the disaster of the Depression. It is not surprising then that William Aberhart and Ernest Manning, the Prophetic Bible Institute, and the Social Credit League were knit together into a single Alberta garment, the knitting being done in part by the weekly Sunday radio sermons delivered by Aberhart and Manning during their tenures as provincial premiers.

To summarize briefly, while the basic denominational profile of the Prairies in 1931 resembled that of Ontario, greater religious diversity existed in the West as a consequence of immigration from continental Europe and the United States. The West became the centre for a variety of cults, sects, and denominational offsprings from the major Protestant and Catholic faiths. Furthermore, religious concerns seemed closer to the surface of political life on the Prairies than they did in Ontario. Religious cleavages still rocked the political system from time to time, many Protestant faiths were galvanized into political action by the Social Gospel movement, and many prairie ministers emerged to play a leading electoral role in both provincial and federal politics. Thus to a modest but significant degree the regionally distinctive political temper of the West was supported by a religious pillar.

E) Prairie Agriculture

Historical studies have placed great emphasis on the role of agriculture in shaping the grievances, values and political movements of the Canadian west. Prairie agriculture was undoubtedly the main pillar supporting a distinctive regional politics. Yet if agriculture was the crucible within which the character of prairie politics was forged, this suggests that the extensive agricultural changes that have occurred in recent decades should have had a substantial impact upon prairie politics. The pursuit of this line of thought requires a relatively extended discussion of the character of prairie agriculture and of the changes that have occurred.

In the early decades of this century wheat was king on the Canadian prairies and a mainstay of the national economy:

> As the annual wheat crop moved from the western farm to the loading ports of the East it served to justify an expensive system of transcontinental railroads, while the proceeds of its sale enabled the farmer in the West both to buy eastern manufacturers, which in turn became the westbound traffic on the railroads, and to pay for the financial services offered him by banks, grain traders, and mortgage companies. Almost the whole Canadian economy was vitally affected by, and organized around, the movement of the annual grain crop into world markets.[38]

The West had attracted settlement by its agricultural potential, and that potential was soon realized. With the introduction of new strains of wheat that would thrive in the relatively harsh environment of the Canadian prairies, wheat crops flourished. Production rose and grain exports, primarily to European markets, climbed steadily. Within the prairie economy the grain farmers' dominance was unquestioned; over half the workforce was employed directly in agriculture and the incomes of most other Westerners were heavily dependent upon agricultural prosperity. Thus the grain economy served to bind the Prairie provinces into a single economic unit within which individuals essentially shared the same interests and environment, and faced the same problems. In the words of V. C. Fowke, the wheat economy supported a "regional way of life."[39] Given the relative homogeneity of economic and occupational concerns the foundations were set for a regionally-integrated political system. The extent to which grain dominated the economies of all three provinces and the extent to which virtually all prairie residents were enmeshed directly or indirectly in the grain economy made the regionalization of political behavior inevitable.

Although wheat had become the new staple upon which Canadian economic development was to be based, it was one encrusted with economic liabilities and uncertainties. John Thompson explains:

> Wheat had become the fourth in the succession of staple products which so heavily influenced Canadian economic development. It had the disadvantages of any other staple product, in that it created an economy in Western Canada that was highly specialized, unable to convert to any other form of

production, and at the mercy of the vagaries of an international market. Unlike Canada's other great staples of fur, fish, and timber, wheat production depended on variable climatic conditions.[40]

The importance of climatic conditions is hard to exaggerate. G. E. Britnell in a classic study of the Depression-era Saskatchewan wheat economy concluded that variability of rainfall during the growing season was the greatest single problem facing wheat producers.[41] Drought is not uncommon on the Prairies, and early frost and hail are constant dangers. Also related to climatic conditions are the hardships of crop disease and insect pests. If western wheat had been sold primarily on the Canadian market poor yields would have been compensated by higher prices. However, this was not the case as Canadian wheat was sold primarily on international markets. Thus variations in the price of wheat were more closely correlated with climatic and production conditions in Europe than in Canada.[42] As a consequence the wheat economy was unstable and subject to recurrent cycles of boom and bust. When high Canadian yields coincided with poor European crops boom conditions occurred, but when poor Canadian yields coincided with good European crops and hence low prices, calamity struck. The farmer was cast upon the fates of not only the temperamental Canadian climate but upon that prevailing in Europe and in Canada's international competitors in the grain market.

Prairie farmers also faced a multitude of other problems. Because grain had to be moved thousands of miles to market the farmer was placed at the mercy of the intervening grain handling, shipping and marketing interests. Being unable to market his produce directly the farmer could be held up for ransom by those who controlled the marketing and transportation of grain. In addition farmers built up large debts as they expanded their holdings during good years, offset operating losses during bad years, and acquired the expensive machinery demanded by the large prairie farms. Debt charges were high, could not always be met when foreign markets collapsed or the weather sabotaged Canadian production, and were collected by eastern-based financial institutions that displayed little willingness to understand or accommodate the uncertainties of the prairie economy.

In short, the position of the prairie grain farmer was precarious. He was a competitive producer, one whose economic well-being varied inversely with the productivity of his neighbours and that of wheat producers around the world. His productivity and profits were largely determined independently of the amount of effort he expended as yields fluctuated tremendously with climatic variations and the price of wheat was determined by overseas market and crop conditions that were wholly outside the control of the Canadian producer. As MacKintosh noted in 1935:

In some fortunate industries the producers can control both their own output and the price at which it is sold; in others the price cannot be controlled but the output can. The farmer who depends mainly on wheat is in a position where he can control neither price nor output.[43]

Kraenzel, incidentally, came to similar conclusions about the economy of the American Plains: "since the economy is chiefly agricultural and without local controls to govern price or volume of production as there are in the case of many industrial areas, the residents are at the mercy of forces outside the region."[44]

Although the prairie farmer was caught up in a larger economic order, the relatively autonomous and individualistic nature of farm work, coupled with the rigours of survival on the prairie frontier, yielded a philosophy of life characterized by rugged individualism. Yet this rugged individualism did not inhibit a pragmatic appreciation of collectivist strategies in politics.[45] From a political perspective the agrarian West was marked more by co-operation and mutual aid than by rugged individualism. Co-operation and mutual aid spawned a plethora of farm organizations which in turn profoundly influenced the nature of prairie politics. Farm organizations sprang up to tackle the manifold economic, social and political problems facing prairie settlers whose lives were tied to the production of grain. Their emergence was ". . . a response to exploitation, or rather, to the inadequacies of individual entrepreneurship in the face of exploitation by outsiders."[46]

In 1901 the Territorial Grain Growers' Association was formed, which became the Saskatchewan Grain Growers' Association in 1906. It was followed by the Manitoba Grain Growers' Association in 1903, the Alberta Society of Equity in 1904, the Alberta Farmers' Association in 1905 and, in 1909, the merger of these latter two into the United Farmers of Alberta. In 1906 the Grain Growers' Grain Company was formed and purchased a seat on the Winnipeg Grain Exchange. At Saskatoon in 1908 the various provincial organizations established the Interprovincial Grain Growers' Council and thereby organizationally cemented a regionally shared set of interests and problems. In 1909 the prairie organizations joined with the Dominion Grange of Ontario to form the Canadian Council of Agriculture and laid the foundation for a national agrarian political organization that was to burst forth 12 years later as the Progressive Party of Canada. The year 1909 also marked the first publication of the *Grain Growers' Guide*, the paper which over the next two decades was to play a major role in integrating prairie farm organizations and in articulating a regional agrarian political philosophy.

In the 1920s farm organizations established wheat pools across the Prairies for the marketing of prairie wheat. The wheat pool movement developed when the Canadian Wheat Board, established through wartime legislation in 1917, was disbanded in 1920. Although the Wheat Board had not been that effective in the 1917-1920 period, the idea of a national marketing board caught hold in western Canada. By 1925 co-operative wheat pools were marketing over 50% of the prairie grain crop.[47] However, the efforts of the pools to market wheat overseas met with financial disaster when the Depression arrived. By 1930 falling wheat prices had driven the pools out of the export business and the federal government stepped in to organize foreign sales. The federally-managed Central Selling Agencies for the Pools had the authority to purchase Canadian grain when world prices were low, store it, and sell it when world prices rose. In 1935 the Canadian Wheat Board was re-established and charged with establishing a floor price for western grain, a price, incidentally, that was below the market price for the first five years.[48] In 1943 the Board was made the sole legal purchaser and seller of wheat, a development that ". . . had been urged by the farm community during the 1930s and was adopted only when it served the needs of the nation as a whole."[49] The Board also became the sole seller of oats and barley on the foreign market in 1948. At the present time the Board maintains its control over foreign sales while the Alberta and Saskatchewan Wheat Pools, the Manitoba Pool Elevators, and the United Grain Growers own almost all private elevator and grain storage facilities in Canada.[50]

While the discussion to this point has emphasized the economic homogeneity that was imposed on western Canada by the wheat economy, this homogeneity should not be exaggerated. The border between Alberta and Saskatchewan was selected in part because that particular median was thought (incorrectly) to divide the Prairies into ranching and grain growing areas.[51] The economic and hence political divide between Alberta and Saskatchewan has been discussed by W. L. Morton:

> To wheatlands Alberta added rangelands, irrigated lands and vast coal deposits. It's economic development was more varied, even in frontier days, than was that of the monolithic wheat economy of Saskatchewan. A diversity of interests, comparatively speaking, characterized the electorate of Alberta, and the organized farmers could not speak for everyone, as in Saskatchewan.[52]

There were also significant differences in the economies of Saskatchewan and Manitoba, with Saskatchewan farms being larger and less diversified than those in Manitoba and the Manitoba economy containing much larger urban and industrialized components than did that of Saskatchewan. Nor should the history of prairie cities be neglected in any discussion of the wheat economy. The cities not only displayed a somewhat divergent political history from the rural countryside—fostering active communist parties that did not spread to the countryside and in Alberta and Manitoba generating much more support for the CCF—but the cities and the non-farm community also produced much of the prairies' political leadership including men such as Woodsworth, Aberhart, Douglas, Coldwell, Knowles, Manning, and Lloyd. The early West, then, was not homogeneous nor was the wheat economy monolithic.

Nevertheless, compared to the contemporary situation, the prairie region prior to the Second World War was *relatively* integrated by the wheat economy. Not only was a majority of the populace engaged in agriculture but they were largely engaged in the same regionally-distinctive form of agriculture and faced common interests, problems and grievances. Reinforcing the regionalizing effects of a common grain economy was a vast social and organizational network of co-ops, wheat pools, farm organizations—many with an overlapping leadership cadre[53]—and publications such as the *Grain Growers' Guide*. Furthermore the economic well-being of people employed outside the grain economy was tied directly to the economic prosperity of the grain farmer. To those in western Canada who serviced the grain economy—the merchants, teachers, clergymen, professionals and civil servants—wheat was the economic focal point of their lives even though they did not work the soil. Outside the West it was wheat that fueled the industrialization and growth of the pre-war Canadian economy. In this sense Easterbrook and Aitken describe wheat as the "keystone in the arch of Canada's national policy"; "its production and sale made possible the construction of transcontinental railway systems and the extension of political control across the continent to the Pacific."[54] It was thus the grain economy that created the foundations for regional politics in western Canada and which left the Progressives, the United Farmers of Alberta and Manitoba, the CCF, and Social Credit as its political legacy.

Despite the setbacks suffered during the Depression, as Canada entered the Second World War agriculture reigned supreme in western Canada, fulfilling the destiny envisioned for it when prairie settlement began in earnest four decades before. Ironically, however, the contributions of prairie wheat to the Canadian economy set in motion economic changes—changes accelerated by the war—that inexorably eroded the importance of wheat to the national economy and thereby indirectly eroded the economic importance of western Canada:

> By 1930, wheat had made its major contribution to Canada's growth. By the drive and momentum it had given the economy, it had drawn the manpower, capital and technology necessary to the beginnings of development on a massive scale of the rich resources of the Canadian Shield. It was only as this shift took on large-scale proportions that the fortunes of wheat producers ceased to exert a decisive influence on the evolution of the economy as a whole.[55]

F) Culture

In the early decades of this century the prairie society lay on the periphery of the Canadian mainstream; the gulf between it and the older, larger society of central Canada was enormous and was bridged in only the most tenuous fashion. The reasons for this gulf are not difficult to delineate, the most important being simple geographical distance. Given the existing forms of transportation travel between the Prairies and central Canada was difficult, time-consuming and expensive; any prospects of intimate social interplay foundered on the barrier of the Canadian Shield. The media of the time offered little compensation for limited personal interaction; there was not, nor could there be, a national media knitting the society together. The absence of electronic media and the undeveloped state of journalistic wire services tended to regionally partition the media. Ironically perhaps, just as the primitive state of communication, travel, and media technologies served to sustain regional cleavages within the Canadian society, it also protected that nascent society from what was later to become an engulfing flood of American mass culture.

If the difficulty of travel, the lack of an integrating media and the simple size of the Canadian nation isolated the prairie society from central Canada, the consequence was the development of culture patterns that were regionally distinctive, patterns which reinforced the economic and political cleavages in the Canadian society and which helped set the Prairies apart from the East. At the same time the region was settled by a polyglot immigrant population, many members of which sought with considerable success to maintain the cultural, linguistic and religious patterns of their homeland. The prairie society was therefore too diverse to foster a unified regional culture, and the efforts of British immigrants to transplant their own cultural patterns intact were only partially successful. The prairie culture that emerged was thus a kaleidoscopic reflection of the region's immigrant base. It was this very heterogeneity that set the prairie region apart from central Canada—out of diversity a regional image of prairie culture was born.

This brings to a close the discussion of the socio-economic pillars supporting political regionalism in western Canada prior to the Second World War. It is now time to turn to political regionalism per se.

POLITICAL REGIONALISM IN WESTERN CANADA

The most distinctive feature of national political behavior on the Prairies has been the electorate's rejection of the traditional two-party system and the concomitant emergence of third parties more or less indigenous to the Canadian plains. The first task, then, is to examine the pre-Second World War patterns of prairie electoral support for the two mainstream political parties of the time, the Liberals and the Conservatives.[56] The second is to examine the patterns of electoral support for the collection of third parties that from 1921 to the Second World War figured so prominently in prairie federal politics.

A) Major Party Support in Western Canada

National politics in Canada have been dominated by two major parties—the Conservatives who reigned almost without interruption over the first three decades of Canadian nationhood, and the Liberals who obtained a solid grip on national office with Wilfred Laurier's victory over the Conservatives in 1896. Both have been aptly characterized as brokerage parties, all encompassing omnibus organizations that have sought, if not always successfully, to include all groups, regions and interests in their pursuit of national office. Since the days of Sir John A. Macdonald party strategists have correctly assumed that narrow group appeals and ideological consistency, or indeed clarity, would prove of little electoral benefit in a country as vast and diverse as Canada.

Because the Liberal and Conservative parties tried to function as national brokerage organizations, electoral support for these parties provides a useful handle on the study of regionalism. To the extent that the Liberals and Conservatives have dominated national electoral politics and to the extent they have pursued brokerage strategies to do so, they have helped knit the country into a relatively integrated political unit. In other words, if the various regions, ethnic groups and classes in Canada find that they can achieve adequate representation and support through one or both of the two major national parties, then a considerable degree of political integration can be said to exist. While the Liberal and Conservative parties have not been wildly successful as vehicles of political integration, they have been more successful in that respect than have been the third parties that challenged them. Conversely, if the major parties are seriously challenged by new, emergent parties based on more narrow sectional, ethnic or class appeals, then the integrative performance of the brokerage parties is brought into question. With respect to prairie regionalism specifically, the degree of electoral support for the two major parties provides a rough index of regional integration into the broader political system. To the extent that the major party organizations held sway in the Prairies the political expression of regionalism was muted. To the extent that the major parties were challenged by third parties, sectional discontent molded distinctive regional patterns of political behavior.

W. L. Morton has argued that "Confederation was . . . a prelude and preparation for the annexation of the Prairies to the Canadian version of continental integration.''[57] In the early decades of western settlement it appeared that the national parties would provide ready assistance to this integration by extending their political dominance to the new region. In Manitoba, a province that only narrowly missed being a fifth partner in the original confederation, the predominantly Ontario settlers brought with them commitments and allegiances to the eastern-based Conservatives and Liberals. The two parties had five decades in Manitoba in which to entrench themselves before the onslaught of agrarian revolt in the 1920s. When Saskatchewan and Alberta became provinces in 1905 the national parties were grafted onto the emergent provincial political systems thereby providing provincial party organizations that were able to sustain federal electoral activity. The Laurier Liberals, acting through their appointment of the new lieutenant governors and in turn through the lieutenant governors' power to call governments of their choosing, were able to establish Liberal provincial regimes that lasted until 1929 in Saskatchewan and until 1921 in Alberta.[58] With respect to national elections, then, we concur with David Smith that ''until the end of the First World War . . . the politics and parties of the Prairie provinces were an integral part of the national political structure.''[59]

Yet beneath the veneer of electoral success the popular underpinnings of the two national parties were less than secure. Agrarian unrest had been simmering since the early days of settlement. In 1883 the first farm protest organization, the Manitoba and North West Farmers' Protective Union, was formed in the wake of crop failures and the collapse of a land boom. The Union's Bill of Rights demanded ''. . . that Manitoba be granted its 'provincial rights', including control of its public lands; that withholding of land from actual settlers by speculation and federal government reserves be ended; that the national tariff be made once more a revenue tariff; that the Canadian Pacific Railway monopoly be ended; that the elevator 'monopoly' be broken; that the government of Manitoba be allowed to charter railways; and that the construction of branch lines be hastened.''[60] Although the Union disbanded four years later it was an important dress rehearsal for what was to follow.[61]

During the first two decades of the 20th century agrarian unrest came to a boil. The focal point of discontent was the National Policy and, more specifically, the tariffs embodied therein. The tariffs were designed to raise revenue for the national government in order to offset government contributions to railway construction, to promote the east/west flow of rail traffic, and to promote the growth of manufacturing in central Canada. From a prairie perspective the National Policy, through its tariffs on imported farm machinery and its flagrantly discriminatory freight-rate structure, imposed an unconscionable financial burden on western grain producers who were being forced to buy the necessities of life and production on the protected domestic market while selling their crops on the open international grain markets.

Coupled with agitation against the National Policy came a host of other grievances including a monopolistic and frequently inefficient grain marketing and transportation system, federal disallowance of provincial legislation, and the national control of crown land in Saskatchewan and Alberta. A particular target was the inequities associated with "standard" elevators, elevators built under concessions at regular intervals along the CPR tracks. Where standard elevators existed the CPR would load grain only through those elevators. Farmers ". . . were convinced that in many cases the monopoly position means lower prices, lower grades, excess dockage, and in certain cases dishonest weight."[62] Western agitation was stronger here than in the case of tariffs, more sustained, much less in opposition to financial and industrial interests in central Canada, and thus much more successful.[63] With respect to the national control of provincial crown land, Ottawa had maintained control of prairie land in order to facilitate immigration and homestead policies thought to be essential for the rapid development of the West. Its wisdom aside, this decision served to reinforce the feelings of Westerners that they had been placed in a colonial position relative to the "landlord Dominion."[64] In retrospect the colonial perceptions of western Canadians do not seem wholly inappropriate; just as Canada was beginning to question its colonial relationship with Britain an internal colony was being developed in the West. Mallory describes the situation:

> The West was, after all, Canada's empire. The expansion of the West provided the lifeblood of eastern Canadian commerce, finance, manufacturing, and transportation. It furnished the market for the goods and services which, by permitting the economies of large-scale operations, made eastern undertakings successful. To put it crudely, as Macdonald did, the Dominion had purchased the West and was entitled to the profits of its exploitation.[65]

The extent of justice inherent in this position was not evident to the settlers of western Canada.

As noted earlier, the precarious nature of frontier agriculture and the hardships of frontier life made western farmers quick to organize against any additional hardships that were politically imposed. Agrarian discontent, moreover, was augmented in the early part of the century by a number of complementary protest movements. The campaign for prohibition, the women's suffrage movement and the Social Gospel all fostered a general climate of reform that infused the agrarian movement with additional energy, personnel and ideological perspectives.[66] The growth of the nonpartisan movement in bordering American states also provided new political ideas that challenged the partisan status quo in Canada. Given the unassimilated immigrant character of the prairie population, the electorate was readily disposed to the new political ideas and organizations that were in the wind.

For movements of political protest the Canadian federal system provides two points of attack; both the national and provincial governments are open to assault. In western Canada provincial governments were unquestionably recast by agrarian unrest as the emergence of the United Farmers of Alberta, the United Farmers of Manitoba, the Saskatchewan CCF and the Alberta Social Credit were to attest. Nevertheless it was the national government that was the initial and primary target of agrarian unrest. This was inevitable in that the principal areas of agrarian grievance—tariffs, agriculture, transportation and finance—were all national or concurrent fields of legislative jurisdiction. Thus if agrarian grievances were to be remedied the cure could only come through the actions of the national government. Western Canadians could not retreat behind the protection of provincial governments as Francophone Quebecers in many cases could. The national government, unfortunately, represented not only the farmers but also other powerful groups within the society whose interests were frequently in conflict with those of the farmers, groups who rendered the national government much less sympathetic to agrarian demands than were provincial governments in the West. The national government was also far more immune from agrarian electoral attack than were the provincial governments in the West.

During the second decade of the 20th century agrarian discontent began to focus more sharply upon the national party system. In 1911 Wilfred Laurier's Liberal government, which had advocated a modest degree of long-awaited reciprocal tariff reductions on Canadian-American trade, was soundly defeated by the pro-tariff Conservative party. Although the Liberals captured six of seven seats in Alberta and nine of 10 in Saskatchewan they only received two of 10 in Manitoba and were swamped 73 to 13 in Ontario. Prairie farmers, sensing that even modest attempts at tariff reduction would be repulsed by the bulk of the Canadian electorate residing in Quebec and Ontario,[67] were placed in a quandary. While continued electoral support for the Liberals looked futile, the pro-tariff Conservatives looked even worse. Agitation thus began to intensify for a break with the traditional party and electoral systems. Believing that western representatives were ineffectual behind the closed doors of cabinet and party caucuses, that eastern financial interests dictated party policy on such critical issues as the tariff, and that the electoral system was inherently prejudicial to their interests, westerners began to advocate new political arrangements. Nonpartisanship, occupational representation, referenda, legislative initiatives, and the voter recall of sitting members of Parliament were all explored as possible mechanisms by which western Canada could free itself of the existing party system and come to enjoy a measure of political power commensurate with its rapidly growing population, its economic contribution to national prosperity, and the undaunted optimism of its citizens.

Although the political discontent of western Canadians grew steadily after the 1911 election any direct challenge to the existing political system was sidetracked by the outbreak of war in 1914. As John Thompson has so thoroughly illustrated in *The Harvests of War*, the First World War had a profound effect on western Canada. Initially western grain producers hoped that the war would end the recession of 1913-1914 and, through handicapping Canada's competitors, stimulate the world demand for Canadian wheat. Prosperity did indeed come with the war but the cost was to be high; "the war's high prices brought temporary prosperity to prairie agriculture, but the scramble for short-term profits led to increased levels of debt, costly damage to the land, and continued overdependence on wheat to the detriment of a more balanced agricultural development."[68] While the war strengthened the region's economic dependence on wheat it also stimulated the industrialization of central Canada and thereby widened the economic gulf between central Canada and the Prairies. For its part the national government made little if any attempt to provide western Canada with even a small share of the wartime bounty of government contracts and industrialization. Thompson notes, for example, that between August 1914 and February 1915 the Militia Department spent $4,755,903 to outfit the Canadian Expeditionary Force. Of this only $25,158 was spent in Manitoba and not a cent was spent in either Saskatchewan or Alberta.[69] Throughout the war the Prairies received only 0.67% of the government funds spent on munitions.[70] Overall government expenditures served to reinforce the concentration of industrialization within central Canada and did so to the detriment of possible economic diversification on the Prairies.

Despite the questionable economic benefits that the war years brought to western Canada the war effort itself was enthusiastically supported by the majority of the prairie population. In that effort Westerners seized their opportunity to become full participants in the national community. As Thompson concludes:

> The emergence of a sense of regional identity in Westerners predated the Great War, but the years of war heightened their feelings of identity. In this sense western Canada "came of age" within the Dominion in the same way that Canada itself matured within the Empire and the international community.[71]

In 1917 Robert Borden's Conservative government faced a serious political crisis. Voluntary military enlistments had failed to keep pace with casualties and an expansion of the Canadian war effort in Europe. As a consequence the government turned to the conscription of military manpower, a move that was as bitterly opposed in Quebec as it was enthusiastically supported in Ontario, except for the Ontario farmers. On the Prairies opinion towards conscription was mixed. Many European immigrants may have opposed conscription as did the French Canadians, but ". . . no one consulted them as to their opinion, and they wisely kept that opinion to themselves.''[72] Among western labour leaders opposition to conscription, based on the fear that it would end collective bargaining, was much more virulent than that expressed by the trade union movement in central Canada, although support for Borden and the war was still present. The union paper *The Federalist*, stated that national registration was advocated by ''all of those interests that have had their fangs of exploitation fastened in the flesh of the workers and that fatten upon the profit sucked from their blood and sweat.''[73] Within the agrarian community conscription was opposed on the more practical grounds that it would reduce the supply of farm labour and thereby weaken the West's agricultural contribution to the war effort. When this objection was taken care of by proposed agricultural exemptions to the draft, support for conscription became widespread. In general sentiment in western Canada towards the conscription issue more closely resembled that in Ontario than it did that in Quebec.

The support for conscription in western Canada was consolidated in the creation of the Union government. Western Canadians, among others, had been agitating for the creation of a national nonpartisan government to direct the war effort and the formation of the Union Government from the amalgamation of the Conservative party and pro-conscriptionist Liberals followed western proposals closely.[74] In gearing up for the 1917 election, furthermore, the Union Government displayed considerable sensitivity to western Canadian concerns. Enough of the Canadian Council of Agriculture's 1916 Farmers' Platform was endorsed that the *Grain Growers' Guide* editorialized: ''it can truly be said that this is the most progressive program put out by a government actually in power in the last 25 years''.[75] When the 1917 election came conscription and the Union government were overwhelmingly endorsed; the Union government received 71% of the prairie popular vote and 95% of the region's seats. However, the Union Government was unable to convert its 1917 success into support for the Conservative party. Traditional Tory defence of the tariff, the suspension of the Crow's Nest Pass Agreement under the authority of the War Measures Act, and the government's April 1918 renege on a promise to exempt farmers' sons from conscription all served to quickly terminate any flirtation between prairie voters and the Conservative party as it emerged from its wartime camouflage as the Union Government. Perhaps the greatest disillusionment for Westerners came from the Union Government's rapid abandonment of nonpartisanship. With Borden's replacement by Arthur Meighen in July, 1920, party labels were again applied to government supporters in the House.[76] To Westerners the abandonment of nonpartisanship combined with the postwar government's disinterest in western concerns was like a slap in the face; ''. . . The farmers were more than ever disillusioned with the old party system.''[77]

The magnitude of the Liberal defeat in 1917 coupled with the party's unrelinquished opposition to conscription effectively destroyed the Liberals' organization and electoral credibility on the Prairies. At the same time, while the Union Government was able to rout the Liberals from western Canada the Conservatives proved incapable of moving into the major party vacuum that had been created. With both major parties prostrate on the Prairies following the war the stage was set for agrarian discontent to move directly to electoral politics:

> Many of the established political landmarks had been swept away during the war, and political parties were adrift as politicians found it hard to get their bearings in the new, uncharted seas of the postwar world. Sectional cleavages were revived with increased bitterness, and for the first time class conflict appeared in the Dominion.[78]

The revolt that had been brewing since the election of 1911, but which had been sidetracked by the war, broke forth in the national election of 1921 with the emergence of the Progressive Party of Canada. The incumbent Conservatives received only 20.1% of the prairie popular vote and no seats while the Liberal party fared little better, capturing two seats with an even smaller proportion of the popular vote, 16.3%. Over 53% of the popular vote and 86% of the prairie seats went to the Progressive Party.

The 1921 election is critical for an understanding of regional politics on the Prairies for it ushered in four decades in which the prairie electorate stood apart in its rejection of the two national parties. As Figure 2:1 illustrates the degree of major party support on the Prairies lagged far behind that in Ontario. From 1921 to 1957 the Liberals and Conservatives together averaged 86% of the popular vote in Ontario but only 59% across the Prairies. Thus the Progressive party introduced a clearly distinctive era of western regional politics. From 1921 to the 1958 sweep of the Diefenbaker Conservatives the prairie region stood sharply apart from the Canadian norm in its relative rejection of the two major Canadian parties. Nevertheless the same two parties continued to dominate the national government despite their rejection by western voters. Thus this period was marked also by the relative weakness of prairie representation at the centre of political power in Canada. By rejecting the major parties the Prairie provinces had drawn a curtain of partisanship between themselves and the national governments, a curtain that could only exacerbate regional discontent and alienation.

It must be noted, however, that rejection of the major parties was not uniform across the three Prairie provinces. In Figure 2:2 it can be seen that from 1921 to 1957 Albertans failed to return a majority of government members in even one of the 10 federal elections. Saskatchewan voters on the other hand returned a majority of government members on four of the 10 occasions with Manitoba voters doing so eight times. In addition, the rejection of the major parties by the prairie voters was

FIGURE 2:1 **Percentage of the Popular Vote Won by the Liberal and Conservative Parties**

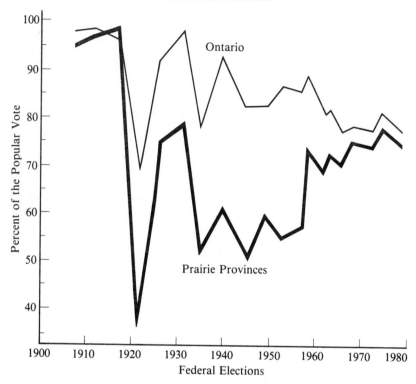

relative rather than absolute; even in lean years the Liberals and Conservatives together picked up more than 50% of the popular vote.

Before leaving Figure 2:2 it is interesting to note the relative propensity of Manitoba voters to support the national government; the contrast between Manitoba and Alberta is very sharp. This east-west gradient, in which Manitoba most closely approximates the national norm and Alberta departs from it most significantly, crops up repeatedly in the analysis of prairie politics. It derives in part, we suspect, from Manitoba's relatively prolonged immersion in the Canadian political system prior to the eruption of agrarian radicalism in the 20th century. Perhaps of even greater importance is the effect of Ontario immigration into Manitoba. Here Rae states that in the waves of Ontario immigration in the 1870s and 1880s Manitoba ". . . was reborn in the image of Ontario."[79] In a similar vein Jackson, commenting upon the 1911 election in which Manitoba voters supported the Conservatives while Alberta and Saskatchewan were swept by the Liberals, describes Manitoba as "a good reflector of Ontario's thought," and refers to the 1911 election outcome in Manitoba as the "afterglow of Ontario's influence."[80] Later

FIGURE 2:2 **Time Periods During Which a Majority of Provincial and Regional M.P.'s were Members of the Party Forming the National Government.**

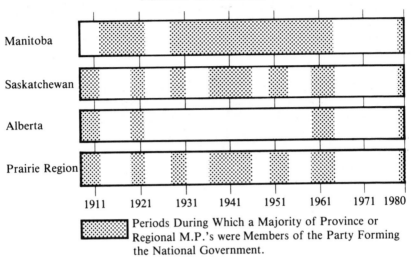

Periods During Which a Majority of Province or Regional M.P.'s were Members of the Party Forming the National Government.

contributions to the weakened regional thrust of Manitoba politics came from the relatively moderate impact of the Depression in Manitoba and the absence of significant natural resources conflict between the province and the national government.

To summarize this discussion of major party support, the 1921 election set in motion a rejection of the two major parties that was to give a regionally distinctive cast to prairie politics until 1958. Although the rejection was not absolute it was sufficient to mark off the prairie region. It must be kept in mind, though, that the fates of the two major parties were by no means similar.

B) Third Parties and Regional Politics

A striking characteristic of prairie politics has been the emergence of 'third parties' which more than once have all but stripped the Liberal and Conservative parties of legislative support from part or all of western Canada. When large numbers of prairie voters abandoned the two major parties in the decades following the First World War they turned to a variety of regionally-oriented parties that by and large placed the articulation of sectional interests ahead of the pursuit of brokerage politics and national office. Not all of these parties were active in national politics; the United Farmers of Alberta, although informally entwined with the Progressive Party of Canada, restricted itself to the provincial stage and the provincial Progressive movement long outlasted the national movement in Manitoba. Other third parties, most notably the Cooperative Commonwealth Federation (CCF) and the Social Credit, were active at both levels of the federal system. It cannot be our pretense here to fully document the evolution, nature and impact of these third parties; the literature that has grown up around them is too rich and extensive to be quickly summarized. All that can be realistically done here is to utilize the third party literature for the light it sheds on regional politics.

The electoral history of third parties is important to the thesis of this book for a number of reasons. In the first place it has already been documented that in the years between 1921 and 1957 prairie voters abandoned the Liberal and Conservative parties in droves; it is now necessary to describe where they went when they left the major party fold. Secondly, electoral support for third parties provides a useful measure of regional sentiment or, conversely, of national political integration. As J. R. Mallory has argued, "the number of political parties, and the distribution of their strength in different provinces, are important indices of the degree of national integration and of the extent to which this integration is modified by strong local pressures."[81] In this light it will be argued that the recent weakening of third parties in western Canada portends the end of one of the most distinctive features of prairie politics and the re-integration of the West into the fabric of national politics. The third reason is closely related to the second. It has been argued that the existence of third parties in western Canada not only represented an expression of western alienation but also served over the long run to sustain and intensify western alienation. By supporting third parties western Canadians isolated their MPs and themselves from the instruments of national power and rendered successive national governments insensitive to western concerns.[82] If this argument holds, the recent decline of third parties should eventually lead to the moderation of western alienation and the political re-integration of the West through the medium of the two major national parties. Any such process, of course, has been complicated by the fact that the prairie electorate, in retreating from third parties, threw its support solidly behind only one party—the Progressive Conservatives—as the country experienced an extended period of Liberal hegemony.

THE PROGRESSIVE PARTY OF CANADA

Of all the radical movements spawned in western Canada the Progressive party merits special attention. It was the Progressive party that in 1921 came the closest of any third party to achieving national power. The 1921 election was the high water mark of agrarian discontent; never before or since was the agrarian community so powerful electorally and so homogeneous in its political expression. Although national office eluded the Progressives they achieved what no other third party has done—the right to form the Official Opposition; the Progressives captured 64 seats compared to 116 for the Liberals and only 50 for the Conservatives. The grievances of western Canada were crystallized in the Progressive movement with a clarity never to be replicated. The Progressives, moreover, broke the electoral ground in western Canada for a succession of protest movements that were to follow in their footsteps: Social Credit, the CCF and the Progressive movement in Manitoba all find roots within the Progressive Party of Canada. Finally, the Progressives were precursors of western political revolt in another sense; their ultimate failure in national politics was to illustrate the inherent political limitations on western revolt, limitations upon which succeeding protest movements would also become impaled.

The Progressive platform in 1921 evolved directly from the 1916 Farmers' Platform put out by the Canadian Council of Agriculture. That platform called for the reduction of the British preferential tariff, acceptance of the 1911 reciprocity treaty, further reduced tariffs on agricultural implements and the necessities of life, a graduated income tax, inheritance and excess profit taxes, and the nationalization of all railway, telegraph and express companies.[83] In 1918 the Farmers' Platform was recast as the New National Policy. The New National Policy sought more than economic reform; it also challenged many basic features of the Canadian political system. As Sharp describes, the twenty year-old "crusade for democracy" found full expression in the New National Policy: "abolition of titles, reform of the Senate, direct legislation, abolition of patronage, removal of press censorship, declaration of ownership of newspapers and periodicals, proportional representation, prohibition, and the admission of women representatives to Parliament—these were demands that had become articles of democratic faith on the Canadian Prairies".[84] When Manitoba's T. A. Crerar resigned from the Union Government in protest over insufficient tariff reductions in the post war budget, he and the eight western Unionists who joined him were endorsed by the Canadian Council of Agriculture as the parliamentary exponent of the New National Policy. By this act the farm organizations threw their hat into the electoral ring and chose one of their own, the president of the United Grain Growers Limited, as their leader. Within a year the Progressives were to dominate electoral politics in western Canada, form the second largest parliamentary contingent in the House of Commons, and redraw the face of Canadian politics.

The Progressive movement embodied the spirit of nonpartisanship that had been popular in the West since the days of the Territorial Assembly. The Assembly had administered local authority in the Northwest Territories prior to the birth of Alberta and Saskatchewan in 1905 and its members were selected and functioned free of partisan entanglements. F. W.G. Haultain, leader of the Assembly, had declared that:

> I stand for non-party government regardless of what any political party or both political parties may decide. To me the welfare and interests of this great Western country are more and always have been more important than the success or convenience of any political party. . . .[85]

In 1921 the Progressives tried to transplant non-partisanship into the heart of the national political system, the House of Commons. However the contest between the innovative western creed and the established partisan norms and procedures of the House was short and one sided. Partisanship was not purged, nor was its grip on national political institutions weakened. As an organizing principle for the national government nonpartisanship was decisively rejected.

The Progressives established the dominant feature of prairie regional politics—the rejection of the major national parties in favour of indigenous third party vehicles of western discontent. Yet when the Progressive movement is examined closely at its electoral peak, it is clear that it encompassed far more than sectional protest emanating from western Canada. The agrarian discontent that formed the central pillar of the movement extended beyond the geographical confines of the Prairies and it was a national organization, the Canadian Council of Agriculture, that first endorsed the Progressives. The rural society at large in English Canada was concerned with the onset of industrialization, the migration of the rural population to urban sources of employment, and the consequential decline in the political and social power of the rural society. Rural depopulation in particular had become a festering sore in the Ontario countryside. In addition to agrarian discontent a number of movements for social and political reform, such as the Social Gospel, the Suffragettes and the Prohibitionists, adhered in a loose informal coalition to the Progressive party. Only the trade unionists were excluded, the Winnipeg General Strike having dashed the hopes for co-operation between farmers and the labour movement.[86] While these complementary movements were very vigorous in western Canada their activities were not restricted to the West nor were their political demands sectional in character. Thus the Progressives, while the archetype for western Canadian political revolt, embodied more than a regional protest. The Progressive movement was comprised of a core of regional protest overlaid with broader movements of agrarian and social protest which, although concentrated in western Canada, spread well beyond the geographical confines of the Prairies.

These conclusions are borne out by a close examination of the electoral record of the Progressive Party set forth in Table 2:3. While the 1921 Progressive vote was proportionately much higher on the Prairies than it

TABLE 2:3

Regional Variations in Electoral Support for the Progressive Party of Canada

Province or Region	Percentage of the Popular Vote				Number of Seats			
	1921	1925	1926	1930	1921	1925	1926	1930
Prairies	53.2	30.2	20.2	12.7	37	22	18	11
—Manitoba	43.7	27.1	11.2	4.0	12	7	4	—
—Saskatchewan	61.0	31.8	15.6	8.1	15	6	3	2
—Alberta	52.5	31.5	38.7	30.4	10	9	11	9
Atlantic provinces	11.7	—	—	—	1	—	—	—
Quebec	3.7	—	—	—	—	—	—	—
Ontario	27.7	9.2	4.1	0.9	24	2	2	1
British Columbia	9.0	6.1	—	—	2	—	—	—
Canada	22.9	8.9	5.3	2.8	64	24	20	12

was elsewhere in Canada, support in Ontario was far from negligible. Building on the earlier provincial strength of the United Farmers of Ontario who were elected to head a minority provincial government in 1919, the Progressives captured 27.7% of the 1921 popular vote and 24 seats. In absolute terms the Progressives captured more votes in Ontario than they did in all three Prairie provinces combined. Without electoral support from beyond the Prairies the Progressives' impact on Canadian politics would have been sharply reduced. The party would have won 37 rather than 64 seats, the Conservatives would have been the second largest parliamentary party, and the Liberal party would have secured its parliamentary majority, robbing the Progressives of the limited bargaining power they were able to derive from the Liberals' minority position in the 1921-1925 parliament. While the Progressive movement undoubtedly served as a vehicle for sectional discontent in western Canada, the movement in its entirety cannot be viewed in narrow sectional terms. Indeed the movement was significant because it transcended purely sectional appeals. It served the triple masters of sectional, agrarian, and social protest, all of which reached unsurpassed levels of intensity in western Canada but only the first of which was restricted to the prairie region.

For a number of reasons the Progressive movement began a rather precipitous decline shortly after the 1921 election. Unable to overcome ideological inconsistencies regarding its form and function as a political party, inconsistencies which approximately paralleled provincial boundaries, and unable to accommodate itself to existing parliamentary practice, the parliamentary party began to collapse.[87] While the Alberta Progressives under the ideological leadership of Henry Wise Wood adamantly rejected partisanship in any guise, the Manitoba wing of the movement was more interested in the reform of the party system, and of the Liberal party in particular, than in the abolition of partisanship. Differences between the Manitoba and Saskatchewan Progressives were noted by Prime Minister King in a letter to J. G. Gardiner during the latter's leadership of the provincial Liberals in Saskatchewan:

> There would appear to be this difference between the Progressives of Saskatchewan and the Progressives of Manitoba. . . . In Manitoba the Progressives have been recruited from the Liberals and are for the most part Liberals at heart. In Saskatchewan the opposite's true. There the ranks of the Progressives have been recruited from and directed by the Conservative forces.[88]

King, it must be acknowledged, was excessively prone to perceive the world in partisan terms. In any event, the Liberally-inclined Manitoba Progressives eventually gave way to the adroit courtship of the Liberal leader whose ". . . persistent pursuit of the goal of the re-integration of western and eastern Liberalism in a composite party was by no means the least of the causes of the failure of the Progressives."[89] One by one the Manitoba pillars of the Progressive movement returned to the Liberal fold. Winnipeg *Free Press* editor John W. Dafoe, who had supported the Progressives as a means of saving the Liberals from the sin of protectionism and who felt that the Progressive movement stood for the Western agrarian way of life against the growing strength of "Eastern industrialism" abandoned the cause.[90] In 1926 Crerar campaigned actively for the Liberals and after the 1926 election Progressive stalwart Robert Forke was brought into the Liberal government as Minister of Immigration.

Outside the party the conditions that had spawned the Progressive movement also gave way. The general movement of social reform, of which the Progressive movement was a part, passed away. The agrarian grievances that had precipitated the 1921 political revolt began to fade as economic prosperity returned to the plains. The Progressives' organizational base was weakened as membership levels in farm organizations began to plummet.[91] Prairie farmers turned to economic action, such as the creation of wheat pools, withdrew from political activity and as a consequence lost much of their reforming zeal.[92] Progressive candidates became harder to find; while 148 ran in 1921, the number dropped to 72 in 1925, 37 in 1926, and only 22 in 1930.[93] Finally, the western Canadian labour movement withdrew its tenuous support of the Progressive party as M. P. William Irvine so indicated in a 1925 speech to the House of Commons:

> I regret to find no bright hopes in the Progressive party so far as labour is concerned, and I abandon my hopes of it very reluctantly. Many forward-looking people today see in the Progressive party as it now is a fitting epitaph for the tomb of a lost opportunity . . . the flood of time has passed, the ebb has now set in, and the Progressive party is now gasping and wriggling like a fish left stranded on the beach before the receding tide. There I will leave them. . . .[94]

Table 2:3 shows that as electoral support fell the Progressives were forced back into a western enclave in the ideological bosom of the UFA. While the three Prairie provinces had contributed only 42.4% of the total Progressive vote in 1921, that proportion rose rapidly to 56.4% in 1925, 70.6% in 1926 and 88.3% in 1930. In 1930, the final election for the Progressives, over half of the Progressive vote came from Alberta alone, an exaggeration of the east-west gradient in Progressive support that had emerged by 1926. Thus as electoral decline set in the Progressives became more exclusively a movement of sectional protest. With the loss of Ontario support it could be little else.

In summary, the Progressive party was an important electoral manifestation of western Canadian regional discontent. Evidence for this conclusion is provided by the relatively high proportion of the popular vote received by the party in western Canada compared to any other province or region, by the dominance of western leaders and MPs, and by the centrality of western populist political thought. At the same time the Progressives were much more than a western Canadian protest party at their peak in 1921. It was the support the Progressives received outside the Prairies that made the movement so important to Canadian political history and it was the rapid dissipation of that external support that reduced the Progressives to a sectional base and political impotence.

A) The Cooperative Commonwealth Federation (CCF)

The history of the CCF, both federally and provincially, has been richly documented elsewhere. Our gaze here is restricted to the regional pattern of electoral support for the CCF and the extent to which the CCF tried to escape from, and was trapped by, political regionalism. Unfortunately the history of the CCF, unlike that of the Progressives, is not neatly encompassed by the time frame of this chapter. Although the party was formed in the 30s and had roots extending back into the radical labour and agrarian politics of the early 20s it remained on the electoral stage for two decades following the start of the Second World War. In 1944 the CCF captured the government of Saskatchewan, in 1945 the national party enjoyed its greatest electoral success (28 seats and 15.6% of the popular vote), and it was not until the 1958 Diefenbaker landslide that the national election board was all but swept clean of CCF players. Thus in the discussion to follow the chapter's time frame will be extended to encompass the life-span of the CCF.

The CCF was a child of the Depression; it took that near-total economic collapse to merge labour and farm groups into a single political organization. In 1929 western labour and socialist parties had established the Western Conference of Labour Political Parties to unify the activities of the affiliated parties. As the Depression bore down, the need for co-operation between conference members and the much larger agrarian community became compelling. The opportunity for co-operation was opened up in 1931 by the retirement of UFA president Henry Wise Wood, the principal ideological opponent of joint farm-labour political action. When the Conference met in Calgary in 1932 the participants included the UFA, the United Farmers of Canada (Saskatchewan Section), the Independent Labour Party of Manitoba, the Canadian Labour Party, the Dominion Labour Party of Alberta, the Socialist Party of Canada, the Independent and Co-operative Labour parties of Saskatchewan, and the Brotherhood of Railway Employees. The ideological catalyst for the gathering was provided by the League for Social Reconstruction, an eastern-based group of academics and intellectuals molded along the lines of the British Fabian Society. Out of the Calgary meeting and the 1933 follow-up in Regina came the Co-operative Commonwealth Federation (Farmer, Labour, Socialist), the appendage to the name reflecting an unease that many participants felt about the amalgamation of such heretofore disparate elements.

It is not uncommon to perceive the CCF as an offshoot of the Progressive movement in western Canada. However, any apparent continuity between the two must not conceal some fundamental differences that on balance outweigh the similarities. As noted above the CCF sprang forth from the fusion of labour and agrarian elements, a fusion that was not achieved within the Progressive movement and which was brought about only by the calamity of the Depression. Thus the participation of nonagrarian interests in the CCF set it sharply apart from Progressives. The change was symbolized by the selection of Woodsworth to lead the new CCF: "the election of J. S. Woodsworth as leader, commendable as it was on all counts, quickened the swing away from the sure agrarian foundations laid in the rural constituencies of Saskatchewan and Alberta towards a greater dependence on urban labour and a further increase of the influence of intellectual socialists."[95]

A more important change, and one that bears directly upon the thesis of this book, is that the CCF turned its back on sectional politics. The malady of the Depression could not be cured by changes in freight rates or the National Policy; the founders of the CCF appeared to confront a collapse of the economic order that could only be corrected through a restructuring of the national, and perhaps international, economy. Thus the sectional concerns that had energized the Progressive movement lost their priority. As Morton comments with regards to the Alberta wing of the movement, "from sectional consolidation and the role of critic in parliament, the UFA was turning to co-operation with other groups in a drive for national power, the only way in which a new economic order could be realized then and there."[96]

The CCF's rejection of sectionalism came through most clearly in the party's intellectuals and in the basic policy documents that guided the party through the early decades of its existence. The programs and philosophy of the CCF were clearly national—the social and economic ills that were addressed were seen as springing from the nature of national and international economic organization and the agrarian-sectional concerns of the Progressive era were downplayed. As the CCF stepped towards socialism it necessarily stepped away from sectionalism; thus the 1933 Regina Manifesto advocated strengthening of the national government as a means of economic planning. The provinces would be relegated to little more than administrative agencies for central programs; what the Regina Manifesto proposed was ". . . a virtual return to Macdonald's conception of what the federal union should be."[97] The Research Committee of the League for Social Reconstruction, in a 1935 publication entitled *Social Planning for Canada*, even advocated limiting regional representation in the federal cabinet. They proposed an inner cabinet in which, "obviously, the selection of the senior secretaries of state would be primarily based upon the capacity of the members of Parliament under consideration, and as little as possible upon the plan of giving representation to sections of the country."[98] As LSR members David Lewis and Frank R. Scott wrote in 1943, regional conflict per se was not the problem; it was simply "the result of the inherent contradictions of capitalism."[99]

The centralist orientation of the CCF was not restricted to the national party. Saskatchewan Premier T. C. Douglas fought any restrictions on the national government's power for fear that a future CCF government in Ottawa might be thwarted in its social reforms by provincial governments controlled by capitalist parties.[100] In general, then, an earnest attempt was made to construct a party platform and ideology that would transcend the narrow bounds of regionalism and provide a national perspective on national problems. Indeed the socialistic base of the CCF precluded any attempt to build a party based upon sectional rather than class, and thereby national, appeals. The attempt to transcend regionalism, however, failed at the polls. The party was a non-starter in Quebec and managed no more than an insecure toe-hold within the Atlantic electorate. In Ontario, where the fate of political parties with national pretensions is won or lost, the CCF also fared poorly. As Figure 2:3 illustrates the CCF received a much lower percentage of the popular vote in Ontario than it did across the Prairie provinces, even given the CCF's chronic weakness in Alberta. Only with the formation of the NDP in 1960 did the pattern change. Of the 112 CCF M.P.'s elected from 1935 to 1958, 71 came from the Prairies; 52 came from Saskatchewan alone compared with only eight from Ontario, four from the Atlantic provinces, and 29 from British Columbia. Thus, although the CCF was not conceived as a regional party it rapidly became one anyway. The Prairies provided by far the greatest proportion of seats and in men like J. S. Woodsworth, M. S. Coldwell, and Stanley Knowles provided the core of the CCF national leadership. The stamp of the West was indelible, from the characteristics of the party's leaders to the titles of its guiding documents—the *Regina Manifesto* and the *Winnipeg Declaration*.

In summary, it can be argued that the CCF represented another chapter in western Canadian regional politics. There are, however, a number of caveats that should be kept in mind. The first is that the CCF strove constantly, even if unsuccessfully, to escape its regional chains; it was regionalized more by accident than by design. Secondly, any characterization of the CCF as a manifestation of western Canadian regional politics runs into the problem that the party was notably unsuccessful in Alberta. There the radical alternative to the existing major parties had been pre-empted by the Social Credit party before the CCF was able to launch an independent campaign and the CCF was never able to sustain any serious electoral challenge in Alberta, federally or provincially. Finally it should be noted that in the 1949, 1957 and 1958 national

FIGURE 2:3 **Percentage of the Popular Vote Won by the C.C.F./N.D.P. in Federal Elections**

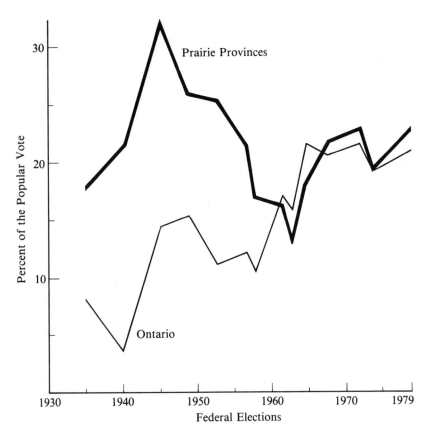

elections the CCF won more votes in Ontario than it did across the three Prairie provincies combined although the proportion of the vote going to the CCF was considerably higher on the Prairies than in Ontario. The Ontario votes, however, did not yield CCF MPs as once again the Canadian electoral system exaggerated regional effects in the translation of votes into seats in the House of Commons.

The National Social Credit Party

In 1935 the Alberta Social Credit party under the evangelistic leadership of William "Bible-Bill" Aberhart swept into provincial office where it was to remain for the next 36 years. Here our concern lies with the national wing of the party which, on the heels of the Alberta victory, captured 15 of the 17 Alberta seats in the 1935 federal election. The separation of the Alberta and national Social Credit organizations, however, should be treated cautiously as up until the early 50s the national party was no more than a pale offshoot of the provincial party and of the Alberta Socred government. Without the sustenance provided by the provincial party and government the national party would not have existed. Furthermore the national Social Credit party, like the CCF, does not fit neatly into the chronological format of this or the following chapter. Although it arose prior to the Second World War the bulk of its electoral history follows the war. At the same time the Social Credit party does not belong to the modern era of prairie politics, the national party being all but destroyed by the Diefenbaker Conservatives in 1958. Because of this the national Social Credit party will be addressed here within the context of pre-World War Two prairie politics.

In the 1935 federal election the seventeen Alberta Social Credit candidates, who have been described as a "covey of doctrinaire nonentites,"[101] captured 47% of the popular vote and 15 seats. Thus, within the same year the Social Credit party established what was to be a long-term stranglehold on both provincial and national politics in Alberta. Although the Socred grip on national politics was slightly looser than in the provincial field, it was nevertheless impressive; between 1935 and 1957 inclusive the party averaged over 39% of the Alberta popular vote in national elections and 71% of the province's federal seats. During this period the Alberta Social Crediters essentially were the national party. Sustained financially and psychologically by its provincial counterpart in Edmonton, the Alberta wing contributed over 86% of the party's national seats (see Table 2:4). As Figure 2:4 illustrates, the great bulk of the Socred national vote in that time period came from the prairie region and, within the region, from Alberta. Success elsewhere on the Prairies was primarily limited to the western border areas of Saskatchewan where the Social Credit party was quite active in its early years. For example, in the 1935 election all but eight of the non-Alberta Social Credit candidates ran in Saskatchewan, where two were elected. In that election the CCF ran ahead of Social Credit in Saskatchewan by only 4% of the popular vote and one of the CCF candidates elected, T. C. Douglas from Weyburn, ran with the endorsement of the Social Credit party.[102] Outside the Prairies the party enjoyed a brief surge of support from Quebec in 1945. Quebec contributed 63,130 Social Credit votes (4.5% of the provincial popular vote) compared to 113,821 Social Credit votes in Alberta, but the Quebec votes failed to elect any members. More importantly, the British Columbia electorate began making a substantial contribution to the Social Credit vote and seat total after the 1953 provincial victory of the Socreds under the leadership of W.A.C. Bennett. British Columbia sent four Socred MPs to Ottawa in 1953 and six in 1957.

Given the concentration of early Social Credit electoral support within

FIGURE 2:4 **Alberta and Prairie Contribution to the Total Social Credit* Federal Popular Vote**

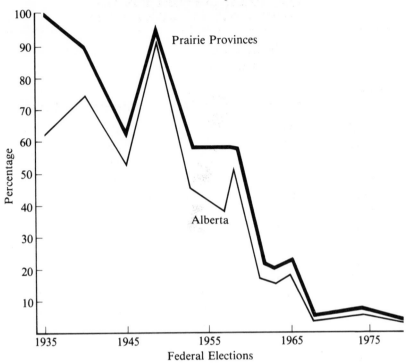

* Including the popular vote for Le Ralliement Des Creditistes

the West and more specifically within Alberta, it might be concluded that Social Credit contributed an important piece to the mosaic of prairie regional politics. Yet there are some serious wrinkles to this conclusion, the first being that electoral support for the national Social Credit party was not regional in scope. Figure 2:4 illustrates the very substantial degree to which Socred electoral support was concentrated in Alberta alone. Secondly there is some debate as to the role played by regional discontent in the emergence of Social Credit. J. R. Mallory argues that the 1935 Social Credit government symbolized a rejection of the National Policy and of the subordinate role of the West.[103] However, the role of regional discontent has been downplayed by others. John Irving, for example, paid little attention to hostility towards central Canada in the events leading up to 1935 and focuses instead on psychological needs arising from the Alberta depression environment—the desire for social context and social meaning, and the satisfaction of basic human needs.[104] In Irving's analysis the contrast is sharp between the social disintegration of the early 30s in Alberta and the more optimistic and bountiful era that spawned the UFA and the Progressives; the contrast leaves little question

TABLE 2:4

**ELECTORAL SUPPORT FOR THE
NATIONAL SOCIAL CREDIT PARTY***

Election Year	Percentage of Popular Vote		Number of Seats	
	Alberta	Canada	Alberta	Canada
1935	46.6	4.1	15	17
1940	34.5	2.7	10	10
1945	36.6	4.1	13	13
1949	37.4	2.3	10	10
1953	40.8	5.4	11	15
1957	37.8	6.6	13	19
1958	21.6	2.6	—	—
1962	29.2	11.7	2	30
1963	25.8	11.9	2	24
1965	22.5	8.3	2	14
1968	1.9	5.2	—	14
1972	4.5	7.6	—	15
1974	3.3	5.1	—	11
1979	1.0	4.6	—	6

* Including Le Ralliement Des Creditistes

as to the relative primacy of regional discontent in the earlier period. To take another example, Harry Hiller has argued that third parties such as the Alberta Social Credit emerge as means to resolve critical problems *within* the regional society, that ". . . the third party could be more preferably viewed as a creative indigenous response to internal social pressures than as a reactionary protest movement to external forces."[105] As the Social Credit movement matured, the role played by regional discontent in sustaining the movement may have declined further. Mallory notes that by the end of 1945 no fundamental conflict remained between the Social Crediters and the eastern financial interests[106] and Young asserts that "by 1952 Social Credit in the West was no longer a vehicle of protest—it was an engine for the protection of the status quo."[107]

In the 1958 and 1962 national elections two important changes took place in the pattern of support for the Social Credit party. In the first election the Diefenbaker Conservatives dealt a knockout blow to the national party in Alberta. Although as Table 2:4 shows the party experienced a very modest resurgence after 1958, its fate within the province had been sealed; Diefenbaker delivered the province to the Conservative camp and there it has stayed. Then in 1962 a new form of Social Credit emerged in Quebec under the leadership of Réal Caouette. As Figure 2:4 demonstrates the 1962 election marked the transfer of the Social Credit phenomenon from Alberta to Quebec, a transfer that was confirmed shortly afterwards when the leadership of the party passed from Westerner Robert Thompson to Caouette. In Alberta the national Social Credit was dead; in Quebec a small but tenacious Social Credit movement survived to elect six MPs in 1979.

To conclude, the Social Credit party in both its Alberta and national guises helped mark off the Prairies as a politically distinct region in Canada. Admittedly there were many factors apart from regional discontent that lay behind the rise of Social Credit, and admittedly the prairie electoral support for Social Credit outside Alberta was weak. Nevertheless Social Credit had a tone and style that embodied many of the enduring features of western Canadian political protest. Also, Albertans' support for the Social Credit further isolated an important sector of the prairie population from the national government and thus in turn enhanced western alienation within the province. With the Conservative victory in 1958, however, this aspect of regional politics was wiped from the prairie slate as far as national politics was concerned.

CONCLUSIONS

During the early decades of this century the Prairies stood apart from the rest of Canada in more than geography and weather. Western Canada formed a relatively distinct and homogeneous socio-economic region within Canada. In terms of ethnic composition, religious affiliation, nativity, rural lifestyle and, most importantly, economic activity, the West was clearly distinct from the rest of Canada. Moreover, the grain economy knit the West together into a relatively homogeneous regional unit by generating a common set of activities, concerns, institutions, grievances and frustrations. The grain economy both integrated the region and set it apart from, and frequently in opposition to, the rest of Canada.

Socio-economic regionalism in the West, accompanied by a regionally-specific set of agrarian grievances and demands, inevitably produced a regional political response. Starting in 1921 western Canadians rejected the Liberal and Conservative parties to a degree unexperienced elsewhere in Canada. In their place indigenous western Canadian parties were created. Although some of these parties secured considerable support outside the Prairie provinces it was on the Prairies that their support was by far the strongest, and it was this support that set the West apart from the mainstream of Canadian national politics. The West became a

CAMROSE LUTHERAN COLLEGE
LIBRARY

political region unto itself and this, coupled with weakness in the House of Commons that came with a relatively small population, served to isolate the West, to prolong the solution of western grievances, and to foster the attitudinal component of political regionalism, western alienation.

The regional economic and political homogeneity that prevailed in the West has been nicely captured by David Smith:

> Across this expanse a one-crop economy predominates, and politicians court peril if they ignore the dictum of John Diefenbaker: "There's only one thing to talk about . . . There's only one thing to say here . . . . Wheat.[108]

Diefenbaker's dictum, however, reflected the historical prairie past much more than it did the contemporary West. By the time of Diefenbaker's electoral triumphs the West was already in the throes of fundamental socio-economic and political change. In fact, many of the changes that were to remake the prairie society in the post-war years were already underway before the Second World War broke out. In the turbulence of Depression-era prairie politics the outlines of new political patterns were emerging:

> The rise of the Social Credit movement and of the Co-operative Commonwealth Federation marked the beginning of a new phase of Canadian political development, a phase of class rather than sectional politics, of urban rather than rural dominance. The period 1910 to 1935 was one of transition in Canada from an agrarian to an industrialized society; with the Progressive movement passed the Canadian, and North American, agricultural frontier. Social Credit and the CCF were the successors of the Progressive movement rather than continuations of it.[109]

Thus even in two of western Canada's most distinctive contributions to Canadian politics the ebbing tide of political regionalism could be detected.

NOTES

1. Vernon C. Fowke, *Canadian Agricultural Policy: The Historical Pattern*, Toronto, University of Toronto Press, 1947, p. 177.

2. The phrase "the last, best west" was used in immigration promotional materials of the period. For a vivid pictorial history of this era see Jean Bruce, *The Last Best West*, Toronto, Fitzhenry & Whiteside, 1976.

3. David E. Smith, "Western Politics and National Unity," in David Jay Bercuson, ed., *Canada and the Burden of Unity*, Toronto, Macmillan, 1977, p. 144.

4. Cited *Ibid.*, p. 144.

5. W. L. Morton, *Manitoba: A History*, Second Edition, Toronto, University of Toronto Press, 1967, p. 163.

AUGUSTANA UNIVERSITY COLLEGE
LIBRARY

6. J. H. Richards, "Retrospect and Prospect," in P. J. Smith, ed., *Studies in Canadian Geography: The Prairie Provinces*, Toronto, University of Toronto Press, 1972, p. 123.

7. Morton, *Manitoba*, p. 254.

8. Prior to 1870 French Canadians formed a majority of the non-native population in Western Canada. B. Y. Card, *The Canadian Prairie Provinces from 1870 to 1950: A Sociological Introduction*, Toronto, J. M. Dent & Sons, 1960, p. 8.

9. W. L. Morton, "A Century of Plain and Parkland," in Richard Allen, Ed., *A Region of the Mind*, Regina, Canadian Plains Studies Centre, University of Saskatchewan, 1973, p. 172.

10. The census statistics on ethnic composition are subject to some serious sources of error and thus the figures presented in Table 2:1 should be treated as approximate only. See Carle C. Zimmerman and Garry W. Moneo, *The Prairie Community System*, Ottawa, Agricultural Economics, The Research Council of Canada, 1971, p. 17, and John Erd Thompson, *The Harvests of War: The Prairie West, 1914-1918*, Toronto, McClelland and Stewart, 1978, pp. 76-7.

11. For example see Walter Young, *Democracy and Discontent*, Toronto, McGraw-Hill, 1969, p. 5, and *The Anatomy of a Party: The National CCF, 1932-61*, Toronto, University of Toronto Press, 1969, pp. 15-16.

12. This argument is also addressed by Robert J. Brym, "Explaining Regional Variations in Canadian Populist Movements," Paper presented to the Annual Meeting of the Canadian Sociology and Anthropology Association, Fredericton, New Brunswick, June 1977, p. 2.

13. *1931 Census of Canada*, Vol. IV, Table 4.

14. M. C. Urquhart and K. A. H. Buckley, eds., *Historical Statistics of Canada*, Toronto, Macmillan, 1965, p. 29.

15. James A. Jackson, *The Centennial History of Manitoba*, Toronto, McClelland and Stewart, 1970, p. 157.

16. *1931 Census of Canada*, Vol. IV, Table 4. In 1921, when the Progressive Party burst forth in western Canada, the proportion of Americans was even higher. In that year 87,000 of the 757,000 Saskatchewan residents had been born in the United States (11.5%), as had approximately 100,000 of the 588,000 Alberta residents (17.0%). Andrew N. Jackson, "Patterns of Hinterland Revolt: Alberta and Saskatchewan in the Inter War Period," Paper presented at the Annual Meeting of the Canadian Political Science Association, Fredericton, New Brunswick, June 1977, p. 15.

17. Harry H. Hiller, "Internal Problem Resolution and Third Party Emergence," *Canadian Journal of Sociology*, 2(1), 1977, p. 67.

18. Cited in David E. Smith, *Prairie Liberalism: The Liberal Party in Saskatchewan, 1905-1971*, Toronto: University of Toronto Press, 1975, pp. 327-328.

19. A. Ross McCormack, *Reformers, Rebels, and Revolutionaries: The Western Canadian Radical Movement 1899-1919*, Toronto, University of Toronto Press, 1977; David J. Bercuson, *Fools and Wisemen: The Rise and Fall of the One Big Union*, Toronto, McGraw-Hill Ryerson, 1978; and

Bercuson, *Confrontation at Winnipeg*, Montreal, McGill-Queen's University Press, 1974.

20. McCormack, *Reformers, Rebels and Revolutionaries*, p. 15.

21. *Ibid.*, p. 67.

22. S. M. Lipset, *Agrarian Socialism*, Berkeley, University of California Press, 1971, p. 43.

23. McCormack, *Reformers, Rebels, and Revolutionaries*, p. 5.

24. *Ibid.*, pp. 9-11.

25. J. E. Rae, "The Roots of Prairie Society," in David P. Gagan, ed., *Prairie Perspectives*, Toronto, Holt, Rinehart and Winston, 1970, p. 51.

26. C. H. Douglas, *Alberta Experiment*, London, Eyre & Spottiswoode, 1937, p. 4.

27. McCormack, *Reformers, Rebels, and Revolutionaries*, p. 35.

28. *Ibid.*, pp. 17, 67.

29. *Ibid.*, p. 74.

30. Cited in Jean Bruce, *The Last Best West*, Toronto, Fitzhenry and Whiteside, 1976, p. 14.

31. See H. Blair Neatby, *Laurier and a Liberal Quebec*, Toronto, McClelland and Stewart, 1973, Chapters 5 and 6.

32. See Richard Allen, *The Social Passion*, Toronto, University of Toronto Press, 1973 and "The Social Gospel and the Reform Tradition of Canada, 1890-1928," in Samuel D. Clark, J. Paul Grayson and Linda M. Grayson, eds., *Prophecy and Protest*, Toronto, Gage, 1975, pp. 45-61.

33. J. H. Thompson, " 'The Beginning of our Regeneration': The Great War and Western Canadian Reform Movements," in *Ibid.*, pp. 87-104.

34. Smith, *Prairie Liberalism*, Chapter Five.

35. See William E. Mann, *Sect, Cult and Church in Alberta*, Toronto, University of Toronto Press, 1955.

36. Allen, *The Social Gospel*, Chapter One.

37. Mann, *Sect, Cult and Church in Alberta*, p. 156.

38. J. R. Mallory, *Social Credit and the Federal Power In Canada*, Toronto, University of Toronto Press, 1953, p. 39.

39. Vernon C. Fowke, *The National Policy and the Wheat Economy*, Toronto, University of Toronto Press, 1957, p. 282. With reference to Fowke, Smith notes that "on the Prairies, more than in any other part of Canada, the economy defines the region. . . ." David E. Smith, "The Prairie Provinces," in David J. Bellamy, Jon H. Pammett, and Donald C. Rowat, eds., *The Provincial Political Systems: Comparative Essays*, Toronto, Methuen, 1976, p. 47.

40. Thompson, *The Harvests of War*, p. 60.

41. G. E. Britnell, *The Wheat Economy*, Toronto, University of Toronto Press, 1939, pp. 59-60.

42. W. A. MacKintosh, *Economic Problems of the Prairies*, Toronto, Macmillan, 1935, p. 25.

43. *Ibid.*, p. 21.

44. C. F. Kraenzel, *The Great Plains in Transition*, Norman, University of Oklahoma Press, 1955, p. 7.

45. Mody G. Boatright, "The Myth of Frontier Individualism," in R. Hofstadter and S. M. Lipset, eds., *Turner and the Sociology of the Frontier*, New York, Basic Books, 1968, p. 62.

46. John W. Bennett and Seena B. Kohl, "Characterological, Strategic, and Institutional Interpretations of Prairie Settlement," in A. W. Rasporich, ed., *Western Canada Past and Present*, Calgary, McClelland and Stewart West, 1975, p. 25.

47. Robert W. Crown and Earl O. Hardy, *Policy Integration in Canadian Agriculture*, Ames, Iowa, Iowa State University Press, 1972, p. 7.

48. *Ibid.*, p. 10.

49. *Ibid.*, p. 14.

50. Barbara J. Genno and Larry M. Genno, *Food Production in the Canadian Environment*, Science Council of Canada, 1976, pp. 8-9.

51. Smith, *Prairie Liberalism*, p. 14.

52. W. L. Morton, *The Progressive Party in Canada*, Toronto, University of Toronto Press, 1950, p. 36.

53. William Phelan, "Radical Politics and Western Alienation," Unpublished M.A. Thesis, University of Calgary, 1976, p. 25.

54. W. T. Easterbrook and Hugh G. J. Aitken, *Canadian Economic History*, Toronto, Macmillan, 1967, p. 476.

55. *Ibid.*, p. 492.

56. The Progressive Conservative party adopted the "Progressive" label in 1942; prior to that time it was known simply as the Conservative Party of Canada.

57. Morton, "A Century of Plain and Parkland," p. 167.

58. See John Tupper Saywell, "Liberal Politics, Federal Policies, and the Lieutenant-Governor: Saskatchewan and Alberta, 1905," in Donald Swainson, ed., *Historical Essays on the Prairie Provinces*, Toronto, McClelland & Stewart, 1970, pp. 179-190.

59. David E. Smith, "Western Politics and National Unity," in David Jay Bercuson, ed., *Canada and the Burden of Unity*, Toronto, Macmillan, 1977, p. 151.

60. Quoted in Morton, *Manitoba*, p. 211.

61. Brian R. McCutcheon, "The Birth of Agrarianism in the Prairie West," *Prairie Forum*, 1(2), November 1976, p. 91.

62. Fowke, *Canadian Agricultural Policy*, p. 244.

63. Easterbrook and Aitken, *Canadian Economic History*, p. 504.

64. The expression comes from Card, *The Canadian Prairie Provinces*, p. 6.

65. Mallory, *Social Credit and the Federal Power*, p. 169.

66. Thompson, "The Beginning of our Regeneration," pp. 87-104.

67. As Thompson comments, "the defeat of reciprocity in 1911 had demonstrated to Westerners that their interests were in some ways irreconcilable with those of central Canada. . . ." *The Harvests of War*, p. 14.

68. *Ibid.*, p. 71.

69. *Ibid.*, p. 51.

70. *Ibid.*, p. 55.

71. *Ibid.*, p. 170.

72. *Ibid.*, p. 28.

73. McCormack, *Reformers, Rebels, and Revolutionaries*, p. 125.

74. See John English, *The Decline of Politics: The Conservatives and the Party System 1901-20*, Toronto, University of Toronto Press, 1977, Chapter Six.

75. Cited in Thompson, *The Harvests of War*, p. 131.

76. Louis Aubrey Wood, *A History of the Farmers' Movements in Canada*, Toronto, University of Toronto Press, 1975, p. 353.

77. Smith, *Prairie Liberalism*, p. 75.

78. Paul F. Sharp, *The Agrarian Revolt in Western Canada*, Minneapolis, University of Minnesota Press, 1948, p. 128.

79. Rae, "The Roots of Prairie Society," p. 47.

80. Jackson, *The Centennial History of Manitoba*, p. 174.

81. Mallory, *Social Credit and the Federal Power*, p. 5.

82. Dale C. Thomson, "The Prairie Provinces and the Canadian Federation," in David Elton, ed., *One Prairie Province?*, Lethbridge Herald, 1970, p. 51.

83. Wood, *A History of the Farmers' Movements*, p. 346.

84. Sharp, *The Agrarian Revolt*, pp. 136-7.

85. C. Cecil Lingard, *Territorial Government in Canada: The Autonomy Question in the Old North-West Territories*, Toronto, University of Toronto Press, 1946, p. 123.

86. Sharp, *The Agrarian Revolt*, p. 141.

87. See Morton, *The Progressive Party*, Chapters Five and Six.

88. Smith, *Prairie Liberalism*, p. 181.

89. Morton, *The Progressive Party*, pp. 270-1.

90. Ramsay Cook, *The Politics of John W. Dafoe and the Free Press*, Toronto, University of Toronto Press, 1963, pp. 286-7.

91. Morton, *The Progressive Party*, pp. 211-212.

92. Wood, *A History of the Farmers' Movements*, p. xxi.

93. J. M. Beck, *Pendulum of Power*, Scarborough, Prentice-Hall, 1968, pp. 160, 174, 188 and 202.

94. Cited in Reginald Whitaker's Introduction to William Irvine, *The Farmers in Politics*, Toronto, McClelland and Stewart, 1970, p. xxv.

95. Morton, *The Progressive Party*, p. 283.

96. *Ibid.*, p. 280.

97. Edwin R. Black, *Divided Loyalties: Canadian Concepts of Federalism*, Montreal, McGill-Queen's University Press, 1975, p. 48.

98. Cited *Ibid.*, p. 49.

99. David Lewis and Frank R. Scott, *Make This Your Canada*, Toronto, 1943, p. 104.

100. Black, *Divided Loyalties*, p. 53.

101. James H. Gray, *The Winter Years: The Depression on the Prairies*, Toronto, Macmillan, 1966, p. 207.

102. Smith, *Prairie Liberalism*, pp. 225-27.

103. Mallory, *Social Credit and the Federal Power*, p. 57.

104. John A. Irving, *The Social Credit Movement in Alberta*, Toronto, University of Toronto Press, 1959.

105. Hiller, "Internal Problem Resolution and Third Party Emergence," pp. 55-6.

106. Mallory, *Social Credit and the Federal Power*, p. 162.

107. Young, *Democracy and Discontent*, p. 105.

108. Smith, "The Prairie Provinces," p. 46.

109. Morton, *The Progressive Party*, p. 287.

CHAPTER THREE

REGIONALISM IN DECLINE: 1940 TO THE PRESENT

Since the Second World War the character of the prairie society has been dramatically transformed. While the contemporary prairie society has deeply embedded roots in the agrarian frontier of the past the resemblances between the two are becoming fewer and fewer. Moreover, the tide of social change has eroded the social and economic homogeneity of the past and in so doing has eroded the regional distinctiveness of the Prairies. As R. M. Burns has stated, the concept of a homogeneous prairie region is more ". . . a heritage of the past than a statement of the present."[1]

The change in the prairie society is analogous in degree to the process of metamorphosis; although the butterfly develops directly from the caterpillar larva the change is of such magnitude that the two seem of different species. The direction of change has moved the prairie society closer and closer to the English-Canadian norm so that in a social and economic sense the Prairie provinces have been losing both their regional distinctiveness and, to a lesser extent, their intra-regional homogeneity. As the regionally-distinctive social and economic underpinnings of political behavior have disintegrated, the political regionalism that characterized prairie politics in the past has also waned. This can be demonstrated through an examination of post-war federal electoral behavior on the Prairies.

PILLARS OF REGIONALISM

A) Population Change

The 1931 census marked the peak of the Prairies' share of the national population. As Figure 3:1 illustrates the percentage of the Canadian population residing on the Prairies has fallen steadily since the onset of the Depression all but ended immigration to the Canadian west. In absolute terms the prairie population continued to inch upwards during the

FIGURE 3:1 **Percentage of the National Population Residing in Ontario and the Prairies**

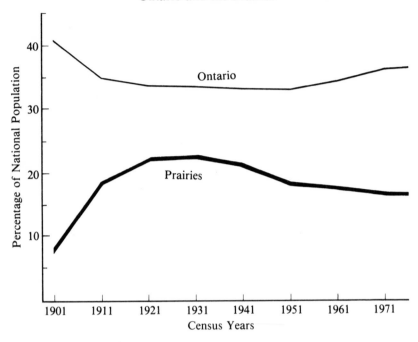

30s and 40s, as Figure 3:2 shows, but growth was largely restricted to the province of Alberta. Even there the growth rate was less than what the natural population increase alone should have produced. From 1931 to 1941 the region experienced a net migration loss of 248,000 people; from 1941 to 1951 the net loss was 268,000 before a modest net gain of 45,000 was achieved during the 50s.[2] The outflow was particularly severe in Saskatchewan where the net emmigration was 158,000 between 1931 and 1941, 199,000 between 1941 and 1951, and 79,000 between 1951 and 1961. The initial onslaught of the Depression, coupled with a process of rural depopulation that has continued unabated through the 1970s, cut Saskatchewan's share of the total prairie population from 39.2% in 1931 to only 24.4% in 1976.

Population growth in the Prairies has been largely confined to Alberta. There the debilitating impact of the Depression was less evident; Alberta's population actually increased by 8.8% in the decade between 1931 and 1941 and then increased again by 18.0% between 1941 and 1951. Since 1951 Alberta's oil-rich economy has fired a rate of population growth that has been rapid relative to Canada as a whole (with only British Columbia experiencing more rapid growth) and even more rapid relative to the other Prairie provinces. From 1951 to 1961 Alberta's population increased by 41.8%; in the same period Canada's population

FIGURE 3:2 **Growth of the Prairie Population 1901-1976**

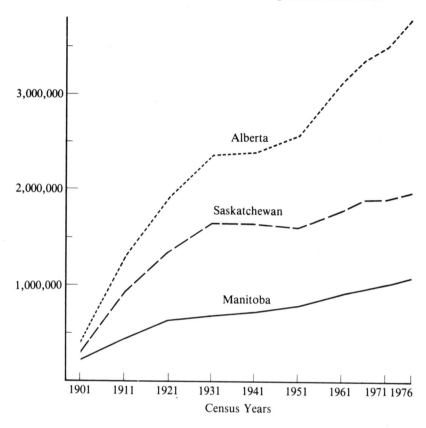

increased by 30.2% while the populations of Manitoba and Saskatchewan increased by only 18.7% and 11.2% respectively. From 1961 to 1976 Alberta's population increased by 38.0% compared to an increase of 26.1% for Canada as a whole. By 1976 Albertans made up 48.6% of the prairie population compared to 31% in 1931. By the end of the 1970s one out of two prairie residents lived in Alberta.

To summarize briefly, the population picture on the Canadian prairies has changed substantially during this century. The early decades were marked by explosive population growth; as Figure 3:1 shows, there was a dramatic westward shift in the distribution of the Canadian population. However, since 1931 the proportion of the Canadian population residing on the Prairies has declined steadily and the gap between the prairie and Ontario populations has progressively widened. Within the prairie region the bulk of growth is occurring within a single province, Alberta. These demographic shifts are charged with political implications, two of which must be touched upon here. The first is that today the prairie population packs less electoral punch in national politics than it did during the peak

years of political radicalism. In 1935 22.4% of the federal seats came
from the Prairie provinces; by 1979 that proportion had shrunk to
17.4%. If the population gap between Ontario and the Prairies continues
to widen, and as the Canadian electoral system imperfectly translates
population shifts into political power through representation in the
House of Commons, the political imbalance between the Prairies and
Ontario will continue to grow. The second implication is that the electoral power of Alberta within the prairie region will slowly eclipse that of
the other two provinces. In 1979 Alberta had 21 seats while Saskatchewan and Manitoba had 14 each. This enhanced electoral power,
coupled with Alberta's economic pre-eminence, will further unbalance
the political character of the prairie region.

B) Urban-Rural Redistribution

The shift in the bulk of the prairie population from first Manitoba and
then Saskatchewan to Alberta is not the only demographic change that
has occurred. An even more dramatic shift has occurred with the urbanization of the prairie population. As Figure 3:3 illustrates the Prairie
provinces, along with Ontario and Canada, underwent rapid urbanization following the Second World War.[3] Given Ontario's lead going into
the war urbanization across the Prairies still falls well short of that in Ontario; in 1971 the Prairies approximated the Ontario situation in 1941.
Nevertheless the distinction between Ontario and the Prairies with
respect to urbanization is being steadily eroded. By 1971 over 67% of the
prairie population was classified as urban. In the next few decades the
rate of urbanization in Ontario can only slacken as the proportion of the
population living in urban areas edges closer to 100%. On the Prairies
the limit to urbanization has yet to be approached. As a consequence the
next few decades should witness a continued erosion of the gap between
Ontario and western Canada.

At present the degree of urbanization is far from uniform across the
three Prairie provinces. The 1971 census classified 73.5% of the Alberta
population as urban, with 55% of the provincial population living in Edmonton and Calgary alone. In Manitoba 69.5% of the 1971 population
was classified as urban while in Saskatchewan the proportion was only
53.0%, 1971 marking the first census in which urban dwellers formed a
majority. Considerable intra-regional variation in the degree of urbanization thus exists although all three provinces have been undergoing
roughly similar rates of urbanization. Between 1961 and 1971 the proportion of the provincial population that was urban increased by 10.2%
in Alberta, 10.0% in Saskatchewan, and 5.6% in Manitoba.

To a considerable extent the prairie population is being not only urbanized but 'metropolitanized'. Winnipeg, the slowest-growing major

FIGURE 3:3 **Percentage of the Population Living in Urban Areas**

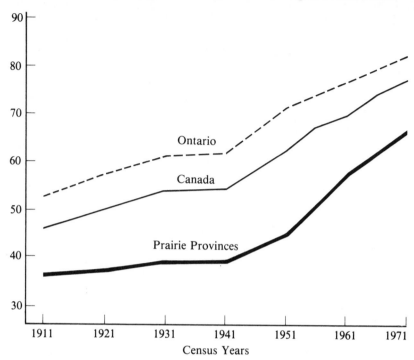

Census Years

centre on the Prairies, contained 54.7% of Manitoba's population in 1971 compared to 46.0% two decades earlier. Regina and Saskatoon have increased their joint share of the Saskatchewan population from 15.4% in 1951 to 28.8% in 1971. In Alberta, Calgary and Edmonton together claimed 55.3% of the 1971 provincial population, a substantial increase from 35.7% in 1951. Calgary, Edmonton, and Winnipeg, it should be stressed, are not only metropolitan centres relative to the surrounding countryside; they are also metropolitan relative to the nation as a whole. The three are the fourth, fifth and sixth largest cities in Canada with their relative rankings being a matter of hot dispute among the competing Chambers of Commerce.

Not surprisingly there is considerable competition among the metropolitan centres for regional dominance, as evidenced particularly by the competition for regional head offices. In the past Winnipeg was the metropolis to the prairie hinterland, the gateway to, and the financial and service centre of, western Canada. Today economic power is shifting further westward. Modern air transportation and telecommunications links between Alberta and central Canada have removed much of the traffic from the Winnipeg gateway. With the development of the oil industry in Alberta the regional financial and head office hegemony of

Winnipeg is being strongly challenged by Edmonton and, in particular, by Calgary. The latter city is now claimed by local residents to be "the financial centre of western Canada," a claim that reflects more than civic pride. In June 1979 the Bank of Montreal announced that it was moving its Chairman of the Board to Calgary and would consolidate its operations in a new office tower, the building to be the tallest structure between Toronto and Hong Kong. The symbolic importance of this move, given the role that financial dependency upon eastern financial operations has traditionally played in western alienation, is difficult to exaggerate.

In bringing this discussion to a close it should be noted that the farm population on the Prairies—the bedrock of the earlier agrarian society—has declined in absolute as well as relative terms. Table 3:1 shows that the decline in the prairie, Ontario, and Canadian farm populations has been almost precipitous. The prairie farm population declined from 50.4% of the regional population in 1931 to only 16.9% in 1971, during which period the actual number of farm residents fell by 587,000. The absolute decline has made it very difficult for rural communities to sustain many of the basic services offered in the past. The decline in population coupled with the increased ease of travel into urban areas has crippled the viability of many local schools, stores, services, and recreational facilities.

As most prairie residents adopt an urban lifestyle little different from that experienced by the residents of Toronto, Vancouver or Hamilton, the West is rapidly losing its regionally distinctive rural character. As a consequence the likelihood of a regionally distinctive political culture being maintained is diminished. As George F. C. Stanley writes:

> It may be argued . . . that the Western scene is changing: that an urban population is taking over from the rural . . . and second—that *an urban population is not exposed to the full impact of the prairie environment.* This, of course, is true . . . In time, the osmotic action that carried the spirit of independence from the countryside to the urban communities may cease and *we will become as the others are.* (emphasis added).[4]

In short, the experiential conditions for a regionally-distinctive political subculture are being eroded by the process of urbanization.[5]

C) Ethnic Composition

While earlier in this century the Canadian West had been a land rich with opportunity and optimism, conditions had changed drastically by the end of the Second World War. Open land was by then scarce, expensive, and generally located in the less hospitable north. The opening of a new farm or the acquisition of an existing one required a large capital in-

TABLE 3:1

Farm Population of Canada, Ontario and the Prairies

Farm Population

Census Year	Canada	Ontario	Prairies
1931	3,223,400	785,600	1,186,600
1941	3,116,900	694,700	1,142,700
1951	2,827,700	678,000	952,700
1956	2,631,600	632,200	890,000
1961	2,072,800	505,700	762,000
1966	1,913,700	481,700	717,100
1971	1,419,800	363,600	599,800

Source: *1971 Census of Canada*, Vol. V—Part 1 (Bulletin 5.1-2), p. 18.

vestment that was beyond the means of most immigrants and indeed most Canadians. The manpower needs of prairie agriculture were being trimmed by extensive mechanization with the consequence that there were insufficient jobs to sustain the existing rural population much less attract immigrants. Moreover as industrial employment opportunities were scarce in the West, employment prospects outside the agricultural sector were little better than within. Finally, years of depression and drought had stripped the prairie residents of their earlier confidence and optimism. Many pre-depression immigrants abandoned the economic collapse that gripped the Prairies and moved on; others were deported as Canadian governments sought to reduce the costs of relief payments.[6] Small wonder that new immigrants looked askance at the prospect of starting a new life in the West.

It was Ontario that became the magnet for post-war immigration to Canada. Of the new immigrants arriving in Canada between 1941 and 1951, 50% named Ontario as their intended destination compared to 17% naming the Prairies.[7] The prairie proportions fell to 13.5% in the 50s and 10% in the early 60s with the Ontario proportion holding at 53% throughout the period. At the time of the 1961 census more than 55% of all post-war immigrants lived in Ontario while only 14% lived on the Prairies. Ontario offered an urban environment and industrial employment opportunities which better suited the skills, talents and inclinations of post-war immigrants than did agricultural pursuits on the Prairies.

The fact that post-war immigration largely bypassed the Prairie provinces has had some important consequences. The first is that the prairie population, while built upon an immigrant base, is now largely native-born. As Figure 3:4 illustrates the native-born component of the

FIGURE 3:4 **Percentage of the Population Born in Canada**

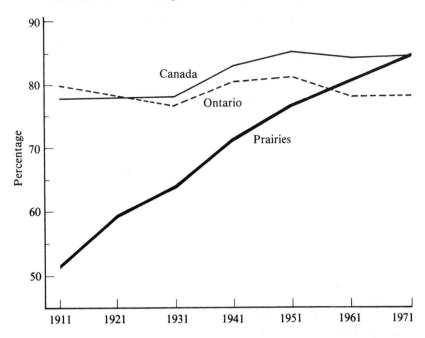

prairie population was by 1961 proportionately larger than in the province of Ontario; by 1971 it had reached the overall Canadian average and had surpassed the Ontario proportion by nearly 8%. The upshot of this change in immigration patterns is that today the prairie population is one of the most indigenous in Canada. Therefore one might speculate that the contemporary prairie population is less open to the allure of radical politics than was the prairie population of the past. At present there is no sizeable immigrant population which, lacking in traditional attachments to Canadian political institutions and actors, can be mobilized behind radical alternatives. To the extent that the immigrant character of the prairie population facilitated radicalism in the past and thereby helped produce a regionally distinctive style of political behavior, that support for regional distinctiveness has been erased from the contemporary political landscape of the Canadian prairies.

The second consequence of the shift in immigration patterns is that the ethnic composition of the Prairies remained crystallized as it had been with the onset of the Depression while that of Ontario continued to be molded by sustained immigration. Table 3:2 compares the 1971 ethnic composition of the prairie region to that of Ontario and to that of Canada as a whole (see Table 2:1 for the 1931 comparison). While in 1971 Ontario still had a much higher proportion of British Canadians than did the Prairies or Canada it also had a much higher proportion of the major post-war immigrant group next to Britons; Italians. The Prairies,

TABLE 3.2
Ethnic Composition of Canada
The Prairies, and Ontario
1971 Census

Percentage of the National, Regional and Provincial Populations Comprised of Each Ethnic Group

	British Isles	French	German	Italian	Ukrainian	Netherlands
Canada	44.6	28.7	6.1	3.4	2.7	2.0
Ontario	59.4	9.6	6.2	6.0	2.1	2.7
Prairies	44.2	6.7	15.1	1.1	9.5	3.2
—Manitoba	41.9	8.8	12.5	1.1	11.6	3.6
—Saskatchewan	42.1	6.1	19.4	0.3	9.3	2.1
—Alberta	46.8	5.8	14.2	1.5	8.3	3.6

	Scandinavian	Polish	Jewish	Asian	Eskimo Indian	Other
Canada	1.8	1.5	1.4	1.3	1.5	5.2
Ontario	0.8	1.9	1.8	1.5	0.8	7.4
Prairies	5.4	3.2	0.8	1.2	3.6	5.9
—Manitoba	3.6	4.3	2.0	1.0	4.4	5.4
—Saskatchewan	6.4	2.9	0.2	0.8	4.4	6.0
—Alberta	6.0	2.7	0.4	1.6	2.7	6.2

however, still contained a higher proportion of residents with a German, Ukrainian, Scandinavian, Netherland's, or Polish ethnic background. Across the Prairie provinces the proportion of non-British, non-French ethnics remains high and in this sense the prairie society is still distinctive from that of Ontario and from that of Canada generally.

Yet the "ethnics" of the Prairies are quite different from those of Ontario. In an analysis of the 1971 census data a distinction was made between "old ethnics" and "new ethnics".[8] Old ethnics were categorized as those individuals who had immigrated to Canada before the start of the Second World War; new ethnics were those who had immigrated after the war. The old ethnics settled largely on the Prairies where they still constitute a disproportionately large share of the regional population while the new ethnics settled largely in Ontario where they too now constitute a disproportionately large share of the provincial population. For example, Table 3:3 presents the regional distributions of three illustrative ethnic groups. Here we see that while 62.6% of the "old" Ukrainian ethnics settled on the Prairies only 35.1% of the "new" Ukrainian ethnics have done so. Far more have settled in Ontario. The same pattern holds for both Polish and German ethnics. As a consequence the ethnic communities on the Prairies tend to be much older than do the corresponding communities in Ontario. Prairie ethnics should thus be more thoroughly assimilated into the Canadian society and its political system than are the ethnics of Ontario. This assumption gains strength by the fact that 28.1% of the new ethnics used neither English or French as their home language in 1971 compared to only 2.5% of the old ethnics.[9] Thus, ". . . while ethnicity may still be a major aspect of differentiation within the society in terms of culture and tradition, assimilation and adjustment to the English language have provided at least a common medium for expression and communication".[10] Today it is Ontario and not the Prairies which forms the crucible of ethnic assimilation. Times have indeed changed.

In the past ethnic cleavages within the prairie society had a marked impact on both provincial and federal politics. In Saskatchewan, for example, ethnic conflict lay at the root of the Liberal government's defeat in 1929 after 24 years in office. Although the immediate impetus for the Liberal defeat came from the Ku Klux Klan which provided some semblance of organization among the disparate opposition groups in the province, the ethnic conflicts upon which the Klan prospered were longstanding.[11] In Manitoba the importance of ethnicity as a factor in provincial politics has been commonly acknowledged.[12] Perhaps only in Alberta has the impact of ethnic cleavages on provincial politics been relatively light.[13] Nationally, partisan divisions in the prairie electorate frequently followed lines of ethnic cleavage, not uncommonly with newer ethnic groups supporting the party—generally the Liberals—which formed the government at the time of their arrival in

TABLE 3:3

Regional Concentrations of "Old" and "New" Ethnics

Ethnic Group	Place of Residence	
	Prairies	Ontario
Ukrainian		
—old	62.6%	22.8%
—new	35.1%	49.8%
Polish		
—old	45.9%	36.4%
—new	20.8%	59.8%
German		
—old	46.3%	32.0%
—new	28.5%	44.6%

Source: John Kralt, "Ethnic Origins of Canadians", *1971 Census of Canada*, Vol: V—Part: 1 (Bulletin 5.17), August 1976, p. 31.

Canada. Finally we should note the related persistence of anti-French Canadian sentiment in the West, sentiment that traces back to early disputes on education and language policies in the North West Territories and which received ample reinforcement from the conscription crises of the two world wars. Prairie residents, seeking to accommodate and assimilate a great variety of ethnic groups, rankled at any special preservation of French Canadian language or educational rights. To the assimilators French Canadian rights constituted an unwelcome shield behind which other groups might try to hide from the pressures of assimilation; to the assimilated they constituted a special privilege to which they themselves were not privy.

Today ethnic cleavages no longer play a significant role in prairie politics. The Great Depression all but removed ethnicity from the political arena in Saskatchewan and replaced it with a set of economic preoccupations that have remained to this day.[14] In Manitoba the rise to power of the provincial New Democrats in the late 60s has been attributed to a change in the major political cleavage from that of ethnicity to that of class.[15] In national politics the importance of ethnicity has also declined although anti-Quebec sentiment remains a significant factor in the western political culture. However, the character of this sentiment has been radically altered over the past few decades and now reflects a phenomenon that is more complex, less ethnically based, and more inherently political and partisan than in the past.

The decline in the political importance of ethnicity can be traced to a variety of factors. First, because large scale immigration ended with the onset of the Depression, the prairie society over the last 50 years has not had to cope with the assimilation of large numbers of immigrant settlers. As a consequence the tensions accompanying assimilation and the frequently abrasive character of contact among culturally and linguistically diverse groups have diminished. Second, the great majority of non-British ethnics on the Prairies are Canadian-born and for these second, third, and fourth generation Canadians ethnic identities compete unequally with newer but well-established identifications with the broader Canadian society. Third, in the past social isolation assisted many ethnic groups in sustaining a distinctive identity: ". . . the settlement of most prairie communities tended to be of a group nature, so that small areas—at least the size of church parishes—became dominated mainly by people of the same ethnic, language and religious backgrounds."[16] Recently, however, the continued advance of urbanization coupled with the decline of economic opportunities in rural areas, the creation of regional school systems and urban centres of advanced education, the vastly improved transportation system linking rural to urban communities, and the penetration of the English-language mass media into the rural countryside have eroded the earlier pattern of ethnic isolation.

The heterogeneous nature of the contemporary prairie city fails to provide a supportive environment for the maintenance of ethnic distinctiveness; the support offered by organizations such as the Danish Canadian Club is frail indeed compared to that provided by a rural community in which one's neighbours, merchants, church and social life all shared and mutually-reinforced distinctive ethnic folkways. The assimilationist pressures of the contemporary society are both more intense and more effective than in the past even though their need has fallen with the decline of immigration onto the Prairies.

To conclude, the ethnic distinctiveness of the prairie region has been eroded since 1931. More importantly there has been a general decline in the importance of ethnicity across the Prairies and a further decline in the political saliency of the remaining ethnic distinctions. Thus the ethnic composition of the Canadian Prairies no longer forms a social base for regionally distinctive politics.

D) Religious Composition

By the 1971 census the religious composition of the Prairies had not been greatly altered since the Depression era. The limited changes that had occurred reflected broad societal shifts such as the increase in the proportion of Catholics attributable to the character of post-war immigration. Thus the pattern noted in the last chapter continues: "the nation's . . . religious composition is a mirror image of those faiths which predominated in the immigrants' countries of origin at the time of their arrival in Canada."[17]

In recent decades the links between religion and political behavior have been all but obliterated and in the process an important prop for a distinctive regional politics has been destroyed. Across Canada there has been a progressive decline in the political importance of religion and religious issues. Church and state have been separated not only institutionally but attitudinally. Religious elements have disappeared from partisan debate and the earlier religious underpinnings of Canadian electoral behavior remain only as statistical artifacts that fail to survive rigorous analysis.[18]

Religious organizations both in the West and elsewhere in Canada are reluctant to become embroiled in the political process. Political activity, of course, is not altogether absent as church involvement in native land claims and the abortion question has demonstrated. However, the degree of political participation falls well below that witnessed in western Canada during the early decades of the century. No longer do Protestant ministers provide a ready cadre of reform politicians. The prospect of another "Bible-Bill" Aberhart transforming a large evangelical following into electoral power is remote in the extreme.

In summary, the distinctive religious composition of the Canadian Prairies was established by the patterns of immigration in the early part of this century and it has been little disturbed since then. However the impact of religious issues, leaders and organizations on prairie politics has declined precipitously. As a consequence the religious distinctiveness of the Prairies, while it remains, can no longer foster or sustain a distinctive regional politics.

E) Prairie Agriculture

Since the Second World War the character of prairie agriculture, and of Canadian agriculture in general for that matter, has been fundamentally altered in two ways. First, the importance of agriculture within the regional and national economies has been sharply diminished despite increased agricultural output and productivity. Second, the nature of the agricultural enterprise itself has changed in many important respects. Let us examine these two components of change in turn.

Changes in the Importance of Agriculture

As Table 3:4 shows the proportion of the Canadian population living on farms has declined sharply since 1941. While the rate of decline has been somewhat greater in Ontario and the nation as a whole than it has been across the three Prairie provinces, it has been very substantial even in the latter case. Even in Saskatchewan there has been not only a relative but an absolute decline in the farm population. On the Prairies the

TABLE 3:4

Farm Population as a Percentage of the Total Population

Population of:	% 1941	1971
Canada	27.4	6.9
Ontario	18.6	5.1
Prairies	47.2	17.0
—Manitoba	34.2	13.3
—Saskatchewan	57.4	25.2
—Alberta	48.2	14.6

Source: R. Daviault, *Selected Agricultural Statistics for Canada*, Ottawa Economics Branch, Agriculture Canada, 1976, P. 6.

number of occupied farms declined from 296,469 in 1941 to 174,653 in 1971, a fall of 41%.[19] During the same period the percentage of all Canadian farms to be found on the Prairies increased from 40.4% in 1941 to 47.7%. Thus from a national perspective agriculture is becoming increasingly concentrated within western Canada while at the same time, somewhat paradoxically, the farm community is becoming a progressively less important segment of the prairie society.

With the decline in the farm population has come a decline in the percentage of the labour force engaged in agriculture. At the turn of the century over 40% of the Canadian labour force was employed in agricultural occupations,[20] and between 1935 and 1939 an average of 33.5% of the national labour force was so employed. Since the war that proportion has fallen steadily to 18.4% in 1951, 11.2% in 1961, 6.3% in 1971 and only 5.1% in 1975.[21] The proportion of the prairie labour force engaged in agriculture, while remaining higher than the national average, has been declining at roughly the same rate. By 1971 only 16.3% of the prairie labour force was engaged in agriculture; 11.8% in Manitoba, 27.4% in Saskatchewan, and 13.0% in Alberta.[22] For both Canada and the Prairies the decline in the agricultural labour force has been not only relative but absolute. Whereas 153,000 farm labourers had been employed on the Prairies in 1941, by 1966 that number had fallen to less than 40,000.[23]

The decline of agriculture as a component of the national economy can be measured in other ways. From 1935 to 1939, while drought and the Depression lingered on, agriculture contributed an average of 19.9% of the total net value of production in Canada; by the 1969 to 1973 period that share had fallen to an average of 8.5%.[24] To take a provincial illustration, agriculture's contribution to the net value of production in Alberta fell from 52.9% in 1931 to 18.7% in 1961 and 16.3% in 1971.[25]

In summary, a host of indicators point to the sharply reduced importance of agriculture within the Canadian and prairie economies. Interestingly, though, Canadian farmers today produce far more than they did in the past despite the reductions in the number of farmers and farms. The Second World War brought a return of agricultural prosperity to the Prairies and a surge in capital expansion. To understand this growth it is necessary to turn to changes that have occurred since the war in the nature of prairie agriculture.

Changes in the Nature of Prairie Agriculture

Although the Prairies experienced an absolute decline in the number of farms, farm operators and farm employees since 1941, the number of acres occupied by farms actually increased from 120,129,000 acres in 1941 to 133,571,000 in 1971, an increase of over 11%.[26] The size of the average prairie farm increased from 221 acres in 1941 to 502 acres in 1971,[27] an increase that was accompanied by a tremendous surge in mechanization. Mechanization made the growth in farm size not only possible but necessary as small-scale farming operations simply could not carry the heavy costs of the new agricultural equipment that was becoming available. Advancements in mechanization had been occurring steadily since settlement began—in the 1880s portable steam engines were introduced for threshing, gas farm tractors appeared around 1910 and combines were introduced in 1925. The pace of mechanization then increased noticeably with the manpower shortages encountered during World War Two. At the war's end the surge of mechanization continued. While the number of farms decreased from 1941 to 1971 the number of trucks increased from 43,363 to 251,377, the number of tractors from 112,624 to 308,475, and the number of combines from 18,081 to 127,509.[28] During the same period rural electrification was being carried out across the Prairies which allowed the introduction of countless labour-saving devices, both domestic and agricultural. Steady advances had also been made in agricultural productivity with the introduction of new crop varieties, pesticides, herbicides and fertilizers. All of these changes, but particularly those relating to mechanization and farm size, led to a sharp increase in the capital value of prairie farms. The average capital value rose from $6,565 in 1941 to $72,805 in 1971, an increase that far outstrips any inflationary devaluation of the Canadian dollar over the same time interval. The increase in capital value has been particularly steep in recent years; between 1971 and 1975 the average capital value of prairie farms increased to $136,537, a rise of 88% in only four years.[29]

In 1976 the *Financial Post* described a farming operation in Manitoba that illustrates, although undoubtedly does not typify, the changes that have taken place. The farmer described in the article had started with half a section of land purchased for $2,500 in 1942. Now he and his four sons run an incorporated business with eight sections of land worth $750,000 and farm machinery worth another $500,000. There are four tractors which are worth $43,000 each, more than the $37,000 Mercedes driven by the father. The yearly operating costs of the farm top $300,000 including $25,000 for weed killer alone. This is indeed a large scale operation.[30]

Mechanization and a growing reliance on fertilizers, pesticides and herbicides have made Canadian agriculture increasingly dependent upon petroleum products that are rapidly escalating in price. Although prairie agriculture is much more energy-efficient than that in Ontario the prairie region still consumes about two-thirds of all agricultural fuel used in Canada.[31]

Another agricultural change that has occurred both nationally and on the Prairies has been the growth of corporate farming. Large corporations have entered the production of food-crops in both a direct and indirect fashion. Apart from corporate-owned farms, "the agricultural system now includes the large food conglomerates who often sell the farm inputs to the farmer through one subsidiary and buy the farm products through another."[32] Although "agri-business" may be more omnipresent in eastern Canada than it is in the Prairies, corporate inroads have been made in western agriculture. The result is that the individualistic and competitive nature of farming has been somewhat diminished.

The expansion of corporate farming highlights a very basic transformation of agrarian life in western Canada. Farming used to be more than a business; it was a different way of life with its own mores, patterns of community organization, and institutional forms. Mutual aid and cooperation were fundamental ingredients of the agrarian frontier and were inevitably extended beyond the local community through the creation of countless co-operative organizations. Donald Willmott has identified five factors which underlay the formation of co-operative organizations: common economic problems; ecological conditions requiring collective labour such as threshing parties, barn-raisings and snow plowing; ecological conditions, such as the large distances between homesteads, that encouraged organized recreation and sociability in place of over-the-back-fence socializing; ecological conditions which required small units of local government; and emergent cultural values which encouraged collective action at the local level.[33] With respect to this last factor Wilmott points out that "the nostalgic accounts which oldtimers gave to pioneer times makes it clear that mutual aid and cooperation were not merely for convenience or necessity alone: they involved an ideology which grew out of, and in turn reinforced, the loyalty and solidarity which the early farmers developed among themselves."[34]

Most of these factors have disappeared or are disappearing from the prairie scene. Collective labour and multitudinous small units of local government are no longer needed while radio, television and vastly more convenient means of transportation and communication have eroded the need for organized recreation and sociability. Willmott also suggests, although the evidence here is inconclusive, that the ideological tenets of mutual aid and co-operation are fading in the prairie community. Agricultural diversification has undercut the degree to which western farmers share a common set of problems or economic conditions. Thus the ecological and economic conditions that in the past fostered co-operative endeavours and a rich infrastructure of formal organizations have been eroded. As a consequence Morton's comment upon an earlier era seems particularly germane to the Prairies today:

> With the Progressive revolt, farming ceased to be a way of life and became simply another occupation. Countryman and city dweller no longer inhabited separate social orders; the city had prevailed over the country. . . .[35]

Changes have also occurred in the crops and products of prairie agriculture. In the early decades of prairie settlement wheat was unquestionably the dominant crop. Its dominance can be attributed to a variety of factors perhaps the most important being the absolute and comparative economic advantage that Canadian grain growers have enjoyed over other major wheat producers.[36] On the world market Canadian wheat has a well-won reputation for its superior baking characteristics, high protein content and low sedimentation. Thus while alternate crop possibilities existed for the prairie farmer none matched the potential profitability of wheat. Thus while prairie agriculture was never a one-crop system, wheat was the export staple; "prosperity and stimulus came through wheat, as did depression and discouragement".[37]

During the 1970s the dominance of wheat was still apparent. Nevertheless there has been a noticeable trend in prairie agriculture towards crop diversification which has reduced the region's dependence upon a single crop and thereby helped to stabilize the regional economy. The precise extent of crop diversification is difficult to determine as the composition of the prairie grain crop will fluctuate with the price and supply conditions for both wheat and alternative crops. The acreage yield for different grain crops will also fluctuate substantially from year to year in response to climatic variability. Although the acreage seeded in wheat seldom varies more than 10% from year to year, price-determined fluctuations can at times be of considerably greater magnitude.[38] For example in 1970 wheat sold at $1.44 a bushel and comprised 34.6% of the total grain crop. By 1973 the price had risen to $4.47 a bushel and, as a consequence, wheat's share of the following year's grain crop rose to 51.9%.[39]

Despite the fluctuating composition of the prairie grain crop it is possible to illustrate at least the rough character of crop diversification by relying on five year averages. Table 3:5 presents the average composition of the prairie grain crop for two five year periods; 1935 to 1939 and 1971 to 1975. While wheat, oats and barley were the dominant crops in both periods their relative shares of the total crop changed considerably. Barley and oats, it should be pointed out, are the most common substitutes for wheat and their acreage tends to vary inversely with the acreage planted in wheat. In the 1971 to 1975 period, when the total prairie grain production was over twice that of 1935-1939, the production of flaxseed, rapeseed, and mixed grains began to reach significant proportions. Although their total output came nowhere near that of the three major grain crops a trend towards diversification is clearly apparent. Prairie grain farmers will continue to increase their crop diversification in order to be more responsive to changing market conditions and to achieve a degree of economic stability that a reliance upon a single crop prohibited.

Another aspect of agricultural diversification has been the expansion of the cattle industry. During the Second World War foreign grain sales declined as the market for Canadian grain was limited to Great Britain. At the same time there was a substantial increase in both the domestic and American demand for beef cattle, and the production of cattle and feedgrains on the Prairies has increased steadily ever since.[40] The number of beef cattle has increased from a 1935-1939 average of 439,000 to a 1971-1975 average of 3,014,400.[41] While Alberta retains the lead in the cattle business, the rate of growth has been more rapid in Saskatchewan and Manitoba.

The diversification of prairie agriculture has followed different paths in the three provinces with the result that it is becoming increasingly difficult to discuss agriculture in *regional* terms. The monolithic regional wheat economy of the past is no more. Today the wheat economy is strongest in Saskatchewan where the acreage in wheat is approximately five times that in Manitoba and three times that in Alberta.[42] While Saskatchewan farmers derive most of their income from wheat, livestock is predominant in Alberta along with barley, tame hay, honey, forage seeds, sheep and sugar beets.[43] In Manitoba flaxseed, buckwheat, peas and sunflowers are the top crops. This variability among the Prairie provinces throws the utility of regional agricultural statistics into question and reinforces the argument that the regional homogeneity of the past is rapidly disintegrating.

Perhaps the most significant agricultural change is the prodigious growth in government involvement that has occurred since the start of the Depression. Prior to that time provincial governments in the West, facing farmer-dominated electorates, had been responsive to agrarian needs to the limit of their jurisdictional responsibilities. Unfortunately for the western farmers, the major problems facing them fell beyond the powers of the provincial governments, and the national government was generally unresponsive to agrarian concerns. In part this can be traced to

TABLE 3:5

Diversification of the Prairie Grain Crop

Crop	1935/39 Average Bushels (000's)	%	1971/75 Average Bushels (000's)	%
Wheat	290,579	51.3	520,400	38.3
Oats for grain	197,325	34.9	245,400	18.1
Barley	67,772	12.0	458,800	33.8
Rye	7,780	1.4	16,247	1.2
Flaxseed	1,424	.3	18,120	1.3
Mixed Grain	1,291	.2	36,940	2.7
Rapeseed	—	—	63,380	4.7
Total	566,171	100.0%	1,359,287	100.0%

Source: R. Daviault, *Selected Agricultural Statistics for Canada*, Ottawa Economics Branch, Agriculture Canada, June, 1976, p. 78.

a general governmental antipathy to intervention in or regulation of the economy. It would take the Great Depression, Keynesian economics, the government's successful management of the economy during the Second World War and a significant political challenge from the socialist left to shift the national government toward a more interventionalist stance. More importantly, the agrarian demands of western Canada represented a direct challenge to the National Policy of tariffs and freight rates used to create and protect a fledgling industrial economy in central Canada. To have met agrarian demands would have meant an abandonment of the National Policy and, it was assumed, a crippling blow to the manufacturing and financial interests of central Canada. Here the prairie voters lacked enough political clout to impose their will upon a national government electorally dominated by central Canada. It should also be pointed out that from an economic standpoint the prairie farmers simply could not be offered the type of protection that the National Policy provided to central Canadian manufacturers:

> The prices of too many prairie commodities are determined by world market conditions for long-term price stability to be possible. Prairie residents often accuse central Canadian manufacturers of hiding behind high tariff walls in order to capture the domestic Canadian market. However, manufacturing oriented to the domestic market is relatively easy to protect whereas export-oriented production is extremely vulnerable to market fluctuations.[44]

There was, of course, some response from the national government to the agrarian demands issuing forth from western Canada: the set of national policies designed to promote immigration and agricultural settlement served the regional agrarian interest.[45] The Manitoba Grain Act of 1900, which broke the standard elevator monopoly and regulated the grading, weighing and dockage of grain, was hailed as the "Magna Carta" of the grain grower. The Canada Grain Act of 1912, passed after the farmers' 1910 "Seige of Ottawa" and the defeat of the Liberal government in 1911, extended government regulation of the handling and grading of grain.

Oddly enough, the piece of legislation that came to symbolize western Canadian political power was the Crow's Nest Pass Agreement (CNPA) of 1897. As part of an arrangement to extend the Canadian Pacific Railway through the Crow's Nest Pass into the booming mineral region of the Kootenays, the CNPA granted a perpetual freight rate reduction of three cents per hundredweight on grain and flour moving from the West to Fort William and eastward. Yet as it turned out the CNPA was of little significance for the first 20 years as freight rates remained below the statutory ceiling. Then when freight rates rose with wartime inflation and the CNPA reductions became appreciable the agreement was suspended in 1918 under the authority of the War Measures Act. Despite continual agitation from western Canada the agreement was not reinstated until 1924. It is thus questionable whether the CNPA is indicative of any significant government response to agrarian grievances or pressure.[46] Nevertheless the Crow's Nest Pass Agreement retained an important symbolic position in western Canada. Eventually it was also to deliver significant economic benefits to prairie wheat farmers although these were not without their detrimental side effects.

It was the Depression that finally triggered sustained and extensive government intervention in prairie agriculture. The Depression, it should be stressed, did not cause many of the problems facing prairie agriculture. Unstable foreign markets, the tariff on farm machinery, oppressive freight rates, and bottlenecks in the storage and transportation of grain were perennial problems in the West. What the Depression did was to so forcefully dramatize the need for assistance that assistance was actually forthcoming. While the effects of the Depression were felt throughout Canada they were particularly catastrophic in the three Prairie provinces. Prairie cities, like those elsewhere in Canada, faced massive unemployment and the near collapse of basic social services. Yet it was in the countryside that the Depression was most severe. Foreign markets for western grain all but disappeared. Where markets could be found prices were abysmally low and in many cases below the cost of production. Between 1926 and 1929 inclusive the gross cash income for all farm products on the Prairies averaged $538,500,000; in the 1930 to 1933 period the average plummeted to $194,000,000.[47] Municipal debt increased from $343 million in 1930 to $507 million in 1937.[48] The West had always been a debtor society because of the heavy public and private borrowing necessary to open up the agrarian frontier, but during the

Depression things got much worse. The debt, furthermore, was largely held outside the region. Thus the dominant political issue became ". . the clash of interests between a class of debtors who lived in the midst of economic ruin and a class of creditors most of whom did not."[49] It was within this context that the Social Credit proposals for monetary reform found their appeal.

Along with these problems came the worst drought ever to hit prairie agriculture. In 1931, 1933, 1934, 1936 and 1937 drought cut wheat production to less than half of the normal yield and swept away decades of backbreaking work in the dust clouds of the 'Dirty Thirties'. Fortunately the effects of the drought were somewhat localized, striking mainly in the infamous Palliser Triangle incorporating south-central Saskatchewan and the adjoining corners of Alberta and Manitoba. Thousands were forced to abandon their homesteads while many of those who remained faced stark destitution; at the height of the Depression and drought one area in south-central Saskatchewan listed 890 persons on relief out of a total population of 895.[50] The resulting despair and disillusionment of the farm population is epitomized in an advertisement picked up by historian James Gray:

> For Sale: 800 acres highly improved stock farm, located on Pelletier Creek. Would sell on cash installment basis. If interested, write Fred Hearsey, Duncairn, Sask. N.B.: I might be tempted to trade this farm for something really useful, say some white mice or goldfish, or even a playful little monkey.[51]

In Ontario the per capita income declined by 44% between 1929 and 1933; in Manitoba the decline was 49% while it reached 61% in Alberta and 71% in Saskatchewan.[52] Even given the enormity of the economic collapse, however, perhaps the greatest long-term damage was that done to the psyche of the prairie population. As historian Gray has so movingly written:

> It was a decade that destroyed men's faith in themselves, mocked their talents and skills, blighted their initiative, and subverted their dedication to the cultivation of their land. It shattered the morals of our inland empire, replaced a whole people's proud search for success with a disspirited search for security.

The "last, best west" had been crossed by the shadows of Depression and drought, and the image of the region held by residents and outsiders alike was never to be the same.

The national government responded to the agricultural depression in a number of ways. In 1930 it stepped in through the creation of the Central Selling Agencies to relieve the faltering wheat pools of the responsibility for foreign sales. In 1935, the year that marked the re-establishment of the Canadian Wheat Board, the national government passed the Prairie Farm Rehabilitation Act which, "using the experimental farms as a nucleus . . . launched a program to construct water-catching dugouts on 50,000 farms, convert 2,000,000 acres of sub-marginal land into community pastures, and change the face of the West with forestation, reclamation, and irrigation.''[54] Other acts included the Debt Adjustment Board Program, the Prairie Farm Assistance Act, and the Farm Creditors' Act, the last of which wiped out more than $200 million in farm debts. All of these programs eased even if they did not eliminate the debt and production-cost problems of prairie farmers. With the start of the Second World War and the resultant efforts of the Canadian government to regulate the economy to a degree not even considered possible much less desirable in the past, the introduction of new government programs and regulatory intervention continued apace. Wartime initiatives included the Feed Freight Assistance Act (1941), the removal of the tariff on farm machinery in 1943, the Agricultural Price Support Act (1944), and the Export Credit Insurance Act (1944).

Today there are a multitude of national and provincial agricultural programs, the number and coverage of which probably surpass the wildest speculations of agrarian reformers in the early decades of this century. In 1975 there were 58 provincial acts in Manitoba that impinged upon agricultural production, 108 in Saskatchewan, and 79 in Alberta.[55] National programs, including the Agricultural Stabilization Act, the Crop Insurance Program, and the Western Grains Stabilization Program, were equally prolific; a 1976 publication listed 78 programs and policies relevant to agriculture in Manitoba, 58 for Saskatchewan, and 69 for Alberta.[56]

At present the financial position of the prairie farmer is still precarious as shown by the story of the Saskatchewan farmer who won a million dollar Lotto Canada draw. When asked what he intended to do, his reply was: "Keep growing wheat until the money runs out." Nevertheless, government policies have both moderated the historical boom and bust cycle of prairie agriculture and provided a minimal financial floor under farm operations. Government intervention has helped to stabilize farm incomes and to make farm profits more secure. However, as a consequence farmers are now enmeshed in a maze of governmental programs and regulations; relations between farmers and government have become increasingly formalized, bureaucratized and institutionalized. A report by the Science Council of Canada has gone so far as to conclude that "the current situation appears one step away from having farmers under contract to the government with an assured stable percentage of profit."[57]

Grain farmers have seen their position as independent commodity producers steadily undercut by increased government intervention, most of which has come at their own insistence. Politically the effects of program proliferation have been double-edged. On the one hand the programs demonstrate a degree of national government concern and support that was not evident decades earlier. On the other hand the government is held responsible for every program that fails or is mismanaged. Given the myriad of programs presently in place there appears to be ample opportunity for continued friction between farmers and the national government.

Discussion

The character of prairie agriculture has changed dramatically since the early decades of this century. It is now more capital intensive, larger in scale, more productive, more diversified, more mechanized, more closely entwined with provincial and national governments and, on balance, more stable financially. Perhaps only the precarious prairie climate has remained impervious to change.

The political implications of agricultural change are almost as sweeping as the change itself. While farmers today produce far more than a much larger agrarian community could manage in the past, tractors and combines cannot vote. As the agrarian community has fallen in numbers it has witnessed a steady decline in its electoral power. There are no longer enough farmers or rural residents to dominate provincial or federal politics on the Prairies. Although this is least true of Saskatchewan even there the electoral power of the agrarian community has been sharply eroded. Diefenbaker's dictum that wheat is the only thing for politicians to talk about on the Prairies no longer applies. In the past farmers shaped the political evolution of the Prairie provinces by their numbers and economic centrality, and in so doing cast prairie politics into a distinctive regional mold. Today this power has been irrevocably lost. Rather than a large, relatively homogeneous agrarian bloc within the prairie electorate there is now a small, relatively heterogeneous bloc. While the agrarian community unquestionably constitutes an important and integral part of the contemporary prairie society, it no longer sits astride the broader prairie society as it did in the past. Moreover, the formerly powerful agrarian bloc has not been replaced by any other large, homogeneous bloc upon which a regional political culture rivalling that of the past could be rebuilt. The network of farm organizations, co-ops, wheat pools, and newspapers, knit together by common economic concerns and grievances, gave the agrarian community in the past a coherence and strength that is unparalleled in the contemporary prairie society.

In light of this argument it is interesting to compare the new Canadian Agricultural Movement with earlier movements of agrarian protest in western Canada. The C.A.M. emerged in Alberta in the early months of 1978 and demonstrated that agrarian radicalism is not yet dead on the Prairies. It was, as many agrarian movements before had been, an offshoot of an American protest movement—the American Agricultural Movement—founded in 1977. Americans, however, played no role in organizing C.A.M.; they simply provided the example and the similarity of agrarian grievances on both sides of the border appeared to demonstrate the Canadian applicability of the American model, a sequence not unlike that preceding the agrarian revolt in 1921. The C.A.M. sought to protect the financial position of farmers through the parity pricing of agricultural commodities. Agricultural prices would be tied to the general cost of living; if 10 years ago a bushel of wheat bought a shirt, C.A.M. supporters argued the same equivalency should exist today.

The C.A.M., like its radical predecessors, adopted a nonpartisan stance. Founder Bert Brown stated that a political party had approached him to back the movement but that the approach had been turned down. "We don't want to offend any one party", Brown said, "we want to offend them all," a remark that echoes the Progressive movement of the early 20s.[58] Yet unlike the Progressives the C.A.M. stands little hope of successful electoral action in the pursuit of its goals. The farm community is too small and the bulk of the prairie electorate relates to agriculture as consumers, not producers. Hence any program that would substantially drive up food prices would be a difficult electoral commodity to sell. The actions contemplated by the C.A.M. more closely follow the examples of trade unionism. They include a reduction in farm production in order to eliminate surpluses and drive up the price of agricultural commodities, the boycotting of new equipment purchases unless absolutely necessary, tractor processions that would tie up the highways and publicize the farmers' plight, and the purchase of advertising time on national television. The option of electoral action that was open to and seized by the agrarian community in the early part of this century is no longer available. While political influence can be sought, political control is now beyond the grasp of the farm community.

To return to the broader argument, there are some important parallels between the analysis presented here and the staple theory of Harold Innis.[59] Wheat, along with fish, timber and fur, was one of the staples that shaped the evolution of the Canadian economy. It also shaped the evolution of the prairie society and forged the relationship between that society and the central Canadian heartland. Then, as the importance of wheat declined within the regional and national economies, its impact upon the political economy of western Canada also declined. The cement of regional integration that it had provided cracked, as did the political power of the agrarian community. Ironically, however, the weakening of agrarian political power was not accompanied by any increase in government indifference or neglect.

The explanation for expanded government support in the face of diminished electoral power is hard to pin down precisely although a number of factors come into play. One is the general expansion of government involvement in the economy that has occurred since the end of the war, an expansion that was unlikely to bypass the agricultural sector. A second factor is that government aid came in part as a result of other more powerful economic sectors desiring greater stability and security in agriculture.[60] A third factor is the farmers' successful entry into interest group politics. In 1935 the Canadian Chamber of Agriculture (later to become the Canadian Federation of Agriculture) was formed. One of its basic objectives was to provide a less sectional voice for Canadian farmers.[61] In so doing the Chamber turned its back on the earlier tradition of electoral politics and moved instead towards the more institutionalized and bureaucratic politics of conventional interest groups. Today well organized agrarian interest groups and close working relationships with an expansionist public service have replaced an earlier and perhaps cruder reliance upon electoral action.

It is interesting to note that increased government support for American agriculture also came at a time when the farm population was on the decline. Richard Hofstadter argues that the decline in the farm population had two paradoxical effects. First it made agrarian-based third parties increasingly futile by undermining their membership base. Second the smaller farm population and the correspondingly larger urban tax base made it easier for the two major parties to "buy off" the farm vote with agricultural subsidies.[62] While the applicability of Hofstadter's thesis to the Canadian scene remains to be demonstrated it should not be written off lightly.

While in the past economic development on the Prairies lay in the expansion of wheat production, the prairie farmland is now close to saturation and the prospects for employment expansion in agriculture seem remote. If wheat is to fuel future expansion it can only come from an upward spiral in world prices, something over which Canadian provinces have no control. Thus today the search is for economic alternatives to an historical over-reliance upon wheat in particular and grain crops in general. Because the prairie region is fragmented into three provincial jurisdictions, the drive for economic diversification has led to economically unsound competition among the three provinces in the agricultural sector.[63] Outside the agricultural sector interprovincial competition flourishes over the location of regional headquarters and resource developments, and the pricing and taxation of natural resources, particularly oil and natural gas. The net result is diminished regional homogeneity within the Prairies.

The push for economic diversification confronts one of the sacred cows of prairie agriculture, the Crow's Nest Pass Agreement. T. D. Regehr points out the conflict that is emerging:

> The Crow's Nest Pass rates have been consistently exempted from successive horizontal rate increases and have in fact become the best transportation bargain on the continent. It is this fact which makes the rate structure

tolerable to many Western grain farmers. Western Canada, however, is no longer the exclusive domain of the grain farmer.[64]

While freight rates in general discriminate markedly against western Canada, grain is moved at statutory rates that are presently below cost. For example, studies published by the Alberta Wheat Pool and the federal government showed a net 1977 loss to the railways of $175 million in the haulage of grain even after all subsidies were taken into account.[65] This situation inhibits economic diversification in a number of ways. Because the rates to ship grain out of the West are so low in comparison to the rates for processed or semi-processed agricultural products, it makes economic sense to locate processing plants and their employment potential outside western Canada. Grain-fed animal agriculture, meat processing, the milling of wheat and the crushing of rapeseed in western Canada are all discouraged. While the railways may be willing to restructure freight rates so that they will be less detrimental to the establishment of secondary industry in western Canada, the prospects of any such change are remote unless the railways are allowed a compensatory increase in the rates for grain. Here, however, ". . . many prairie grain farmers are determined to resist any tampering with the Crow's Nest Pass rates, and a rural-urban, agricultural-industrial cleavage on this issue seems inevitable."[66] It should also be noted here that the Crow's Nest rates have inhibited the efficient transportation and marketing of prairie grain even though the cost has been kept down. Since the 1950s when the railways began to lose money in transporting grain they have been understandably reluctant to maintain grain lines, provide more grain cars, and so forth. The more grain that was moved the more the railways stood to lose. Thus some substantial revision of grain rates may be a necessary condition for the improvement of a transportation system that falls well short of maximizing Canada's grain export potential.

On September 19, 1977, newly appointed Trade and Commerce Minister Jack Horner told a Calgary audience that his top priority would be more industrial development for western Canada. Any success in this respect will have two consequences germane to the thesis of this book. The first is that the prairie economy—and the prairie society in general—will edge closer in character to those of Ontario, thus further eroding the regional distinctiveness of the Prairies. The second will be intensified economic conflict among the western provinces and, more importantly, among competing sectors of the prairie economy. The first consequence will erode regional distinctiveness, the second regional homogeneity. Both will inflict considerable damage upon the increasingly frail economic foundations of political regionalism.

To conclude, the grain economy in the past provided the economic underpinnings for a regional politics by encompassing a majority of the prairie workforce, a majority sharing common economic interests and grievances. While agriculture today is still a major economic force on the Prairies, the vast majority of the labour force is engaged in non-agricultural pursuits. There is no longer a common set of economic interests and grievances to integrate the prairie electorate. Thus there is no longer a sound economic underpinning for regional politics. While other bases of regionalism may still exist their ability to integrate political behavior across the Prairies is markedly weaker than that of the grain economy in decades past. In essence this conclusion is a logical extension of C. B. Macpherson's classical study of Alberta politics.[67] Macpherson argued that for a competitive party system to exist there has to be supporting differentiation among social classes. In Alberta, however, the political system was dominated by a single, homogeneous class of wheat farmers,[68] and given the absence of significant class differentiation there was little need or electoral support for more than one party at any given time. If we extend the broad outline but not the detail of Macpherson's argument to the present, our expectation would be that increased economic diversification and the end of the economic hegemony of grain growers should yield increased differentiation and political conflict both within and among the Prairie provinces.

F) Cultural Change

Although the cultural changes that have occurred within the prairie society may be evident to longtime residents of the region they are elusive to documentation or quantification. Nevertheless, it seems clear that the cultural distinctiveness of the prairie society has diminished over time. The factors that sustained cultural distinctiveness in the past have all but disappeared; travel outside the region has become easy and relatively inexpensive, the strength of earlier ethnic identifications has faded, isolated ethnic settlements of the past have by and large been assimilated into the anglo-Canadian mainstream, and inter-personal contact across regions has been greatly facilitated by inexpensive long-distance telephone networks. More importantly there now exists an electronic media that inexorably works to tear down regional distinctiveness in the pursuit, both intentional and unintentional, of national and continental cultural homogeneity.

The impact of radio was already being felt within the prairie region during the Depression years: "It broke the barrier of isolation that had held the prairie West in its grip for almost fifty years."[69] When the Canadian Broadcasting Corporation was formed in the 1930s the first step was taken towards the establishment of a national communications system that would serve as a conscious tool for national integration or, conversely, for the dismemberment of cultural regionalism. The C.B.C., the

Canadian Radio, Television and Telecommunications Commission, national wireservices, large newspaper chains and Canadian content regulations have all helped create a national culture, frail though it may be in the face of American competition. As a consequence the media that confronted the residents of Calgary or Winnipeg in the 1970s differed little in substance from that confronting their counterparts in Toronto, Vancouver or St. John's. The prospects for a media-supported regional prairie culture, on the other hand, are bleak. There is no regional infrastructure for the prairie media, no regional equivalent of the C.B.C., the C.R.T.C., Southam News or the Canadian Press wireservice. Media outlets on the Prairies are either locally based or tied into national networks and affiliates. There is, in other words, no media infrastructure through which a regional culture can be promoted or sustained. With respect to magazines and television particularly, prairie residents are plugged into national and continental cultural patterns in the face of which any pre-existing regional culture can only atrophy. Regionally distinct cultural forms that might emerge outside the mass media face intense competition from the engines of national culture in Canada and even greater competition from the American culture that flows almost unchecked across the Canadian border.

In the early part of this century the prairie region was an economic and cultural frontier. Today the frontier is gone, having been replaced by a complex, multifaceted and predominantly urban society. The television and films watched, the radio programs listened to, the magazines read, the food eaten, the consumer goods purchased, and the leisure activities pursued differ little from one part of English Canada to the next. The western Canadian from Edmonton or Saskatoon who lives in a highrise, works for the Royal Bank, drives a Ford, shops at Canada Safeway, travels to Hawaii for holidays, reads Time and Playboy, goes out to the disco, watches the N.F.L. game of the week on television, and collects the records of Elton John and Carole King is pursuing a lifestyle that is scarcely distinguishable from that of other Canadians. Certainly it is not different enough to nurture a distinctive prairie culture. If cultures reflect life-circumstances, urban Westerners will gravitate towards cultural patterns that are shared and created by their central Canadian and American counterparts.

If there is one thing that western Canadians share alone and in common it is the prairie climate. Regional historians such as W. L. Morton have been inclined to place considerable emphasis on the role of climate in the evolution of prairie society,[70] although this emphasis has not gone unchallenged.[71] Today, to the prairie suburbanite shopping in a climate-controlled mall in the dead of winter, playing tennis under a plastic bubble, or enjoying a summer walk in a mosquito-free park, even the climatic frontier is dead.

I should stress in conclusion that the loss of a distinctive prairie culture, or the lost opportunity to create a distinctive prairie culture in the future, is not being bemoaned. There is little to indicate that the prairie culture of the past was in any sense superior and there is even less to indicate that the prairie region alone could foster and sustain culture patterns of any enduring value. Given the immense difficulties in sustaining a distinctive English Canadian culture in the face of American competition, the prospects for a regional culture unbuttressed by linguistic distinctiveness are bleak in the extreme. The argument presented above is not meant to rail against the cultural integration that has been occurring across English Canada and across the continent. Rather it is to point out that in yet another way the distinctiveness of the prairie region is being undercut.

POLITICAL CHANGE SINCE THE WAR

In the chapter thus far I have shown that the prairie society has been radically altered in the decades since the Second World War and that the direction of change has been such as to erode the regional distinctiveness and homogeneity of the Prairies. Implicit throughout has been the argument that the decline in social, economic and cultural regionalism has been accompanied by a corresponding decline in political regionalism. It is now time to address political regionalism directly by examining federal political behavior across the Prairies from the Second World War to the end of the 70s.

The end of the Second World War did not mark any sudden change in the political patterns that had been established on the Prairies by agrarian revolt and the Depression. However, in the decades that followed the war substantial changes were to occur. With the victory of the Diefenbaker Conservatives in 1958 the major party share of the prairie popular vote was restored to a share roughly equivalent to that received by the two major parties in Ontario. As Figure 2:1 illustrates the last two decades have brought a convergence of major party support in the Prairies and Ontario. With respect to this particular indicator the regional distinctiveness of the Prairies has evaporated. This conclusion, though, glosses over the fact that the pattern of initial major party success, then collapse, and finally revitalization on the Prairies conceals important and striking differences between the Liberal and Conservative parties. Although both parties were subject to the challenge from agrarian revolt, their histories prior to, during, and subsequent to that revolt display few similarities. Thus to bring the analysis of major party support into closer focus and to open up the discussion of post-war political change let us first turn to the electoral history of the Liberal Party.

A) The Liberal Party in Western Canada

During the early years of prairie settlement the Liberal party enjoyed substantial success, capturing 59 of the 96 western seats in the five national elections held between 1896 and 1911. The party was particularly successful at the edge of the frontier taking 42 of the 52 seats in Saskatchewan and Alberta compared to only 39% of the Manitoba seats. The success of the Liberals can be attributed to both pull and push factors. Looking first at the former, the Laurier Liberals formed the national government during the great settlement boom in western Canada and the Liberal party shone in its reflected light. In addition, many new immigrants acquired a natural affiliation with the party holding office at the time of their immersion into Canadian politics, a factor that helped the Liberal party significantly on the Prairies. Liberal policies including support for low tariffs and provincial rights were popular in the West. Finally, the Liberal party was able to capitalize on holding national office in 1905 by using the power of the new Lieutenant-Governors in Saskatchewan and Alberta to entrench Liberal provincial organizations which in turn sustained the national party in the two provinces.

The principal push factor in the Liberals' electoral success came from the character of their opposition. The Conservative party, firmly wedded to the National Policy and its central pillar of tariff protection for central Canadian industry, was inherently unattractive in western Canada. Its vigilance over Canada's British connection had a limited appeal to the flood of non-British immigrants settling in Saskatchewan and Alberta. Only in Manitoba, where the party had been successfully entrenched during the long national tenure of the Macdonald Conservatives and where the population had strong familial and historical ties to central Canada, did the Conservatives enjoy more than a modicum of electoral success.

The demise of the Liberals on the Prairies began with the conscription election of 1917 in which the party won only two of 43 western seats with 27% of the regional vote. Although that election yielded gains in future contests by propelling eastern and central European immigrants even further into the Liberal camp,[72] these modest future gains were more than offset in the short run by catastrophic losses elsewhere on the Prairies. In 1921 the Liberals' share of the popular vote slumped even more and, as Figure 3:5 illustrates, it was to remain below the party's Ontario vote in every subsequent election save that of 1926. Figure 3:5 also demonstrates that the Liberal vote in the West tended to oscillate in tandem with the party's vote in Ontario even though the western vote remained comparatively small. This parallel movement in electoral support for the Liberals is indicative of national effects on electoral behavior while the sustained gap between the two levels of support demonstrates the impact of regional effects.

FIGURE 3:5 **Electoral Support for the Liberal Party**

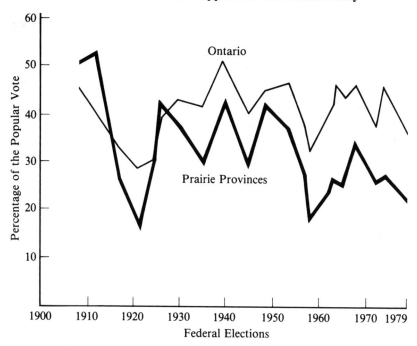

Figure 3:5 shows that the gap between Liberal support in the West and in Ontario has been growing over recent years. In the 10 elections from 1921 to 1957 the Liberals averaged 33.9% of the prairie vote compared to 40.6% in Ontario, the average gap being 6.7%. In the eight elections dating from Diefenbaker's landslide victory in 1958 the Liberals have marginally increased their average share of the Ontario popular vote to 41.3%. At the same time their share of the prairie popular vote dropped to an average of only 25.6% thus increasing the average regional gap to 15.7 per cent. The Trudeau Liberals were unable to break the party's drought in western Canada in part because of the government's preoccupation with national unity issues, a preoccupation accompanied by an apparent disinterest in long-standing regional grievances in western Canada. Trudeau's forays into the West were frequently marred by misunderstandings and bad publicity, as George Radwanski reports: "When Trudeau went to a Liberal dinner in Winnipeg in December [1968] and began his response to a question about selling wheat by saying, "Well, why should I sell the Canadian farmers' wheat?", that incautious opening sentence stuck in the public's mind and quite overshadowed the serious exposition of federal wheat policies that followed; thus began Trudeau's losing of the West."[73] To the intense frustration of western Canadians, however, the Liberals seemed able to write off the

West without serious risk to their hold on national power. The electoral impotence of the West was starkly revealed in the 1974 national election when the Liberals were only five seats short of a majority government before the polls had even closed west of the Ontario border. The five seats that the Liberals eventually did win on the Prairies were electoral gravy for even without a single prairie representative the Liberals would have secured a majority government. Solid support in Quebec, reasonable support in Ontario, and the partisan fragmentation of opposition to the Liberals outside Quebec proved to be a reliable recipe for Liberal electoral success, a recipe in which prairie support was an unnecessary ingredient. In 1979, however, when Liberal support in Ontario buckled, the party's weakness in the West was fatal.

Liberal support on the Prairies has been subject to considerable variation not only over time but also across the three provinces. In Figure 3:5 we have already witnessed the shrinkage over time in the Liberals' share of the regional popular vote. In Table 3:6 the analysis is extended by looking at provincial variations within the regional vote and by examining the number of prairie seats won by the national Liberal party since 1921. Looking first at provincial variations it is apparent that there is little to differentiate between Liberal electoral support in Saskatchewan and Manitoba. Although the periods of Liberal strength in the two provinces do not perfectly coincide, over the long haul there has been little difference between the two provinces. With respect to the number of seats won by the Liberal party the edge goes to Saskatchewan although this is attributable solely to the larger number of seats that have been up for grabs in Saskatchewan during the period under examination. Proportionately, the Liberals captured 33.1% of the Saskatchewan seats in the 18 elections while winning 34.1% of the Manitoba seats. It is Alberta that has proven particularly barren soil for the federal Liberals. The Liberal share of the popular vote in Alberta was less than that received in either Saskatchewan or Manitoba for every period save that from 1968 to 1979; over the 18 elections the Liberal vote in Alberta trailed that in the other two provinces by an average of almost 7%. The relative weakness of Liberal electoral support in Alberta is magnified in the distribution of parliamentary seats. Over the 18 elections only 35 Liberal MPs were elected in Alberta.

Surprisingly, across the region the Trudeau Liberals rebounded somewhat from the debacle of the Pearson years when the party captured only 3.1% of the prairie seats. Compared to the Pearson era the Liberals under Trudeau increased their average share of the popular vote by over 40% although the 1979 vote fell below the average of the Pearson era. The proportionate increase in the number of Liberal seats was even greater although Alberta reverted to a Liberal wasteland; while there were four Liberal MPs elected in Alberta in 1968 there were none elected in 1972, 1974 or 1979. In April 1977 the Liberals gained a temporary

TABLE 3:6

Electoral Support for the Liberal Party

Percentage of the Popular Vote

National Elections By Liberal Leader	Number of Elections	Manitoba	Saskatchewan	Alberta	Region
King: 1921-45	7	32.8	40.2	25.5	31.1
St. Laurent: 1949-57	3	38.1	37.1	32.5	35.9
Pearson: 1958-65	4	29.4	22.6	19.4	23.4
Trudeau: 1968-79	4	30.9	26.2	26.9	27.8
Total: 1921-79	18	32.5	32.7	25.6	30.2

Number of Liberal Seats

National Elections by Liberal Leader	Number of Elections	Manitoba	Saskatchewan	Alberta	Per cent of Regional Seats
King: 1921-45	7	56	75	20	40.8
St. Laurent: 1949-57	3	21	23	10	36.2
Pearson: 1958-65	4	4	1	1	3.1
Trudeau: 1968-79	4	11	6	4	11.4
Total: 1921-79	18	92	105	35	25.1

foothold in Alberta when Conservative Jack Horner crossed the floor of the House of Commons to join the Liberal party and the federal cabinet as a Minister Without Portfolio. In a September 1977 cabinet shuffle Horner was promoted to Minister of Trade and Commerce. In style, mannerisms, and beliefs Jack Horner is the archetypical if not stereotypical prairie politician, and members of his immediate family are politically active throughout the prairie provinces. He is more distinctly cut from western Canadian political cloth than either Otto Lang, the Trudeau governments' principal western Canadian cabinet representative or Joe Clark, the Albertan leader of the national Progressive Conservative party. Nonetheless Horner's contribution to the Liberal party was cut short in the 1979 election when he was trounced by Conservative Arnold Malone; Horner received only 5,947 votes (18.2%) in the Crowfoot constituency compared to 25,202 (77.1%) for Malone. Following the 1979 election the very survival of the Liberal Party in western Canada is open to serious question.

B) The Conservative Party in Western Canada

If the record of the federal Liberal party on the Prairies has been dismal since 1921, that of the Conservative party was even worse until John Diefenbaker captured the party's leadership in 1956. In the minds of western voters the Conservative party was historically linked with central Canada, Bay Street, the National Policy and steadfast support for high tariffs. As the designers and most avid advocates of the National Policy the Conservatives paid a heavy political price on the Prairies.

Apart from brief electoral successes such as those in 1917 and 1930 the party's early track record was little short of disastrous. Even the few successes served in the long run to further weaken the party. In this respect the 1917 election has already been touched upon in the last chapter. After the 1921 election in which the Progressive party won 64 seats to the Conservatives' 50, the adroit Liberal leader Mackenzie King was able to woo many Progressives back into the Liberal fold while the more vitriolic leadership of Conservative Arthur Meighen effectively blocked any prospects of a Progressive fusion with the Conservative party. Here Wood cites a March 1921 speech in the House by the Conservative leader in which the Progressive leaders were described as "servile tools and minions" of the Liberal party, "ready to do whatever they are bid to do"; indeed, they were merely a "delapidated annex" of the Liberal party.[74] It was a speech that fell somewhat short of providing common ground upon which co-operation between the Conservatives and the Progressives could be based, and strategically the speech is in marked contrast to King's description of the Progressives as "Liberals in a hurry." In 1930 the Conservatives gained office under a western Canadian leader, R. B.

FIGURE 3:6 **Electoral Support for the Conservative Party**

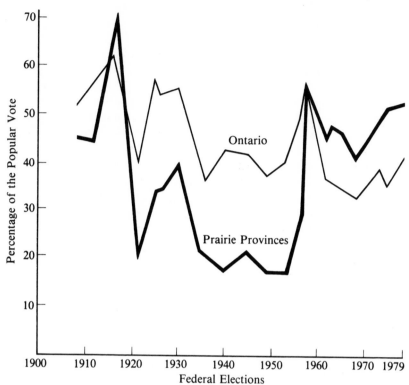

Bennett, only to have the country plunge further into its worst-ever economic crises, leaving the Conservatives little in the West but the derisive epitaph of the "Bennett-Buggy." While in 1930 the Conservatives won 23 prairie seats compared to the Liberals' 18, in 1935 they won but three compared to 31 for the Liberals.

Figure 3:6 illustrates the bleakness of the 1921 to 1957 period for the Conservative party on the Prairies. Throughout that time the party fared much worse in western Canada than it did in Ontario. It also fared much more poorly on the Prairies than did the Liberal party during the same period. In the 10 federal elections from 1921 through 1957 the Conservatives elected only 69 MPs with an average of 24.8% of the prairie popular vote while the Liberals elected 205 members with an average 33.9% share of the popular vote. Even the selection of western Canadian leaders did little to improve Conservative fortunes. R. B. Bennett bolstered the party in both Ontario and the West in 1930 but the continued depression wiped this modest gain and more from the electoral slate. In 1942 the Conservatives chose John Bracken to replace Arthur Meighen, who had recently gone down to a York South byelection defeat at the hands of the CCF. Bracken had been the Progressive Premier of

Manitoba since 1920 and in Meighen's mind he had much to offer the Conservatives: "Mr. Bracken appealed to me because I was convinced that only the farming population of Canada could save this country from the C.C.F. avalanche which was growing at that time very rapidly, and that the leader should be a man who in a high degree had the confidence of the farmers of Canada."[75] As a condition of his acceptance of the Tory leadership the party's name was changed from the Conservative Party to the Progressive Conservative Party in an unsuccessful attempt to link the party to the legacy of the western Progressive movement. That the impact of both Bracken's leadership and the name change was minimal is suggested by the extremely modest bulge in the party's 1945 vote, illustrated in Figure 3:6. In general the post-Bennett Tory slide continued unabated until the party reached its prairie low-point in the election of 1953 when it received only 17.0% of the popular vote.

The Conservatives had the misfortune of being in office going into the two elections that marked the heydays of agrarian revolt, 1921 and 1935. Even when in opposition, however, the Conservative party was unable to capitalize on western antagonism towards the national government. Protest was channeled through third parties which effectively neutralized the Conservatives as a vehicle for western discontent. Eventually, however, this changed as David Smith explains:

> By the early 50s, the protest parties of the West had become 'provincialized'. Prairie voters who wanted to vent their wrath at Liberals and who also hoped to change government policies had to look elsewhere. Eventually, they focused on the one party that had never been popular in the West, the Progressive Conservatives.

The improvement of Conservative fortunes on the Prairies and the transformation of the Conservative party into a vehicle for western political protest began with the 1956 resignation of George Drew from the Tory leadership and the subsequent accession of John Diefenbaker. During the late 30s Diefenbaker had led the Saskatchewan Conservative party, a thankless job at a time when Jimmy Gardiner's Liberal machine dominated national and provincial politics in the province. Diefenbaker nevertheless persevered and in the late 40s and early 50s served as the Conservative's sole Saskatchewan representative in Ottawa. When he became national leader in 1956 he offered the prospect of a long-sought bridge between the Conservative party and the prairie electorate. Not only was he a near native son of western Canada, but his style and rhetoric found resonance in the past half century of western progressive radicalism. Yet it is critical to note that the Conservatives had earlier experimented with western Canadian leaders—including Bracken with his impeccable Progressive credentials—who had been incapable of guiding the party out of the western electoral wilderness. In Diefenbaker's case national success did not follow nor was it prompted by a surge in electoral support across the Prairies. To the contrary it was Conservative success in the central Canadian heartland that propelled Diefenbaker and his party into national office. Diefenbaker and through him the Conservative party were to emerge as champions of the West not in victory but in defeat. Let us examine this contention in some detail.

Although the St. Laurent Liberals did not look particularly vulnerable going into the 1957 election campaign, post-election analyses have tended to emphasize Liberal weaknesses as much as Conservative strengths. David Smith, for example, maintains that the Liberals were hurt in the West by their inability and apparent disinclination to move a huge accumulating surplus of prairie wheat.[77] More generally John Meisel writes that ". . . it appears that the major cause of the Liberal defeat was a widespread feeling that the government had become too powerful, too arrogant and careless in its relations with Parliament, and that government fiscal policies had aroused considerable hostility."[78] Meisel attributes the 1957 Conservative victory to adroitness in exploiting Liberal weaknesses rather than to the positive appeal of either the Conservative party or leader. As is commonly the case governments are more prone to beat themselves than to be beaten by opponents, and in 1957 Tory success hinged upon the prior alienation of the electorate from the incumbent Liberal administration. Here it must be stressed, however, that this alienation was pervasive throughout Canada although it may have been accentuated on the Prairies by the wheat surpluses.

The role played by the Prairie provinces in the Conservative victories of 1957 and 1958 appears to have been marginal. It can be seen from Table 3:7 that between 1953 and 1957 the Conservatives increased their share of the prairie popular vote by more than 11%. However their increase was almost as great in Ontario, where the party captured nearly half the 1957 popular vote compared to less than 29% across the Prairies. The Conservatives, starting from such a low share of the regional popular vote in 1953, captured only 14 of 48 prairie seats in 1957, an increase of eight from the last election. In Saskatchewan, Diefenbaker's home province, the party took only three of 17 seats. In Alberta, soon to become a Conservative bastion, the party also took only three seats with a meagre 27.6% of the popular vote, slightly less than that received by the Liberal party. The Conservatives had faced three formidable federal opponents in the two western-most Prairie provinces: Jimmy Gardiner's patronage-based Liberal machine, Saskatchewan's popular CCF provincial administration led by Tommy Douglas, and the Social Credit Party in Alberta backstopped by Ernest Manning's seemingly invincible Social Credit provincial government. While the Conservatives came close to expelling the Liberals from the Prairies the collapse of the two provincially-sustained opponents would have to wait until 1958.

It was central Canada that delivered the national government to the

TABLE 3:7

Conservative Share of the Popular Vote, 1953-1962

Percentage of the Popular Vote

Region	1953	1957	1958	1962
Atlantic	39.5	48.6	54.5	45.4
Quebec	29.4	31.1	49.6	29.6
Ontario	20.3	38.8	56.4	39.3
Prairies	17.0	28.6	56.2	44.9
British Columbia	14.1	32.6	49.4	27.3
Canada	31.1	38.9	53.6	37.3

Conservatives in 1957. The Conservatives captured 61 of the 85 Ontario seats, up from 33 in 1953. In Quebec the Conservatives received a larger share of the popular vote, albeit five fewer seats, than they did across the Prairies. Thus it cannot be argued that the Diefenbaker Conservatives rode to national power on a wave of western Canadian electoral support. The prairie electorate had a minor role, played with little enthusiasm, in the 1957 victory.

In 1958 Diefenbaker again led his party into a general election, this time to win the largest legislative majority in Canadian history. Prairie voters swung decisively into the Conservative camp electing 47 of the party's 48 candidates. As Denis Smith observed, "the Prairies had not shown such unanimity since 1917 and 1921; and ironically, it was the Conservative party, against which the venom of Prairie discontent had been concentrated in the decades before, that now captured the West more completely than the Progressives and the Liberals had ever been able to."[79] However, in swinging into the Conservative camp the prairie voters were by no means alone. As Table 3:7 demonstrates the Conservatives' share of the prairie popular vote was only slightly above the party's national average. The Conservatives won a larger share of the popular vote in Ontario than on the Prairies, and in Quebec the party's vote was only 4% from the prairie average. The 1958 Conservative win was a national landslide in which the prairie electorate played only a proportionate part. Although the election was to initiate a Conservative hegemony on the Prairies it was not an election in which regional factors came to the fore.

Support for this conclusion comes from several sources. Beck's description of the election concludes that "because voting behavior was virtually uniform across the country, national rather than regional or local factors must be regarded as the primary determinant of the 1958 result."[80] In a review of the election written for the *Political Science*

Quarterly, Dennis Wrong argued that the results represented ". . . the final emergence of the nationalization of politics", that ". . . for the first time in its history, Canada has given a truly national mandate. . . ."[81] On a more technical note, the cross-provincial variance in the winning party's share of the popular vote was smaller in 1958 than in any national election from 1908 to 1979. The regional variation in the 1958 Conservative popular vote was smaller than has been the case for any winning party over the last 70 years.

During the 1957 and 1958 campaigns Diefenbaker gave little attention to the regional concerns of western Canada; if any region came in for special emphasis it was not the West but the far north. His speeches were tailored for national audiences and contained little regional flavour.[82] A 1958 speech quoted in the Ottawa *Journal* resembles the political oratory of Martin Luther King more than it echoes prairie populism:

> Catch the vision! Catch the vision of the kind of Canada this can be! . . .
> I've seen the vision; I've seen the future of Canada. I ask you to have faith in
> this land and faith in our people.[83]

As Diefenbaker notes in his memoirs, " 'One Canada' was my message in 1957; 'One Canada' was my message in 1958."[84] Diefenbaker's memoirs also pay little attention to western Canada, western Canadian themes, or sectional grievances; the focus of the memoirs and the man is unquestionably national rather than regional. In election campaigns "One Canada" could not provide a vehicle for the forceful articulation of sectional concerns; the latter had to give way to broader national themes. Diefenbaker became the champion of the little man generally and of the new Canadian irrespective of his regional residence. As John Meisel notes, "under Mr. Diefenbaker's leadership the Conservative party ceased being identified with eastern financial interests, it professed to have become the champion of the underdog, and it had made a much stronger appeal to those Canadians whose origin was neither British nor French."[85] This latter appeal was enhanced by Michael Starr's appointment as Minister of Labour, making him the first Ukrainian-Canadian to serve in the federal cabinet. In a similar vein Diefenbaker has been described by H. S. Ferns as a genuine outsider: "a man with a non-Anglo-Saxon name in a predominantly Anglo-Saxon party; a Conservative in a Liberal or a Socialist province; a lawyer in a small town far away from the centre of big business; a Baptist in a country where most people are Catholic, United or Anglican; a man with a law degree from a prairie college in a nation where the leading bureaucrats get their degrees from big-name universities."[86]

Denis Smith has made the argument that Diefenbaker's appeal to pan-Canadian themes, while apparently subordinating regional concerns, at the same time captured an important component of western Canadian political aspirations:

He gave to the Prairies for the first time in their history the same sense of dynamic and central participation in nation-building that his predecessor, John A. Macdonald, had given to central Canada after 1867 . . . John Diefenbaker's policies, when he came into power in 1957, were policies of national integration that typified the Prairie conception of Canada. His emphasis upon 'unhyphenated Canadianism' reflected 50 years of watching the new community in its efforts to find its own character by assimilating its disparate national elements into a single, dominant, English-speaking personality.[87]

It was unfortunate that Diefenbaker was to run up against a resurgent Quebec pursuing a very different vision of Canada and Canadianism.

To a degree the anti-establishment tone of the Diefenbaker government reflected populist sentiment and as such it was a source of appeal in the West and suspicion in the East. Nevertheless in the early years of his leadership Diefenbaker was at best an incidental spokesman for western Canada. It was not until his administration came under sustained attack and Diefenbaker came to see himself vilified by the press, establishment and politicians of eastern Canada that the regional aspects of Diefenbaker's style and electoral appeal came increasingly to the fore. It began to appear both to Diefenbaker and to many of his western Canadian supporters that the Conservative leader had been cast in the time-honoured role of the prairie leader pilloried by central Canada. It is in defeat that we see Diefenbaker as an embattled champion of western Canada; the mistake to be avoided is to assume that this role played a significant part in the Conservative victories of 1957 and 1958. At his peak Diefenbaker was a leader who rose above his region to stand astride the nation as a whole.

The significant point about the Diefenbaker years is not that the prairie electorate swung into the Conservative camp, for so too did the rest of the country in 1958. Rather it is that the Prairie provinces stayed in the Conservative camp when the rest of the country more or less returned to the Liberal fold. In this respect Flanagan labels the 1958 election as a *realigning* election in western Canada whereas it is more appropriately termed a *deviating* election elsewhere in the country.[88] The sustained prairie support for the Conservatives had a great deal to do with the party's agricultural policies. The 1957 election results suggest, of course, that the Conservative agricultural platform did little to stampede prairie voters into the Conservative camp; at best it reinforced other factors eroding support for the Liberal party. It was the performance of the Diefenbaker government in terms of agricultural legislation, not campaign promises, that won and retained the West. Under Diefenbaker's leadership very significant advances were made on the agricultural front. These included the Agricultural Stabilization Act, cash advances on farm-stored wheat (The Prairie Grain Advance Payments Act), the 1961 Agricultural Rehabilitation and Development Act, the South Saskatchewan River Dam and, under western agricultural minister Alvin Hamilton, the 1961 initiation of wheat sales to communist countries. Diefenbaker was justly proud of his agricultural record.

At long last prairie grain producers had found a national government sympathetic and responsive to their plight, and these traits were perhaps as important as agricultural legislation in winning the West. As Smith points out about the Tories, "it was not that they were initially more successful at dealing with the old problems—they were not—but their publicized open-door to farmers, leading directly to the Prime Minister, who was himself a Westerner, assuaged the Prairies' desire for attention, which in the 50s the Liberals seemed more often to withhold than to give".[89]

The transformation of the Conservative party into a vehicle for western Canadian political discontent accelerated with Diefenbaker's fall from power in 1963. The new Liberal government under Lester Pearson became increasingly preoccupied with problems emanating from Quebec, a preoccupation that derailed any serious attention to the concerns and grievances of western Canada. As a consequence the Liberals were unable to make any electoral headway in western Canada against the Conservative party led by a native son; the Liberals won two prairie seats in 1962, three in 1963, and only one in 1965. Failure in the West, however, did little to weaken the Liberals' grip on national office and Westerners, locked into support for the Conservative party, became increasingly frustrated as that support went for naught. No matter how many seats the Conservatives won in the West national office remained elusively beyond the party's grasp. While western Canadians were thus frustrated at their inability to oust the incumbent Liberals their rejection of the Liberals led to a muted western Canadian voice within the national government. The national government in turn became ever less sensitive to western Canadian concerns and a vicious cycle was spawned. Just as prairie support in the past for the Progressives, the CCF, and the Social Credit served to isolate the region from the centres of national political power, so too did near-monolithic support for the Conservatives in the late 60s and 70s.

It is important to note here the role played by Canada's electoral system. The West's rejection of the Liberal party has been far more complete with respect to seats than it has been in terms of the popular vote. For example, in the six federal elections held between 1962 and 1974 the Liberals received an average of 27.4% of the regional popular vote but picked up an average of only 9.0% of the prairie seats. To take an even more extreme example, in both the 1972 and 1974 federal elections the Liberals took 25% of the popular vote in Alberta but failed to win a seat either time. Thus as Alan Cairns has demonstrated in a more general context, the Canadian electoral system distorts regional representation within the House of Commons and in doing so exacerbates regional tensions beyond what one might expect as a consequence of the division of the popular vote.[90]

At least within the Alberta electorate a strong relationship existed in the mid-seventies between levels of western alienation and partisan identifications with the Conservative party. However, it remains unclear whether alienated Westerners gravitated toward the Conservative party or whether identification with the Conservative party enhanced pre-existing levels of alienation. One could argue, for instance, that alienated Westerners turned to the Conservative party as the most viable means of expressing their discontent with the incumbent government, which happened to be Liberal in complexion. Since 1963 the Conservative party had been the Official Opposition and its electoral support in western Canada may have reflected opposition to the national government as much as it reflected any affection for Conservative ideas, policies, or personnel. Here we might note what David Smith calls a "floating radicalism that knows no partisan attachment," a spirit of political revolt and alienation that over the region's history has attached itself to a variety of expressive movements.[91] On the other hand there is every reason to have expected Conservative supporters to become increasingly alienated from the national government, both because that government was Liberal and because the Conservative party remained shut out of national office. In this sense partisan discontent may have appeared as regional discontent due to the disproportionate number of Conservative supporters in western Canada.

Even given the chicken-and-egg relationship between western alienation and Conservative strength on the Prairies, it is clear that in recent years the Conservative party has served as an expressive vehicle for regional discontent. It should be noted, though, that the support for the Conservatives became regionalized only as the party's grip on national office began to weaken in the 1960s. In addition, the change from regional political protest expressed through the creation of indigenous protest parties to that expressed through the oldest national party in Canada should not be lightly dismissed in its significance. Also, to state that the Progressive Conservative party has become a vehicle for regional discontent in western Canada is not to state that the party has become a western protest party. The distinction between a vehicle for western discontent and a western Canadian protest party can be made by examining Figure 3:7 which presents the proportion of the total Conservative popular vote that has come from the prairie electorate since 1908. Two observations are immediately apparent. The first is that since the accession of Diefenbaker the western Canadian contribution to the Conservative popular vote has increased substantially and to this extent the Conservative party has been regionalized during the last two decades. The second observation is that even over the last two decades fewer than one Conservative voter in four has lived on the Prairies. In 1979, for ex-

FIGURE 3:7 **Percentage of the Total Conservative National Popular Vote Coming from the Prairie Provinces**

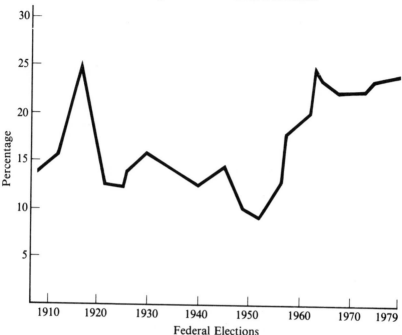

ample, 23.9% of the Conservative votes came from the Prairies. While the prairie component of the Conservative popular vote has increased the bulk of the party's vote still comes from outside the region. The Conservative party therefore cannot be considered a western regional party in the same genre as the Progressive Party, the Social Credit or the CCF. The Conservatives originated outside the West and indeed emerged before there was a western Canadian electorate, and has drawn the vast majority of its support from outside the prairie region. It is not a regional party but rather a national party that is currently employed as an expressive vehicle for regional discontent.

The strong regional support that the Conservative party has received from the Prairies has been the source of considerable intra-party tension arising from several sources. While prairie seats were an important stepping stone to national office the prairie electorate could not by itself deliver that office to the party. To the extent that the Conservative party publicly accepted the regional mantle of western protest its electoral prospects were impaired elsewhere in the country. For the Conservative party, even more so than for the Liberals, southern Ontario remained the primary campaign target and in southern Ontario the cloak of western regional protest generated little electoral enthusiasm. Hence in the 1974 national campaign Conservative leader Robert Stanfield appeared reluctant to endorse or even empathize with Alberta's energy position. To have done so would have hurt the party in southern Ontario while Alberta's 19 seats were already in the bag for the Conservatives. Similarly Joe Clark's early tenure as Tory leader was marked by Clark's determined efforts to appear as a national figure rather than as a sectional spokesman reflecting his Alberta roots. During this period there was considerable speculation that Jack Horner's departure from the Conservative party had been engineered in part by Conservative campaign strategists who felt that the removal of Horner would enhance the party's image in southern Ontario. Thus while many western Canadians may have utilized the Conservative party in order to express their dissatisfaction with the national government, that party was reluctant to provide unequivocal leadership for western concerns. To have done so, it was feared, would have doomed the party to electoral marginality as it has doomed other western-based parties in the past.

The 1979 election may well have been a signal event in the political evolution of western Canada. In only four previous elections—1908, 1917, 1958 and 1962—has the party winning the election received a larger share of the prairie popular vote than that of the country as a whole. During the 11 post-war elections running from 1945 to 1974 the party forming the national government averaged only 34.5% of the prairie popular vote compared to an average 45.2% of the Ontario popular vote. Yet in 1979 the prairie electorate endorsed the winning Conservatives with 53.0% of the popular vote compared to 41.8% for the Conservatives in Ontario and 35.9% across the country as a whole. The Conservative party, led by a Westerner strongly backed by the prairie electorate and containing 38 prairie MPs, had returned from the political wilderness into which it had been driven following Diefenbaker's defeat in 1963.

In putting together his first cabinet Joe Clark if anything de-emphasized the western base of his party; far more attention was paid to bolstering the party in Quebec. Clark himself, moreover, has few characteristics that are readily identified with either the Prairies or prairie politics. As Jack Horner observed following the 1979 election, "Clark isn't a Westerner—he can't even ride a horse!" Joe Clark is a national politician who just happened to grow up in Alberta; he is not a prairie politician in any traditional sense. Given Clark's electoral success on the Prairies and given the magnitude of Horner's personal defeat in 1979, one is tempted to argue that the 1979 election represents a significant shift in the style of prairie politics, a shift that reflects the continued nationalization and de-regionalization of prairie electoral politics. Whether such a shift persists will depend upon the future electoral fortunes of the Conservative party and upon the success of future governments in grappling with long-standing elements of western alienation.

C) Provincial Variance in Major Party Support

While it has been demonstrated that the prairie region has been relatively distinct in its patterns of electoral support for both the Liberal and Conservative parties, the degree of cross-provincial homogeneity in electoral behavior has not been addressed. Of particular concern is whether or not there has been any long-term secular change in electoral variability within the prairie region. Thus we might ask whether the three Prairie provinces are converging—becoming more homogeneous—in the degree of support for either or both of the two major parties, a trend that would be indicative of increased regionalization. Alternatively electoral behavior across the three provinces could be increasingly heterogeneous, a trend that would be indicative of increased regionalization.

Changes in the degree of regional homogeneity or heterogeneity in electoral behavior are not easy to pin down. The measure of homogeneity adopted here is the range in the Liberal and Conservative shares of the national popular vote across the three Prairie provinces. For example, the range in the Liberal vote is calculated by subtracting the smallest share of the popular vote won by the party in any of the three provinces in a given national election from the largest share. The greater the range in the popular vote the more heterogeneous the region is in its political behavior; the smaller the range the more homogeneous. Although the range is generally considered to be a poor measure of variability because it utilizes only the two extreme scores, this is not a serious shortcoming when only three provinces are under examination. The range alone, however, is a flawed measure in that it is affected by the overall size of the popular vote received by a party in the region. If the Conservative party received an average of 50% of the popular vote across the region an inter-provincial range of 10% would not be all that significant. On the other hand a range of 10% could be indicative of considerably more heterogeneity if the party's share of the regional popular vote averaged only 10% to 15%. It is for this reason that the Regional Homogeneity Index presented in Figure 3:8 divides the range by the percentage of the regional popular vote won by the party under consideration. The resultant index score, while not meaningful in an absolute sense, provides a useful measure by which to assess changes in the homogeneity of regional electoral support for the Conservative and Liberal parties.

Turning then to Figure 3:8 it can be seen that there has been no dramatic change in the homogeneity of regional political behavior over time. There has, however, been some change. The Liberal share of the popular vote across the three provinces has tended to become more homogeneous; the average index score for the first 10 elections (1908-1945) was .48, compared to an average of .30 for the last eleven (1949-1979). If we look only at the range of the Liberal vote without any correction for the size of the popular vote, the range dropped from an

FIGURE 3:8 **Regional Homogeneity in Federal Electoral Support for the Liberal and Progressive Conservative Parties**

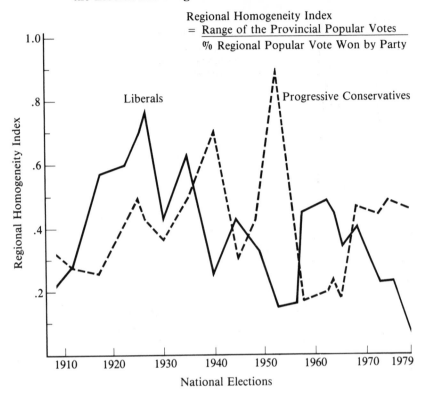

Regional Homogeneity Index

$$= \frac{\text{Range of the Provincial Popular Votes}}{\% \text{ Regional Popular Vote Won by Party}}$$

average of 16.3% for the first 10 elections to only 11.8% for the last 11. In 1979 the range was only 1.7%. The intra-regional variability in the Liberal popular vote has been illustrated earlier in Figure 1:1. Referring back to that figure it can be seen that while the party's share of the vote in the three provinces has tended to fluctuate to a regional and indeed national rhythm it has done so at markedly different levels of provincial support. Of particular note here is the relatively low level of support that the Liberal party received in Alberta from the mid-1920s to the end of the Diefenbaker government. On balance, however, Figure 1:1 supports the conclusion that the Liberal vote is becoming more homogeneous across the Prairie provinces—the three lines representing the party's provincial shares of the national vote appear to be converging over time. Thus for the Liberal party there is evidence of increased homogenization over time and particularly in the past 15 years, a homogenization that has come hand in hand with a secular decline in the Liberals' share of the regional popular vote.

The variability in the Conservative popular vote had undergone less

FIGURE 3:9 **Percentage of the Popular Vote Won by the Conservative Party in Federal Elections**

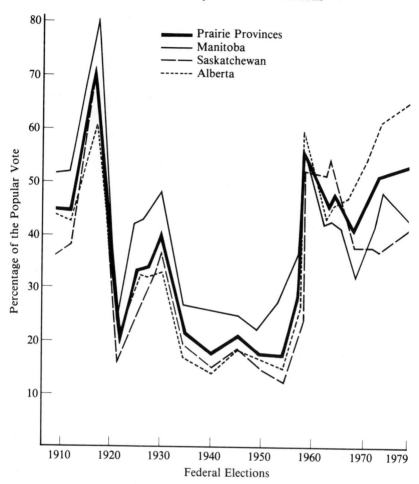

change over time. The mean regional homogeneity index score was .41 for the first 10 elections in Figure 3:8 and .40 for the last 11. Figure 3:9 illustrates the intra-regional variability of the Conservative vote in more detail. Generally speaking the Conservative share of the popular vote across the three Prairie provinces moved in a rhythmic fashion until the end of the Diefenbaker governments. Admittedly rather consistent interprovincial differences have existed in the level of popular support as witnessed by the historical Conservative strength in Manitoba. Nevertheless the party's provincial shares of the national vote have tended to oscillate together; the orchestration provided by the Diefenbaker years is particularly striking. Since the early 1960s, however, the Conservative popular vote has been marked by increased heterogeneity, a pattern quite the converse of that observed for the Liberal party. Any trend towards increased regional homogenization appears to be restricted to the Liberal vote.

D) The CCF and the New Democratic Party

The 1958 election remade the face of prairie federal politics. It brought into regional dominance a party that had languished at the very margins of prairie politics for the previous 50 years, and in doing so brought back the integrative, brokerage politics of national party organizations to the prairie electorate. That election also destroyed the prairie base of the CCF. The 1957 contingent of 10 CCF MPs from Saskatchewan and five from Manitoba was reduced to a single Saskatchewan representative. CCF luminaries M. S. Coldwell and Stanley Knowles both lost their seats. In its last national election the CCF for the first time captured more seats in Ontario than on the Prairies. The shift was prophetic of changes that were to follow.

The 1958 debacle strengthened the resolve of the Canadian Labour Congress to create a new party of the political left, a party that could speak for the interests of labour, a party ". . . not burdened with the image of the old CCF. . . ."[92] In 1960 the CLC, urban social democrats, and the remnants of the CCF launched the New Democratic Party, a party that was to be based on social democratic ideas and which was to direct its appeal toward the urbanized working and middle classes. In some respects the NDP was a continuation under a different label of the older CCF. Certainly the 1961 selection of Tommy Douglas, the CCF Premier of Saskatchewan, as the first NDP national leader helped cement the continuity in the public mind. Yet in more important ways the NDP differed significantly from its predecessor. In the new party trade unions provided the organizational mainstay that farm organizations had provided for the CCF in the past. The shift to a trade union base recognized the direction of social change in Canada; the older agrarian base of the CCF was disappearing and a new urban, industrialized working class was emerging, one that was thought to lack adequate representation within the two major parties.

On the Prairies, the creation of the NDP was not accomplished without acrimony and the alienation of many long-term CCF supporters who felt out of place in the new party. The principal problem lay with the labour base of the NDP. Farm-labour relations had never been easy on the Prairies despite a number of political coalitions between the two groups. As B. Y. Card explains:

> In relation to the region's total culture, the labour movement was something of an urban side-show beside the main agrarian attraction. Although labour

followed the same general plot of revolt against eastern dominance, the relationships between its actors and those of the agrarian show were characterized by indifference and antagonism.[93]

It is thus not surprising that many of the farm organizations that had helped the CCF refused to join the NDP, and that the trade union aura of the NDP did little to lure prairie voters away from their new-found attachment to the Conservative party led by John Diefenbaker. The Saskatchewan farmers, the backbone of the CCF, correctly feared that they would be overshadowed in the new party by a labour movement they viewed with unease, suspicion and even hostility.[94] In Alberta where the small CCF contingent was ". . . controlled by exponents of a branch of socialism so extreme that it made most British Columbia 'leftists' seem mildly liberal,"[95] Relations between the CCF and labour were little better. Among the three Prairie provinces opposition to the new party was weakest in Manitoba where it came predominantly from young urban party activists rather than from the agrarian wing of the CCF.[96]

The trade union support for the new party, the lack of enthusiasm on the Prairies, and the conscious effort of the NDP leadership to reorient the party to the urban working class all led to a shift in electoral support away from the prairie heartland of the CCF to Ontario and British Columbia. By the 1965 national election the federal council of the NDP was convinced that ". . . the turnabout had begun, that the farmers had been left behind, and labour support was the new fact of life."[97] Figure 2:3 in the previous chapter demonstrated that the NDP has done proportionately as well in Ontario as it has done across the Prairies, a sharp reversal of the CCF pattern depicted in the same figure. Figure 3:10 shows that by far the largest bloc of NDP voters is to be found in Ontario; in 1979 42.6% of the total NDP vote came from Ontario as opposed to 20.8% from the Prairies and 8.5% from Saskatchewan. The pattern is drastically altered from the early years of the CCF. Finally Table 3:10 shows that the proportion of NDP members elected from the province of Ontario has increased almost five-fold over the previous history of the CCF whereas the proportion of NDP members elected from the Prairie provinces stands at little more than a third of the CCF proportion.

Electorally, then, the NDP is very different from the CCF. Its electoral base, although weak in the Atlantic provinces and barely existent in Quebec, is national rather than regional. Its prairie component in terms of votes or elected members is only proportionate to the prairie share of the Canadian population. Ideologically the party has shed the CCF's forced concern with agrarian issues and now concentrates on those arising from urbanization, industrialization and unionization. Finally, the leadership of the party has shifted from the Prairies to Ontario with David Lewis and Ed Broadbent replacing J. S. Woodsworth, M. S.

FIGURE 3:10 **Percentage of Total CCF/NDP National Vote Coming From Ontario, Saskatchewan and the Prairie Provinces.**

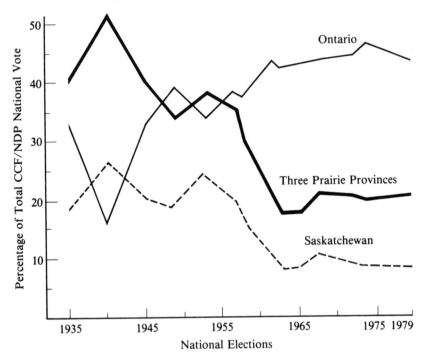

Coldwell and Tommy Douglas. In retrospect it seems that Douglas was a questionable choice as the first leader of the NDP even though he was the pre-eminent left-wing electoral success in Canada and an inspired campaigner. Douglas represented the collapsed Saskatchewan powerbase of the older CCF. In 1962, in his first national campaign as NDP leader, Douglas was beaten in his bid for election in Regina. He ran up against an informal Liberal-Conservative coalition mobilized by the Saskatchewan medicare dispute and was beaten handily; the Conservative candidate received 22,164 votes compared to 12,674 for Douglas. A November byelection put Douglas into the House as the MP from Burnaby-Coquitlam in British Columbia. Then in 1968 Douglas was beaten in the redistributed riding of Burnaby-Seymour by Liberal Ray Perrault, although his campaign efforts in Saskatchewan led the NDP to seven seats there. In 1969 Douglas won a Vancouver Island byelection to represent the riding of Nanaimo-Cowichan-The Islands. His electoral exodus to the west coast symbolized the transformation of the NDP powerbase. The NDP picked up the heritage but not the electorate of the CCF. The shift in leadership and electoral support from the agrarian west to the union strongholds of Ontario and British Columbia completed the

TABLE 3:8
Regional Distribution of CCF and NDP Members of Parliament

	CCF (1935-1958)		NDP (1962-1979)	
	#	%	#	%
Atlantic	4	3.6	4	2.6
Quebec	—	—	—	—
Ontario	8	7.1	52	34.2
Prairies	71	63.4	37	24.3
—Manitoba	19	17.0	20	13.2
—Saskatchewan	52	46.4	17	11.2
—Alberta	—	—	—	—
British Columbia	29	25.9	56	36.8
Yukon/N.W.T.	—	—	3	2.0
Total	112	100.0%	152	100.0%

process of electoral change that the Diefenbaker Conservatives had so forcefully begun in 1958.

Whereas the CCF was inadvertently a regional party, the carrier of a western creed of sectional discontent and agrarian distress, the NDP has been nationalized. In program, personnel and electoral support (west of Quebec) the NDP has shed the regional character of its predecessor. Given this nationalization, support for the federal NDP within the prairie electorate can no longer be considered a manifestation of regional politics. In the evolution of the CCF into the NDP an important feature of regional politics in western Canada has been erased.

CONCLUSIONS

Two broad arguments have been advanced in this chapter. The first is that the socio-economic character of the prairie society has been fundamentally transformed in the decades following the Second World War and that the direction of this transformation has been such to erode the regional distinctiveness of the prairie society. The evidence here is incontestable although there is room for debate concerning the degree of distinctiveness that remains.

The second argument, that socio-economic change has been accompanied by political change and that the political change has been in the direction of declining regionalism, is incontestable in part. Unquestionably the political face of the Prairies has changed. Many of the issues that had charged prairie politics in the past—prohibition, the separate school question, female suffrage, the Social Gospel, the provincial control of public lands and the Depression—have left the political agenda. The distinctive western Canadian parties of the past—the UFA, the Progressives, the Social Credit and the CCF—have fallen by the wayside. It was the Diefenbaker Conservatives who were the direct agents of the most dramatic political changes, re-establishing at least one of the major parties on the Prairies, obliterating the western wing of the national Social Credit party, and destroying the western base of the CCF, leaving that party to be replaced by a resurgent New Democratic Party that has effectively shaken off the regional roots of its predecessor. Thus the regional distinctiveness that characterized prairie politics in the past has been largely dispelled; the rejection of the national political parties and the creation and support of regional third parties belong to the past.

There are, however, two wrinkles in the argument that political regionalism is on the decline in western Canada. The first is that social change may have produced greater homogeneity within the prairie region at the same time that it rendered the Prairies more homogeneous with the rest of Canada. Nationalization, in other words, may appear to enhance regional homogeneity in its wake. Here we might refer back to the decreasing regional variability in the Liberal popular vote noted in Figure 3:8. Also, the collapse of the Social Credit party has moved Alberta's electoral behavior into closer step with that of Saskatchewan and Manitoba, and to a somewhat lesser degree the disappearance of the CCF has diminished the electoral uniqueness of national politics in Saskatchewan. Thus the spread of Conservative hegemony in the wake of the disappearance of third parties has increased the political homogeneity of the Prairies. Yet the more important change, I would argue, is the decline in regional distinctiveness.

The second and more serious wrinkle is the fact that of the two major parties only the Progressive Conservatives have re-established themselves on the Canadian prairies. In addition, the prairie support for the Conservatives has been so substantive and so pervasive across the three provinces that one might argue that political regionalism has not been submerged but that it has simply changed in form and is now being expressed through solid regional support for the Progressive Conservative party. Nevertheless, if prairie support for the Conservative party does reflect regionalized politics it reflects a radically altered style of regionalism than existed in the past. The Conservative party has not abandoned its image and aspirations as a national party and indeed secures the great bulk of its popular vote outside western Canada. Nor has the Conservative party served as an articulator of regional concerns in the manner of indigenous third parties in the past; while the electoral support of the Conservatives may have been substantially regionalized the party itself has not been. More importantly, even if western concerns and frustrations are being expressed through monolithic electoral support for the Conservative party it is of great significance that a national party is now being used as the vehicle for regional discontent, particularly when that party forms the national government. This reflects a greater degree of integration into the national political system than existed in the past and a consequential decline in political regionalism.

NOTES

1. R. M. Burns, "Prairie Union—Implications for Canadian Federalism," in David K. Elton, ed., *One Prairie Province?*, Lethbridge Herald, 1970, p. 66.

2. Warren E. Kalbach and Wayne W. McVey, *The Demographic Bases of Canadian Society*, Toronto, McGraw-Hill, 1971, p. 86.

3. It should be noted that census definitions of "rural" and "urban" have changed substantially over time and thus Figure 3:3 presents an approximate picture only. For a discussion see *1971 Census of Canada*, Vol. V—Part 1 (Bulletin 5.1-2).

4. George F. G. Stanley, "The Western Canadian Mystique," in David P. Gagan, Ed., *Prairie Perspectives*, Toronto, Holt, Rinehart and Winston, 1970, p. 25.

5. For a counterargument see J. M. S. Careless who argues that metropolitan growth within provinces and the devolution of major government functions onto provincial governments may have increased provincial struggles with the federal government and hence regional cleavages. "Limited Identities in Canada," *Canadian Historical Review*, L, No. 1 (March 1969), pp. 1-10.

6. James Gray notes that nearly 10,000 people were deported between 1932 and 1933 alone. *The Winter Years: The Depression on the Prairies*, Toronto, Macmillan, 1966, p. 131.

7. Kalbach and McVey, *Demographic Bases*, p. 93.

8. John Kralt, "Ethnic Origins of Canadians," *1971 Census of Canada*, Vol. V—Part 1 (Bulletin 5.1-7), August 1976.

9. *Ibid.*, p. 37.

10. Harry H. Hiller, *Canadian Society: A Sociological Analysis*, Scarborough, Prentice-Hall, 1976, p. 23.

11. For a discussion see David E. Smith, *Prairie Liberalism: The Liberal Party in Saskatchewan, 1905-1971*, Toronto, University of Toronto Press, 1975, Chapter Five.

12. For example see T. Peterson, "Ethnic and Class Politics in Manitoba," in Martin Robin, ed., *Canadian Provincial Politics*, Scarborough, Prentice-Hall, 1972, pp. 69-115.

13. For a discussion of ethnicity in Alberta see Thomas Flanagan, "Ethnic Voting in Alberta Provincial Elections," *Canadian Ethnic Studies*, December 1971, pp. 139-164.

14. Smith, *Prairie Liberalism*, p. 198.

15. Peterson, "Ethnic and Class Politics," pp. 113-15.

16. Carle C. Zimmerman and Garry W. Moneo, *The Prairie Community System*, Agricultural Economics, Research Council of Canada, 1971, p. 18.

17. Jack Scott, "Canada's Religious Composition,"*1971 Census of Canada, Vol. V—Part 1 (Bulletin 5.1-10), May 1976, p. 13.*

18. William P. Irvine, "Explaining the Religious Basis of Canadian Partisan Identity: Success on a Third Try," *Canadian Journal of Political Science,* September 1974, pp. 560-563.

19. R. Daviault, *Selected Agricultural Statistics for Canada*, Ottawa, Economics Branch, Agriculture Canada, 1976, p. 7. Daviault notes, however, that the 1941 and 1971 census figures are not strictly comparable due to changes in the census definition of a farm.

20. Kalbach and McVey, *Demographic Bases*, p. 74.

21. Daviault, *Selected Agricultural Statistics*, p. 136.

22. *Canada Year Book*, Ottawa, Statistics Canada, 1975.

23. John Stahl, "Prairie Agriculture: A Prognosis," in David P. Gagan, ed., *Prairie Perspectives*, Toronto, Holt, Rinehart and Winston, 1970, p. 67.

24. Daviault, *Selected Agricultural Statistics*, p. 112.

25. Alberta Bureau of Statistics, *Alberta Industry and Resources*, 1973.

26. Daviault, *Selected Agricultural Statistics*, p. 9. During the same period in Ontario the number of acres *decreased* by 28.7 per cent.

27. *Ibid.*, p. 14.

28. *Ibid.*, p. 40.

29. *Ibid.*, p. 51.

30. *Financial Post*, July 17, 1976, p. 6. The article points out that this is not a typical Manitoba farm; 72% of Manitoba's 35,000 farmers earned less than $3000 in 1971.

31. Barbara J. Genno and Larry M. Genno, *Food Production in the Canadian Environment*, Ottawa, Science Council of Canada, 1976, p. 27.

32. *Ibid.*, p. 53.

33. Donald E. Willmott, "The Formal Organizations of Saskatchewan Farmers, 1900-65", in Anthony W. Rasporich, ed., *Western Canada Past and Present*, Calgary, McClelland & Stewart West, 1975, p. 39.

34. *Ibid.*, p. 39.

35. W. L. Morton, *The Progressive Party of Canada*, Toronto, University of Toronto Press, 1950, p. 293.

36. Gerald I. Trant, David L. MacFarlane, and Lewis A. Fischer, *Trade Liberalization and Canadian Agriculture*, Toronto, University of Toronto Press, 1968, p. 8.

37. W. A. MacKintosh, *Economic Problems of the Prairies*, Toronto, Macmillan, 1935, pp. 7-8.

38. Trant, *Trade Liberalization*, p. 12.

39. *Canada Year Book*, Ottawa, Information Canada 1975, p. 471.

40. Robert W. Crown and Earl O. Hardy, *Policy Integration in Canadian Agriculture*, Ames, Iowa, Iowa State University Press, 1972, p. 13.

41. Daviault, *Selected Agricultural Statistics*, pp. 83-85.

42. Bruce Proudfoot, "Agriculture," in P. J. Smith, ed., *Studies in Canadian Geography: The Prairies*, Toronto, University of Toronto Press, 1972, p. 61.

43. *Calgary Herald*, January 18, 1977, p. 27.

44. Brenton M. Barr, "Reorganization of the Economy Since 1945," in Smith, *Studies in Canadian Geography*, p. 81.

45. Vernon C. Fowke, *Canadian Agricultural Policy: The Historical Pattern*, Toronto, University of Toronto Press, 1947, p. 186.

46. V. C. Fowke and Donald Fowke, "Political Economy and the Canadian Wheat Grower," in Norman Ward and Duff Spafford, eds., *Politics in Saskatchewan*, Don Mills, Ontario, Longmans Can. Ltd., 1968, p. 216.

47. D. A. MacGibbon, *The Canadian Grain Trade, 1931-1951*, Toronto, University of Toronto Press, 1952, p. 9.

48. *Ibid.*, p. 10.

49. J. R. Mallory, *Social Credit and the Federal Power in Canada*, Toronto, University of Toronto Press, 1954, p. 60.

50. Gray, *The Winter Years*, p. 165.

51. *Ibid.*, p. 164.

52. Walter Young, *Democracy and Discontent*, Toronto, McGraw-Hill, 1969, p. 45.

53. Gray, *The Winter Years*, p. 6.

54. *Ibid.*, p. 166.

55. A. R. Jones, Compiler, *Provincial Legislation Pertinent to Agriculture in Manitoba, Saskatchewan, Alberta and British Columbia*, Ottawa, Economics Branch, Agriculture Canada, 1975.

56. A. R. Jones, Compiler, *Policies and Programs for Agriculture: Manitoba, Saskatchewan, Alberta, British Columbia*, Ottawa, Economics Branch, Agriculture Canada, 1976.

57. Genno and Genno, *Food Production*, p. 21.

58. *Calgary Herald*, January 10, 1978, p. A1.

59. For a useful overview of Innis in this context see Abraham Rotstein, "Innis: The Alchemy of Fur and Wheat," *Journal of Canadian Studies*, Winter 1977.

60. Fowke, *Canadian Agricultural Policy*, p. 210.

61. Helen Jones Dawson, "An Interest Group: The Canadian Federation of Agriculture," *Canadian Public Administration*, Vol. III, No. 2 (June 1960), pp. 134-149.

62. Richard Hofstadter, *The Age of Reform*, New York, 1955, p. 95.

63. Donald Baron, "Regional Development—Agriculture," in Elton, ed., *One Prairie Province*, p. 367.

64. T. D. Regehr, "Western Canada and the Burden of National Transportation Policies," in David Jay Bercuson, ed., *Canada and the Burden of National Unity*, Toronto, Macmillan, 1977, p. 132.

65. *Calgary Herald*, January 5, 1979, p. A2.

66. Regehr, "Western Canada," p. 134.

67. C. B. Macpherson, *Democracy in Alberta: Social Credit and the Party System*, Toronto, University of Toronto Press, 1953.

68. Macpherson's assumption here has been quite rightly challenged. See Thomas Flanagan, "Political Geography and the United Farmers of Alberta," in S. M. Trofimenkoff, ed., *The Twenties in Western Canada*, Ottawa, National Museum of Man, 1972, pp. 138-169.

69. Gray, *The Winter Years*, p. 53.

70. Carl Berger, "William Morton: The Delicate Balance of Region and Nation," in Carl Berger and Ramsay Cook, eds., *The West and the Nation: Essays in Honour of W. L. Morton*, Toronto, McClelland and Stewart, 1976, p. 13.

71. J. F. Conway, "From Petitions to Politics: The Agitation for the Redress of Prairie Agrarian Grievances, 1880-1930," Paper presented at the 1977 Annual Meetings of the Canadian Sociology and Anthropology Association, Fredericton, New Brunswick.

72. Conrad Winn, "Elections," in Conrad Winn and John McMenemy, eds., *Political Parties in Canada*, Toronto, McGraw-Hill Ryerson, 1976, p. 116.

73. George Radwanski, *Trudeau*, Toronto, Macmillan, 1978, p. 242.

74. Louis Aubrey Wood, *A History of Farmers' Movements in Canada*, Toronto, University of Toronto Press, Republished 1975, p. 354.

75. J. L. Granatstein, *The Politics of Survival: The Conservative Party of Canada, 1939-1945*, Toronto, University of Toronto Press, 1967, p. 138.

76. David E. Smith, "Western Politics and National Unity," in Bercuson, *Canada and the Burden of Unity*, p. 156.

77. David E. Smith, "Grits and Tories on the Prairies," in Hugh G. Thorburn, ed., *Party Politics in Canada*, 4th edition, Scarborough, Prentice-Hall, 1979, p. 279.

78. John Meisel, *The Canadian General Election of 1957*, Toronto, University of Toronto Press, 1962, p. 274.

79. Denis Smith, "Liberals and Conservatives on the Prairies, 1917-1968," in Gagan, *Prairie Perspectives*, p. 40.

80. J. M. Beck, *Pendulum of Power*, Scarborough, Prentice-Hall, 1968, p. 297.

81. Dennis H. Wrong, "Parties and Voting in Canada," *Political Science Quarterly*, LXXIII, No. 3 (September 1958), pp. 408-409.

82. John Meisel supports this point with an analysis of Diefenbaker's 1957 television speeches. *The Canadian General Election*, pp. 285-289.

83. Beck, *Pendulum of Power*, p. 316.

84. John G. Diefenbaker, *One Canada: The Years of Achievement, 1957-1962*, Toronto, Macmillan, 1976, p. 226.

85. Meisel, *The Canadian General Election*, p. 271.

86. H. S. Ferns, "The New Course in Canadian Politics," *Political Quarterly*, XXIX (April 1958), p. 116.

87. Smith, "Liberals and Conservatives," p. 41.

88. Flanagan, "Political Geography and the United Farmers of Alberta," p. 148.

89. Smith, "Grits and Tories," pp. 281-2.

90. Alan C. Cairns, "The Electoral System and the Party System in Canada, 1921-1965," *Canadian Journal of Political Science*, March 1968, pp. 55-80.

91. David Smith, "Conclusions," in Gagan, *Prairie Perspectives*, pp. 92-95.

92. Gad Horowitz, *Canadian Labour in Politics*, Toronto, University of Toronto Press, 1968, p. 204.

93. B. Y. Card, *The Canadian Prairie Provinces from 1870 to 1950: A Sociological Introduction*, Toronto, J. M. Dent and Sons, 1960, p. 22.

94. Frank Cassidy, "The New Party Movement, the Democratic Left, and the Birth of the NDP," Paper delivered at the Annual Meeting of the Canadian Political Science Association, Fredericton, New Brunswick, June 1977, p. 17.

95. Horowitz, *Canadian Labour*, p. 223.

96. *Ibid.*, p. 216.

97. *Ibid.*, p. 219.

CHAPTER FOUR

PRAIRIE PROVINCIAL POLITICS

In a federal system, political regionalism may manifest itself in provincial as well as national politics. While Chapters Two and Three looked at national politics on the Prairies, here the analysis shifts to the provincial realm. The central question is the following: to what extent have provincial politics in Manitoba, Saskatchewan and Alberta been stamped from the same regional mold? To what extent has the common regional setting shaped the three provincial political systems such that they share common characteristics that are distinctive to the West?

The building blocks for a comparative analysis of prairie provincial politics will be provided by brief electoral histories of the three Prairie provinces. Once these have been sketched in the analysis can proceed to commonalities across those provincial histories and then to a comparison of provincial electoral behavior on the Prairies with that in other Canadian provinces. Through this latter analysis aspects of prairie politics that are potentially distinctive to the region, such as the prominence of third parties, the prevalence of one-party dominant electoral systems, and the provincial rejection of parties affiliated with the national government, can be examined.[1]

PROVINCIAL ELECTORAL HISTORIES

A) Manitoba

When Manitoba became a province in 1870 there were fewer than 12,000 people in the new province. The residents had no experience with self government, and the political and social institutions of the territory were only just finding their feet. M. S. Donnelly concludes that ". . . the conferring of provincial status was unwise and premature—it was not, for many years, a source of satisfaction to those people who lived in the province or to the federation as a whole."[2]

Perhaps because of the province's underdeveloped state, pre-1900 Manitoba provincial politics became a stage upon which national conflicts were played out. In this sense Manitoba was to W. L. Morton the 'most Canadian of all provinces', the 'microcosm of all Canada', the 'storm centre of the Canadian past.'[3] The conflicts between English and French, and between Protestants and Catholics, and the rivalries between Ontario and Quebec were the forces that shaped early provincial politics. This last factor and the ultimate victory of Ontario were of particular importance. Morton states that the 1888 provincial election ". . . marked the triumph of Ontario over Quebec in Manitoba,"[4] and that in the Manitoba School Question "the old drive of Ontario to possess the West was prevailing over the counterclaim of Quebec that the West should be the dual heritage of French and English."[5] What Morton has called the 'triumph of Ontario democracy' had a long-standing effect on Manitoba politics; Donnelly maintains that the ". . . preponderance of Ontario influence gave a conservative cast to rural Manitoba, in contrast to the more radical nature of farmers' movements in Saskatchewan and Alberta".[6]

Electoral politics in Manitoba have not been characterized by stable partisan opponents. Rather the history of the province has been marked by quite distinct electoral epochs across which the constellation of party forces has varied considerably. Prior to 1900 party organizations were weak and party lines unclear, although at least some partisan framework was created by the legislative leaders. In 1878 John Norquay established a Conservative administration that was to last for a decade. Then in 1888 the Liberals under Thomas Greenway came to power and remained in office until defeat in 1899. During the boom years from the turn of the century to the start of the First World War Premier Rodmond P. Roblin led the province to prosperity and the Conservative party to dominance in the polls. The Conservative party eventually went into eclipse in 1915 following charges of corruption, bribery and dishonesty, much of it centred on the construction of the new legislative buildings. The Conservatives were replaced by the Liberal party backed in 1915 by an informal coalition of reform groups including the temperance movement, many of the Protestant churches associated with the Social Gospel, the League for the Taxation of Land Values, the Direct Legislation League, the United Farmers of Manitoba, and groups seeking compulsory unilingual education.[7] As Table 4:1 demonstrates the eclipse of the Conservative party lasted until 1958; in the interim the Conservatives retained substantial electoral support but failed to form the government.

Table 4:1 must be treated cautiously as the partisan character of Manitoba provincial politics became extremely confused between 1922 and the mid-50s. The confusion began in 1922 when anti-party sentiment was sweeping the Prairies. Twenty-eight United Farmers of Manitoba candidates, lacking a leader or even a platform, were elected to form the provincial government. John Bracken, president of the Provincial College of Agriculture, was subsequently chosen as premier, a post he held until leaving for the national Conservative party leadership in 1942. In

TABLE 4:1

Provincial Politics in Manitoba
Candidates Elected

Election Date	Total Seats	Lib.	Con.	CCF/ NDP	S.C.	Farm Parties[1]	Other
1907	41	13	28				
1910	41	13	28				
1914	49	20	28				1
1915	47	38	5				4
1920	55	21	7			12	15
1922	55	9	7			28	11
1927	55	7	15			29	4
1932	55		10			38	7
1936	55	23	16		5		11
1941	55	27	15	3	3		7
1945	55	25	13	10	2		5
1949	57	30	14	7			3
1953	57	33	12	5	1		6
1958	57	19	26	11			1
1959	57	11	36	10			
1962	57	13	36	7	1		
1966	57	14	31	11	1		
1969	57	5	22	28	1		1
1973	57	5	21	31			
1977	57	1	33	23			

[1] Farmer candidates (1920), United Farmers of Manitoba (1922), The Progressives (1927), and the Liberal-Progressives (1932). From 1936-1961, Liberal-Progressive Candidates coded as Liberals in this Table.

Source: Loren M. Simerl, "A Survey of Canadian Provincial Election Results, 1905-1976," in Paul W. Fox, ed., *Politics: Canada,* Fourth Edition, Toronto, McGraw-Hill Ryerson, 1977, pp. 622-625.

1927 farmer candidates, now running under the Progressive label, again formed the government.

As the Depression settled in on Manitoba, and with the national defeat of the Liberal party in 1930, a move began to merge the Manitoba Liberal party and the Progressive movement. In 1931 three Liberals were appointed to the Bracken cabinet, in 1932 the Liberals, under pressure from federal leaders,[8] entered a formal coalition with the Bracken Progressives and shortly after the label Liberal-Progressive was adopted by both groups. The coalition barely survived in 1936; a deferred election produced a one-seat majority after efforts to entice Conservative, Social Credit, and CCF members into the coalition failed. The Social Credit members were eventually absorbed nevertheless and in 1940, with the outbreak of the Second World War, an all-party nonpartisan government was formed with cabinet seats apportioned according to the share of the popular vote won by the various parties. Although the CCF withdrew from the arrangement in 1942 the Conservatives stayed until 1950. Thus party lines were blurred even further. It was not until 1959 when the Conservatives had captured the government that the Liberal-Progressives became simply the Liberal party and more conventional party labels came to dominate Manitoba provincial politics.

Although assessments of the Progressive-Liberal/Progressive era differ there is one point of common agreement—Progressive government did not mean progressive policies. J. A. Jackson discusses what he terms the "so called" Progressive period as follows: "the Progressive Party underwent several changes of name and two of leader; but it never was, nor did it ever pretend to be, anything more than a careful and cautious custodian of the public purse".[9] Morton's evaluation is much sharper:

> The Bracken Government was not only without politics; it was even without ideas. It turned back the new political movements of the Co-operative Commonwealth Federation and Social Credit, but the strains it suffered in doing so forced it slowly towards that catchall of Canadian politics, the Liberal party.[10]

In 1958 the Conservative party returned to power after 43 years. Leader Duff Roblin, grandson of Sir Rodmond Roblin, had withdrawn his party from the non-partisan coalition in 1950 and in so doing began to provide the first effective opposition voice in years. Then in the aftermath of Diefenbaker's prairie sweep in 1958 the Conservatives came to power in Manitoba. The Conservative victory started a Liberal slide that continued unabated through to 1977 when the Liberals won only one seat. During the 60s the opposition banner passed slowly to the New Democratic party and in 1969, shortly after the retirement of Conservative Premier Duff Roblin and the election of MP Edward Schreyer to the leadership of the provincial New Democrats, the NDP slipped into power. The NDP secured a one-seat majority through the support of Larry Desjardins, Liberal MLA for St. Boniface. In 1973 the NDP hold on office was strengthened but in 1977 a resurgent Conservative party under the leadership of Sterling Lyon swept back into power. The Conservatives polled 48.9% of the popular vote, the largest proportion received by any party since the First World War. The Liberal share of the popular vote continued to slide from 34% in 1966, 25% in 1969 and 19% in 1973 to only 12% in 1977.

The 1977 election has been subject to quite different interpretations. Manitoban historian Michael Kinnear, for one, perceived little disruption in the continuity of Manitoba politics; while many voters changed sides they did so for very pragmatic reasons, and the election represented primarily a commonplace vote against the incumbent government.[11] To others the election represented an intensification of the class polarization that had set in with the NDP victory in 1969.[12] The decline in the electoral importance of ethnicity[12] hurt the Liberal party in particular; in an ideologically-based electoral conflict the Liberals found themselves outflanked on the left by the NDP and on the right by the Conservatives. The middle ground was small and difficult to hold. Conservative leader Sterling Lyon had travelled to British Columbia in 1976 to study the tactics of polarization used by the Social Credit party to oust the NDP government in 1975, and the 1977 Manitoba Conservative campaign was closely modeled on the British Columbia experience. While the future of Manitoba politics is difficult to predict at this point, it seems clear that any continuation of the NDP-Conservative polarization will make the future prospects of the provincial Liberal party bleak indeed.

In drawing this brief electoral history to a close it should be noted that other political actors have also been active on the Manitoba provincial stage although they have not achieved office. Labour candidates running primarily in the working class districts of Winnipeg had notable success during the 1920s and 1930s. Following the emergence of the provincial CCF in 1941, working class support shifted gradually to the CCF and by the late 50s labour had all but disappeared as an independent electoral force in the province. Elsewhere on the political spectrum the Social Credit party spilled over from Alberta in 1936 and captured five seats in the northern part of Manitoba. The movement, however, was largely absorbed by the Bracken government in the late 30s and although the odd Social Credit candidate won election in subsequent years the Social Credit party failed to materialize into a significant electoral force in Manitoba.

B) Saskatchewan

Compared to the electoral history of Manitoba that of Saskatchewan has been relatively straightforward. Only two parties—the Liberals and the CCF/NDP—have experienced significant electoral success and the importance of the Liberal party throughout Saskatchewan's political history provides a thread of continuity that is absent in both Manitoba and Alberta. As Table 4:2 shows the Liberals enjoyed commanding legislative majorities from 1905 to 1929; during that period they captured over 77% of the seats compared to less than 14% for the opposition Conservatives. The provincial Liberals gained an initial advantage in 1905 when the Laurier government in Ottawa installed a Liberal lieutenant-governor. Prior to the first provincial election the lieutenant-governor appointed an interim government composed almost entirely of Liberals and thus bestowed the advantages of incumbency upon the Liberal party.[19] G. W. G. Haultain, leader of the now-defunct Territorial Government, took himself out of the running for the premier's position by openly opposing the federal government's position on minority language instruction in the school system.[13] Instead Liberal Walter Scott became Saskatchewan's first provincial leader.

The Liberals were able to maintain their domination through the early 1920s when agrarian radicalism destroyed the Liberal party in Alberta, temporarily drove it from office in Manitoba, and all but eliminated federal Liberal representation from the three Prairie provinces. In Saskatchewan the Liberals were able to accommodate and absorb agrarian radicalism, and to deflect its attack upon the traditional party system to the federal level. In part this occurred because the one-crop economy in Saskatchewan ensured that any provincial government would be sensitive to agrarian needs and demands. The Liberals had been careful to include members of the Saskatchewan Grain Growers' Association in cabinet, and the Liberal administration ". . . came to be referred to and regarded as a farmers' government. . . ."[14] The Saskatchewan Grain Growers' Association refrained from electoral politics even though farm organizations in neighbouring Manitoba and Alberta had thrown their hats into the electoral ring. Thus as Courtney and Smith argue, "the differences between the politics of Saskatchewan and those of other Prairie provinces are largely traceable to the Saskatchewan farmer's rejection of direct political action and to the fact that all provincial parties since 1905 have found it profitable to cater to him."[15]

In their successful effort to stave off an agrarian uprising, the provincial Liberals moved to disassociate themselves from the federal Liberal party.[16] However, when the agrarian threat subsided close ties with the federal party were soon re-established. Jimmy Gardiner and Charles Dunning worked vigorously for the federal party and Saskatchewan once again became a major factor in the success of the federal Liberals. After the 1925 federal election in which Saskatchewan voters elected 15 Liberals Mackenzie King stated: "if the day has been saved to Liberalism in Canada it is becoming increasingly apparent that it is Saskatchewan that has saved it."[17]

In the provincial election of 1929 the Liberals once again captured more seats than any of their opponents but this time failed to secure a legislative majority. The Conservatives, with 24 seats to the Liberals' 28, were able to put together a coalition government with the five Progressive and six independent members. While there was no single reason for the Liberal defeat, a number of contributory factors can be identified: the flareup of religious and ethnic cleavages that had been more successfully managed by the Liberals in the past, the agitation of the Ku Klux Klan with respect to such cleavages, a weakened Liberal party machine, and a weakened party grip on the farm movement.[18] The Klan was able to bridge the gap between the Progressives and the Conser-

TABLE 4:2

**Provincial Politics in Saskatchewan
Candidates Elected**

Election Date	Total Seats	Lib.	Con.	CCF/ NDP	S.C.	Other
1905	25	17	8			
1908	41	27	14			
1912	53	45	8			
1917	59	51	7			1
1921	63	45	2			16
1925	63	50	3			10
1929	63	28	24			11
1934	55	50		5*		
1938	52	38		10	2	2
1944	52	5		47		
1948	52	19		31		2
1952	53	11		42		
1956	53	14		36	3	
1960	55	17		38		
1964	59	32	1	26		
1967	59	35		24		
1971	60	15		45		
1975	61	15	7	39		
1978	61		17	44		

* Farmer-Labour Party

Source: Loren M. Simerl, "A Survey of Canadian Provincial Election Results, 1905-1976," in Paul W. Fox, ed., *Politics: Canada,* Fourth Edition, Toronto, McGraw-Hill Ryerson, 1977, pp. 626-629.

vatives, and between the latter and the farm organizations. Its principal contribution to the Liberal defeat, then, came from uniting opposition to the Liberals ". . . by successfully holding them responsible for the non-English problem."[19]

The Liberal fall from electoral grace turned out to be short-lived. With the onset of the Depression the religious and ethnic controversies that had contributed to the 1929 upset were driven from the political stage and the underpinnings of the anti-Liberal coalition collapsed.[20] The Conservatives, saddled with the misfortune and responsibility of being in office as Saskatchewan entered a devastating depression, failed to elect a single member in 1934 as the Liberals captured 50 of the 55 seats. The decimation of the Conservative party, which had provided the opposition mainstay to the Liberals since 1905, was not short-lived; the Conservatives failed to elect another provincial candidate until 1964 and did not elect more than one until 1975. The Conservatives were replaced in 1934 by the newly formed Farmer-Labour Party—soon to be the CCF—which captured five seats under the leadership of M. S. Coldwell, although with a smaller share of the popular vote than that received by the Conservative party. The 1934 election thus marked a major transformation of Saskatchewan provincial politics. The two-party system of the first three decades was replaced by a new two-party system in which the Liberals and the CCF/NDP would wrestle for power over the next 40 years. While two-party competition and the Liberal party both endured, the nature of the second party and the ideological character of Saskatchewan politics were both transformed.

By the 1938 election the Farmer-Labour party had adopted the banner of the CCF and picked up 10 seats although with 3% less of the popular vote than it received in 1934. The CCF was becoming well-established in the province, particularly among the relatively prosperous British protestant farmers who had formed the core of earlier agrarian movements in Saskatchewan. But the key to the eventual success of the CCF lay in its ability to push beyond this traditional base; "the opportunity to act upon discontent came only when the organized farmers joined with labour to form a new party that eschewed the organized farmers' traditional reluctance to seek non-Anglo-Saxon support."[21] In 1941 T. C. Douglas became leader of the party and in 1944, as Saskatchewan voters pondered the shape of the post-war and post-depression society, the CCF rolled to victory with 53% of the popular vote and 90% of the legislative seats. For the next 20 years the CCF retained power and the Liberals dominated the opposition. This confrontation was scarcely disrupted by other parties. Only the Social Credit party captured any seats, winning three in 1956. From 1944 to 1960 the Conservatives failed to win a seat and averaged less than 7% of the popular vote.

As an aside it is interesting to note that the weakness of the provincial Conservative party continued virtually unabated when Diefenbaker swung the Saskatchewan electorate into the national Conservative camp. Under Diefenbaker's leadership the Conservative party did very well in Saskatchewan; across five elections from 1957 to 1965 the national party averaged more than 45% of the popular vote. Yet during the same period the provincial party averaged only 13% of the popular vote in three provincial elections. As Courtney and Smith have pointed out, federal and provincial party politics have been remarkably detached from one another in Saskatchewan, ". . . in no small part because many recent provincial politicians have . . . deliberately eschewed formal organizational and supportive links with their federal counterparts."[22] In the case of the Conservatives, national leaders, including John Diefenbaker, at the same time made little effort to help the provincial Conservative party.[23] This division of Saskatchewan partisanship is illustrated in a 1967 provincial election speech by Liberal premier Ross Thatcher:

I say to my Conservative and to my Social Credit friends—if you are for private enterprise, then look at the Liberals. Cough a couple of times, but put your X in the Liberal column. We do it for you federally. You do it for us provincially.[24]

The CCF period from 1944 to 1964 was marked by frequently intense ideological conflict. In the 1948 campaign, to cite but one example,

CCF administrative policies and reforms were denounced as Leninist, dictatorial, and calculated to lead to a 'police state'. Socialism was depicted as a bridgehead to communism, and Saskatchewan was compared to Czechoslovakia, which had recently disappeared behind the Iron Curtain.[25]

Given such statements it is easy to exaggerate the degree to which the Saskatchewan CCF represented an ideological departure from the mainstream of prairie or even of Canadian politics. S. M. Lipset's application of the term "agrarian socialism" to the CCF has had the unfortunate result of over-emphasizing the socialistic character of the party. Shortly after its electoral debut in 1934 the CCF dropped its land nationalization plank and downplayed references to socialism; Peter Sinclair has gone so far as to say that the 1934 election marked the end of the socialist phase for the Saskatchewan CCF.[26] The policies of the CCF once in power "... represented principally a continuation of accepted policies of public ownership of utilities, and of grass roots co-operation in marketing of agricultural products and the sale of consumer goods, policies pursued by farmer-based parties and movements in other prairie political units, both north and south of the border."[27] The co-operative base of CCF policies did not directly challenge the capitalist system, as co-operatives represented the joint entrepreneurship of individuals. Thus the departure of the Saskatchewan CCF from the political mainstream was not that pronounced.[28]

In 1964 the Saskatchewan electorate returned the government to Liberal hands. The Liberals were then led by Ross Thatcher who had left the CCF in 1955 and lost twice as a federal Liberal candidate in 1957 and 1958 before becoming leader of the provincial Liberals in 1959. Ironically the provincial Liberals were helped by the formation of a national Conservative government, as the provincial Liberals could no longer be held responsible for the policies of the federal government. Thatcher concentrated his attack on the administrative and economic inefficiencies of the CCF government and in doing so moved his party to the ideological right. The CCF government, campaigning in 1964 with a new leader, Woodrow Lloyd, and caught in a bitter controversy over the introduction of medicare in the province, went down to defeat. The Liberals were returned to office with 54% of the seats.

The Liberals held power from 1964 to 1971. Despite the free-enterprise rhetoric of premier Ross Thatcher, no serious attempt was made to dismantle the legacy of CCF social programs. The period was one of considerable growth and prosperity and in 1966 Saskatchewan moved from the "have-not" to the "have" provinces. During this time there were major developments in the province's natural resources, particularly with respect to potash and oil, and as a consequence federal-provincial acrimony over the control, development and taxation of natural resources began to heat up, something that continued into and indeed intensified during the late 70s. Coupled with this acrimony was a growing schism between the Thatcher and federal Liberals, a schism that flowed in part from ideological differences between the two camps and in part from the electoral strategizing of the Saskatchewan party.[29]

In 1970 Allen Blakeney became leader of the Saskatchewan NDP and focused the opposition attack on the natural resources policies of the Liberal government. When a provincial election was held one year later the NDP captured the government winning 45 of the 60 seats. Thatcher died shortly after the election and was replaced by D. G. Stewart, the first Catholic to serve as Liberal leader. In 1975 the NDP retained power albeit with a slightly reduced majority. The surprise of the 1975 election was the resurrection of the provincial Conservative party. The Conservatives captured seven seats, their best showing since 1929, and received nearly 28% of the popular vote, only 4% less than that received by the Liberals. After the election the Conservative resurgence continued, spearheaded by leader Dick Collver. By 1978, by-election wins and Liberal defections, including that of the son of the late Ross Thatcher, had given the Conservatives 11 seats, the same number held by the Liberals. It thus appeared that the Conservatives were on the verge of making a clean sweep of the three prairie provincial governments. In the fall of 1978, however, the New Democrats were returned to power with 44 of the province's 61 seats. The Conservatives took the remaining 17 seats, all but one of which were rural. In the late days of the campaign the NDP had been assisted by two Supreme Court rulings relating to provincial taxation policies on potash and petroleum. Blakeney was able to use the decisions to campaign against the federal government, a strategy that has been dear to the heart of western provincial governments since the settlement of the West. The NDP was also helped by the fact that the Conservative leader was embroiled in law suits relating to his personal business affairs, law suits that raised questions of financial impropriety.

The most significant outcome of the 1978 election was the destruction of the Liberal party. For the first time the Liberals failed to win a single seat. The party received only 14% of the popular vote, down from 43% in 1971. After the election Liberal leader Ted Malone put the results in their most optimistic light by saying although "it's not the end of the Liberal party, it's obviously a very, very formidable setback to us."[30] While electoral crystal-ball gazing is hazardous at best, it does appear that the Liberal era in Saskatchewan has been brought to an end. While the party may have been the "taproot" of Saskatchewan politics in the past[31] it no longer draws sustenance from the soil of Saskatchewan provincial politics.

C) Alberta

Since the creation of the province in 1905 the government of Alberta has changed hands only three times. In each case the change marked a fundamental alteration in the provincial party system. Unlike neighbouring Saskatchewan, Alberta politics have been characterized neither by partisan continuity nor by enduring two-party competition. Instead there have been abrupt shifts in the party system followed by long periods of single-party dominance.

In 1905 the provincial Liberals took advantage of their party's hold on national office, as the provincial Liberals had done in Saskatchewan, to form Alberta's first provincial government, one that was subsequently sustained when the Liberals won 22 of the 25 seats in the 1905 provincial election. Although the Liberal party was popular in the Canadian west at the time, the size of the 1905 Alberta win should not be taken as evidence of any deep-seated Liberal partisanship in the electorate. Nor was Conservative support well-established; L. G. Thomas concludes that those who voted Conservative in 1905 and 1909 supported the non-partisanship of territorial times and were voting against Liberal partisanship rather than for Conservative principles.[32] Partisan affiliations would be a long time taking root in Alberta.

As Table 4:3 shows the Liberals enjoyed a comfortable hold on office through the election of 1917. By 1921, however, circumstances had altered considerably. The already weak partisan dispositions of the Alberta electorate had been weakened further by the Union government experiment in Ottawa. Furthermore, after years of high grain prices during the war agricultural prices fell disastrously in 1920 and 1921, spurring agricultural unrest.[33] Finally, the powerful United Farmers of Alberta had decided to enter the electoral arena. In the past the UFA had shunned direct political action although its ties with the Liberal government were close; ". . . the UFA Convention had more to say in the determination of the policy of the Liberal government than the provincial legislature."[34] Henry Wise Wood, UFA president since 1916, was adamantly opposed to electoral action but the pressure from falling prices and from the political excitement being generated by the national Progressive movement became too great. Despite the objections of Wood the UFA entered the 1921 provincial election and won 38 of the 61 seats. The Alberta voter had rejected both old-line parties; ". . . the conventional patterns held no allurements for him, the unconventional no terrors."[35]

Whereas the Saskatchewan Liberals were able to successfully weather the agrarian revolt of the early 1920s, the Alberta Liberals were blown away by it. They were never again to achieve provincial office. In this they established an important precedent; no party in Alberta has regained office once having lost it. Although remaining the principal opposition force until the late 60s the Liberals never won more than a quarter of the legislative seats and from 1921 averaged less than 16% of the popular vote. Since the accession to power of the provincial Conservatives in 1971 the Liberals have all but disappeared from the provincial scene, abandoning the opposition to the NDP and the remnants of the Social Credit party.

Apart from the rural area north of Edmonton and particularly where French Canadian and Ukrainian voters were concentrated,[36] the UFA had established a secure base in the rural countryside and easily dominated the provincial elections of 1926 and 1930. Interestingly the UFA made no attempt to expand beyond its rural powerbase. As Flanagan explains:

> . . . the Farmers kept very closely to their occupational theory of representation, according to which their organization was not a party in the normal sense, but a representative of a specific class or economic group. Such a theory, strictly applied, made it unthinkable for the U.F.A. to contest urban, industrial, or mining seats, except in exceptional cases of a personal nature. . . .[37]

The political power of the rural heartland was sufficent enough that the self-imposed restrictions of the UFA posed no serious problems. However, the onslaught of the Depression found the UFA government wanting as indeed it found virtually all provincial governments. In addition the UFA premier, John E. Brownlee, was driven from office by a civil suit in which a young woman and her father accused Brownlee of seduction.

Yet the most serious threat to the UFA came from the emergence of the Social Credit movement. Earlier the UFA had had the opportunity to absorb the nascent Social Credit movement through the adoption of Social Credit monetary policy. In the late 20s the UFA had explored the possibility of monetary reform and had thereby provided much of the initial publicity and subsequent legitimization for Social Credit doctrines. When the Social Credit movement began to grow rapidly in the depression-enriched soil of Alberta, repeated efforts were made by its organizers to have the UFA adopt Social Credit monetary theories. Like the UFA before it, the Social Credit movement was reluctant to take the step of direct electoral action. Eventually, though, when the Social Credit overtures were finally rejected by the UFA, the Social Crediters entered the electoral fray under the charismatic leadership of William "Bible Bill" Aberhart. Prior to the final UFA rejection Social Credit

TABLE 4:3

Provincial Politics in Alberta
Candidates Elected

Election Date	Total Seats	Lib.	Con.	CCF/ NDP	S.C.[1]	U.F.A.[2]	Other
1905	25	22	3				
1909	41	36	2				3
1913	56	38	18				
1917	56	34	19				3
1921	61	15	1			38	7
1926	60	7	4			43	6
1930	63	11	6			39	7
1935	63	5	2		56		
1940	57	1			36		20*
1944	57			2	51		4
1948	57	2		2	51		2
1952	61	4	2	2	52		1
1955	61	15	3	2	37		4
1959	65	1	1		62		1
1963	63	2			60		1
1967	65	3	6		55		1
1971	75		49	1	25		
1975	75		69	1	4		1
1979	79		74	1	4		

[1] Social Credit
[2] United Farmers of Alberta
* Coalition of Conservatives, Liberals and some UFA Candidates

Source: Loren M. Simerl, "A Survey of Canadian Provincial Election Results, 1905-1976," in Paul W. Fox, ed., *Politics: Canada,* Fourth Edition, Toronto, McGraw-Hill Ryerson, 1977, pp. 630-633.

supporters had been active in UFA locals throughout the province. When the Social Credit movement opted for direct political action many UFA supporters and indeed entire local organizations deserted the UFA for Social Credit. Through its initial entertainment of Social Credit theories the UFA had been undermined and then crippled from within. In the 1935 election the outcome was not even close; Social Credit took 56 seats with 54.2% of the popular vote while the UFA, with only 11% of the vote, failed to elect a single candidate. Following the election the UFA withdrew from electoral politics thus ending the second distinct phase in Alberta provincial politics.

The role that Social Credit theory played in the 1935 election is open to question. Social Credit originated with Major C. H. Douglas, whose thought has been described by humorist Stephen Leacock as "certain profundities of British fog impossible for most people to understand which in sunny Alberta, by force of prayer, turned into Social Credit."[38] Douglas clashed repeatedly with Aberhart over the latter's utilization of his theory. Writing in 1937 Douglas argued, and in the view of this author argued correctly, that "it would be impossible to claim at any time that the technical basis of Social Credit propaganda was understood by [Aberhart], and, in fact, his own writings upon the subject are defective both in theory and in practicality. . . ."[39] Whether Aberhart is to be condemned or congratulated for this weakness is another question. Given Aberhart's bastardization of his theory Douglas was also unwilling to concede that the theory as advanced by Aberhart was responsible for the 1935 victory: "I am confident . . . that it was at no time Mr. Aberhart's economics which brought him to power, but rather his vivid presentation of the general lunacy responsible for the grinding poverty so common in a province of abounding riches, superimposed upon his peculiar theological reputation."[40] When in power Aberhart appointed Douglas as Principal Reconstruction Adviser and then proceeded to ignore the British economic thinker and his ideas.

William Aberhart possessed a number of attributes which when turned to political action made him a formidable force. He was an extremely effective speaker and an early master of radio, a technological innovation of great importance to isolated prairie farms. He was a superb organizer and in effect contributed the Calgary Prophetic Bible Institute as an organizational base for the Social Credit movement. As principal of Crescent Heights High School, Aberhart occupied a position of considerable social stature, a position that honed his already plentiful organizational skills. Furthermore Aberhart had the advantage of not only being but appearing to be non-partisan and even apolitical, characteristics that found favour in an Alberta electorate where partisan politics were suspect. Finally, ". . . Aberhart was able to transform his large personal religious following into a political force—and succeeded, moreover, in identifying the philosophy of Social Credit with Christian fundamentalism, offering Social Credit as a 'Divine Plan' for the salvation of society."[41] As S. D. Clark has written, "it was to Aberhart, the man of God, that people turned in these times of trouble rather than to Aberhart, the expounder of a new economic doctrine."[42]

After winning the 1935 election the Social Credit party stayed in office for the next 36 years. During that time the party faced only two mildly serious electoral challenges, one from a coalition of Liberal, Conservative and UFA-related opponents in 1940 (the Independent Movement) and the second from a resurgent Liberal party under J. Harper Prowse in 1955. Apart from these aberrations the Socred hold on office was solid in the extreme; in the nine provincial elections from 1935 to 1967 inclusive the party won almost 84% of the legislative seats by polling an average 51% of the popular vote. (If the 1940 and 1955 elections are excluded the Socreds averaged 90% of the seats.) To the extent that small opposition parties survived they did so because of a system of proportionate representation in Calgary and Edmonton (abolished by 1959) which prevented a Socred sweep in either centre.

The party's hold on office was sustained through careful political management and fortuitous development of the province's natural resources. The political management came from Ernest Manning who came to lead the party after Aberhart's death in 1943. Manning had been Aberhart's lieutenant in the Prophetic Bible Institute and the relationship continued when Aberhart became premier; Manning became Provincial Secretary in 1935. After Aberhart's death Manning assumed both the political and religious mantels left by his mentor. As it turned out Manning not only possessed Aberhart's organizational skills and the ability to run an efficient and corruption-free provincial administration, but he was far more politically attuned than was Aberhart. As John Barr notes, while Manning preached the doctrine that politics has no place in public life he was astute enough not to practise it.[43] When oil and natural gas revenues began to flow into the provincial treasury in the late 40s and early 50s Manning was able to greatly expand the level of social services supplied to Albertans without increasing the tax burden. In 1971 Alberta's budget was 36 times what it had been when oil was discovered at Leduc in 1947.[44] The Social Credit government was able to preach the rhetoric of free enterprise and small government, to campaign against socialism and statism in any form, while at the same time creating a well-financed welfare state. Whereas in other provinces citizen demands for more services and fewer taxes inevitably collided, in Alberta they did not because revenues from natural resources filled the gap between a low tax rate and high levels of government expenditures. Oil revenue placed the government in an almost inassailable position. In the words of W. L. Morton:

> . . . Social Credit promised an easy and a sweeping reform, without socialism. The Albertan turned to it, and, aided by the war boom and the oil boom, achieved utopia. If it be objected that he did not thereby achieve a new society, it must be admitted that he has attained a new complacency. If one must travel to Nowhere, there is no more comfortable way than on a tide of oil.[45]

Yet eventually Social Credit lost power. Defeat came on the heels of socio-economic change that had been transforming Alberta, slowly making the Socreds strangers in their own province. In an article that parallels the general theme of this book the Palmers argue that the Conservative victory in 1971 ". . . was not based primarily on superior campaigning or on issues, but was more an indication of provincial trends of

urbanization, secularization, increasing geographical mobility and af-
fluence.''[46] The rapid economic growth of Alberta had attracted a steady
flow of immigrants from other regions of Canada, immigrants who had
no basis for identification with Social Credit. These new Albertans settled overwhelmingly in the rapidly growing cities, cities in which Social
Credit was historically relatively weak and cities which were to receive at
last a majority of the legislative seats in a major redistribution preceding
the 1971 election. John Barr lays out the dilemma Social Credit faced
and in doing so echoes the central argument of this book:

> . . . by the mid-1960s the old Alberta was passing: the small towns were
> dying and with them the certitudes of smalltown life. Social Credit knew how
> to speak to the farmers and the people in small towns. But how to reach the
> new Alberta, an Alberta of secular prosperity, big cities, a growing class of
> professions and managers and intellectuals, a province increasingly
> dominated by young people who did not remember the Depression and new-
> comers who were not schooled in the ancient rituals of voting Social Credit
> because it was the only hope of good government? *Alberta had become more
> like the rest of Canada, and was losing its regional distinctiveness.* (emphasis
> added)[47]

It is an accolade to the Social Credit government that when it was challenged by the Lougheed Conservatives, the Conservatives were on the
whole complimentary of the Socred performance. In essence the Conservatives sold themselves to the Alberta electorate as younger, more tech-
nocratically-skilled, more urban-oriented, and more dynamic Social
Crediters. The Conservatives did not advocate any significant redirection
of the Alberta society or economy. The path established by Social Credit
would be followed; "the Conservatives offered the electorate continued
free-enterprise conservatism, but with the added bonuses of urban
middle-class respectability, a comfortably vague social conscience and a
little political excitement."[48]
Historically the Conservative party had been extremely weak in Alberta. From 1921 to 1963 the party averaged only 9% of the popular vote
and won only 19 seats in 11 elections. Thus when Lougheed assumed the
party's leadership following the 1963 election the party was so moribund
that he was able to build his own party apparatus from the ground up
without worrying about the encumbrances of old party hands and loyalties. In this sense he created a new party, the Lougheed party, that had
few ties in the public mind to the provincial Conservative party of the
past. At the same time it should be kept in mind that the federal Conservative connection, de-emphasized as it may have been, was nonetheless a
critical asset. The Lougheed Conservatives were able to draw from the
50% of the Alberta electorate that had been voting Conservative federally since 1958. Diefenbaker had already moved the electorate into the
federal Conservative camp; Lougheed had only to draw it the rest of the
way by assuring voters that a Conservative government would not upset

the comfortable status quo. This Lougheed was able to do with consummate skill. He was aided by the concurrent attempts of Ernest Manning to realign Canadian partisanship by merging the atrophied national Social Credit party and the Conservative party into a single entity.[49] As Manning had already been telling Albertans that there were few significant differences between the national Conservative and Social Credit parties, Lougheed simply had to extend Manning's argument to the provincial arena.

The Progressive Conservatives won the 1971 election with 49 of the 75 provincial seats, out-polling the Socreds in the popular vote by a margin of 46.4% to 41.1%. The Socreds retained 25 seats, mostly in the rural and southern parts of the province. One New Democrat, leader Grant Notley, was elected and the Liberal popular vote collapsed from 11% in 1967 to only 1% in 1971. In 1975 only four Social Credit candidates were elected and the party's share of the popular vote fell to 17.8%. The Conservatives rolled up 69 seats and over 62% of the popular vote to achieve the largest electoral landslide in Alberta's history. In 1979 the Conservatives rode a slightly reduced share of the popular vote to victory in 74 of the 79 provincial constituencies. Social Credit support increased marginally in the south while NDP support increased marginally in the north. Liberal support remained scarcely detectable. The opposition vote thus remains small and fragmented, and the prospects for an early Conservative demise are remote.

The present Conservative government represents a departure from traditional Alberta politics in that the major parties (Liberals and Conservatives) had been shut out of office from 1921 to 1971. Yet in other ways the Conservative party is an old Alberta wine in a new bottle. Once again one-party dominance has been established and no serious threat to its continuance has appeared on the political horizon. As the Conservative popular vote in 1975 prompted *Maclean's* columnist Alan Fotheringham to comment, "Alberta voters do not pick and choose—they stampede."[50] In addition, the ideology of the Conservative government has not departed substantially from that of former Social Credit governments. The verbal commitment to free enterprise, small government and individualism is still coupled with a strong interventionalist stance in the resource sector that enables the government to provide extensive public services through the country's lowest individual tax loads. The contradictions within Alberta political conservatism have not been that apparent to observers outside the province. There has been a tendency to pay too much attention to the rhetoric of Alberta politicians and thus to characterize the province as being atypically conservative and right-wing. However, when the very significant degree of government intervention in the resource industry and the rapid expansion of government services are taken into account, political conservatism in Alberta is not that different from the ideological positions of other Canadian governments. To quote

Robert Blair, president of Alberta Gas Trunk Lines and the mammoth Foothills natural gas pipeline project, "Peter [Lougheed] is Western conservatism at its best, and Western conservatism is often exactly the same thing as federal Liberalism. . . ."[51]

COMPARISONS AMONG THE PRAIRIE PROVINCES

At first glance it is difficult to imagine a more diverse set of electoral histories than those presented by the three Prairie provinces. We find, for example, that the Alberta Social Credit party held uninterrupted power for 36 years during which time Social Credit was a fringe element at best in the electoral politics of Saskatchewan and Manitoba. In Saskatchewan the Liberal party was a mainstay of provincial politics, although not always in office, from 1905 to the mid-70s whereas it has been somewhat weaker in Manitoba and much weaker in Alberta since 1921. Also in Saskatchewan we find 20 years of CCF government from 1944 to 1964 while at the same time the Alberta CCF was extremely weak and in Manitoba an NDP government was not formed until 1969. In Manitoba farmer parties swept to power in the early 20s, in Alberta the United Farmers of Alberta held power for fifteen years after 1921, but in Saskatchewan the Liberal party successfully fended off agrarian protest parties until the election of the CCF in 1944. All told, then, there appear to be few commonalities in the partisan electoral histories of the three Prairie provinces. Figure 4:1 reinforces this conclusion with a year-by-year comparison of the partisan complexion of prairie provincial governments. From this figure it can be seen that only from 1915 to 1921 was the same party in power in all three provinces. Apart from that brief interlude the partisan histories have not converged and indeed it has not been at all unusual for three different parties to concurrently hold provincial office.

In comparisons such as this, however, we must be wary of attaching too much importance to the fact that provincial governments share or do not share the same party label. It may well be the case that government parties of different names respond in much the same way to essentially the same set of problems and that differences in party names mask important similarities. Conversely it cannot be assumed that governments with the same party name necessarily share the same political outlook, ideology, or goals. As examples here we might point out the frequent conflicts that arise between provincial and national parties of the same name and the contemporary conflict over energy pricing between the Conservative governments of Alberta and Ontario. In summary, then, we must be careful that a partisan correspondence among governments does not blind us to important political differences or that a lack of correspondence does not blind us to important similarities across provincial governments.

FIGURE 4:1 **Partisan Complextion of Prairie Provincial Governments, 1905-1978**

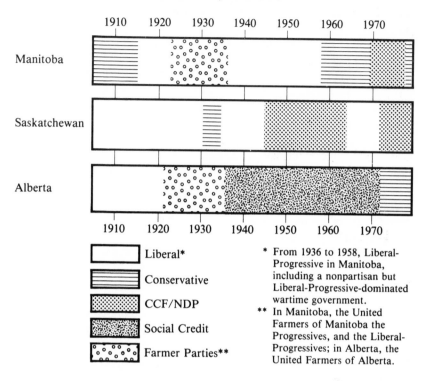

	Liberal*
	Conservative
	CCF/NDP
	Social Credit
	Farmer Parties**

* From 1936 to 1958, Liberal-Progressive in Manitoba, including a nonpartisan but Liberal-Progressive-dominated wartime government.

** In Manitoba, the United Farmers of Manitoba the Progressives, and the Liberal-Progressives; in Alberta, the United Farmers of Alberta.

This latter possibility has been problematic in comparisons between Social Credit in Alberta and the CCF in Saskatchewan. In Canadian political science it has been common practice to locate these two parties at opposite ideological poles; the CCF has been placed at the far left relative to the Canadian political experience and the Social Credit at the far right, again relative to the Canadian political experience. This ideological gulf has given rise to one of the more curious puzzles of prairie politics and one of the more troublesome problems for regional analysis—the near simultaneous rise to power and political dominance of the Social Credit in Alberta and the CCF in Saskatchewan. The puzzle comes from the apparent similarities between Alberta and Saskatchewan at the time; both shared a similar although not identical economic base, both faced severe systemic strain from the Depression, both were western provinces holding similar grievances with the national government, and the two were neighbours. Yet despite such similarities the political histories of the two provinces have been very discrepant ideologically. Several attempts have been made to explain the discrepancy. Brym, for example, isolated significant differences in the occupational structures of the two provinces, noting that "the fact that there were considerably more wheat farmers and less ranchers in Saskatchewan than in Alberta goes a long way toward explaining why the CCF took root so easily in Saskatchewan and Social Credit met with such success in Alberta."[52] Johnson argues that the failure of the CCF in Alberta can be explained by accidental factors that do not necessitate any assumption about significant ideological differences between the Alberta and Saskatchewan electorate.[53]

If we accept that an ideological gulf existed between the Alberta Social Credit and the Saskatchewan CCF the existing explanations seem inadequate. Yet this acceptance itself should be questioned. Admittedly there were differences; anti-communism and anti-semitism, for example, were at times important ingredients in the Alberta Social Credit movement whereas they were largely absent in Saskatchewan.[54] In other ways, however, the differences between the two are harder to establish. Conway has described both as "populist responses to the Canadian national policy."[55] Sinclair also encapsulated both within the concept of populism: "Although the CCF began as a Socialist party and the Social Credit League was eventually transformed into a conventional Conservative party, the conclusion is warranted that from 1934 to 1944 both were populist parties, advocating reform wherever necessary to protect or restore the way of life of the petite bourgeoisie."[56]

The Saskatchewan CCF, despite its ideological location on the political left, spurned the term socialism in its pursuit of power. Lipset states that between 1936 and 1938 the campaign literature of the CCF avoided the term socialism: "the party leaders were trying to popularize the CCF by speaking in the traditional language of agrarian radicalism. . . ."[57] To support his case Lipset quotes a revealing radio speech by the then provincial leader of the CCF, George Williams:

> My friends, is it not fairly obvious that the only way to get people into office who will do something for the *West* is to elect men and women of a *western* party, such as the CCF, who are not continually looking for a cabinet position in Ottawa and willing to sell out their *western* principles in order to get it. . . . Elect a truly *western* government that will really fight for Saskatchewan and it will be done.[58]

Significantly, at this time the Social Credit government in Alberta was replacing the radical Social Credit economics of Major Douglas with sound, conventional fiscal conservatism. It is also interesting to recall that the public policies of the CCF ". . . did not represent the sharp departure from the practices of its predecessors or the neighbouring provinces which was sometimes pictured."[59] Saskatchewan's advance towards the welfare state was well to the rear of the CCF's ideological rhetoric while in Alberta the Social Credit government, behind the smokescreen of ideological conservatism, moved towards many of the same goals at a similar pace. Neither party found its ideological principles to be that amenable to the pursuit and sustenance of political power, and as both adjusted accordingly their paths converged.

One area in which the three prairie electorates have differed is in the character and intensity of political partisanship. In Alberta the notion that partisan cleavages within the electorate are a sign of health in the democratic body politic was slow to win acceptance. The popularity of the non-partisan territorial government prior to 1905, the infusion of American populist advocacy of non-partisanship into a provincial electorate with extensive American ties, the electoral centrality of federal-provincial conflict coupled with the resultant de-emphasis of intra-provincial political cleavages, and the relative homogeneity of the province's economic base all contributed to a deep-felt mistrust of party politics in any form. As C. B. Macpherson has argued, both the UFA and the Social Credit represented an assault on the partisan organization of political life; "the radicalism of both movements consisted not so much in the extent of their economic demands (which were not extreme) as in their conviction, born of repeated frustration of these demands, that the economic subordination from which they were suffering was an inherent part of eastern financial domination and of the party system".[60] Macpherson goes on to argue that Alberta, rather than approximating the two-party and multi-party models of democratic societies elsewhere, had at best a "quasi-party" system in which a single party overtly modelled along non-partisan principles effectively dominated but did not proscribe fragmented and electorally impotent opposition parties.[61] Although Macpherson's analysis dealt primarily with Alberta politics prior to the Second World War, the pattern he describes is in many ways still descriptive of the contemporary scene. The current electoral dominance of the Progressive Conservatives is as great as that of any party in the past, and while in theory they accept the partisan organization of electoral politics, their campaign strategy is still one of de-emphasizing internal provincial cleavages and stressing the threat external foes pose to interests common to all Albertans. While the ideological opposition to partisanship that provided an important element in both the UFA and Social Credit movements has disappeared the non-partisan temper of Alberta provincial politics has not been substantially altered.

In many ways the Manitoba experience with partisanship parallels that of Alberta. The victory of the United Farmers in 1922 ushered in a period of non-partisan, coalition government that extended until the 1958 Conservative victory. During this period party lines and partisan identifications were blurred and the democratic necessity for a competitive party system was thrown into doubt. The parallels with Alberta, however, should not be pushed too far. The election of the United Farmers in 1922 did not signal the same break in the evolution of Manitoba politics as did the victory of the United Farmers of Alberta one year earlier. As Peterson explains, the 1922 election marked a more modest departure:

> Party government was apparently ended. Yet the reality was little changed: the new group was substantially the same as the old—farmers of British

origin from the southwest of the province supported by businessmen of British origin in south Winnipeg. This durable alliance now governed under a new name.[62]

Secondly, the rejection of partisanship in Manitoba was not accompanied by the extensive ideological critique that had been popularized in Alberta, in part because the Manitoba electorate was more isolated from non-partisan sentiment emanating from south of the border. The justifications for non-partisanship that were current in Manitoba tended to draw more from the experience of municipal government than from a critique of the role that parties had played in the economic subjugation of western Canada.

Despite statements like the above, partisanship had become well engrained in Manitoba prior to the agrarian unrest of the 20s and it was not easily removed from the political culture. Indeed there is reason to suspect that the coalition governments were little more than a veneer beneath which the provincial Liberals maintained a firm grip on the levers of power. Peterson's history of Manitoba politics, for example, traces a steady movement of politicians between the coalition governments and the national Liberal party in Ottawa. Kinnear goes so far as to state that from the 1920s until 1958 the Liberals, either alone or in some combination with some other group, won every election.[63] While Kinnear's statement is perhaps too sweeping, the coalition governments did come to be viewed, first by the CCF, then by the Conservatives and finally by the electorate, as equivalent to Liberal provincial governments.

An even sharper contrast to Alberta comes from neighbouring Saskatchewan. As David Smith notes, ". . . Saskatchewan has always enjoyed, in every sense of the term, partisan politics."[64] The strength of partisanship in Saskatchewan has been coupled with a competitive two-party system, again in contrast to the pattern of one-party dominance in Alberta. Thus across the three Prairie provinces the character of provincial partisanship and the acceptance of party politics within the electorate have differed sharply. In this respect the prairie region is fragmented into three very distinctive political cultures.

These political cultures have also differed with respect to the underlying political cleavages that have shaped them. While ethnic, religious, class and urban-rural cleavages have been present in all three provinces their mix and importance varied considerably. In Alberta ethnic cleavages have played a modest role at best in electoral politics,[65] and in Saskatchewan ethnic cleavages were all but swept off the political stage by the Depression. Conversely, ethnicity has played a central role in the society and politics of Manitoba from the formation of the province to the recent past. Politically, only in the last decade has ethnicity been supplanted by other factors.[66]

The trend towards more class-based electoral politics in Manitoba has not yet been echoed in the other two Prairie provinces. While in Saskatchewan ideological disputes among the parties have been sharp, the socio-economic structure of the province has not been such as to encourage class cleavages within the electorate. Perhaps the new middle class that is being created in the wake of resource development, a class similar to that which reshaped Alberta in the 60s and 70s, will be a source of change. Yet in Alberta where the socio-economic structure may be more amenable to class-based politics, issues based on social class or income disparities have been all but absent in the provincial arena. Issues centring upon resource development and federal-provincial relations have effectively dominated electoral politics.

In the past religion played a significant role in prairie politics although the nature of that role varied across the three provinces. Manitoba was the stage upon which major national religious controversies were played out and religious cleavages, interwoven with those of ethnicity, were of considerable importance in the early decades of Manitoba provincial politics. Religious controversy in Saskatchewan, again interwoven with ethnic conflict, was central to the emergence of the Ku Klux Klan and the minority victory of the provincial Conservatives in the late 20s. Fundamentalist and evangelical sects in Alberta helped set the ideological tone of the province and contributed significantly to the electoral success of the Social Credit party. However as Engelmann and Schwartz point out, Social Credit was never specifically a religious party despite the leadership provided by Aberhart and Manning.[67] Nor did the other Alberta parties align themselves along religious cleavages. More recently on the Prairies there has been a progressive and steep decline in the political importance of religion.

All three Prairie provinces have experienced the progressive urbanization of previously rural societies and we might expect that urban-rural cleavages would be common to all three provincial electorates. Yet here again the pattern is irregular. Manitoba has the West's oldest urban metropolis, Winnipeg, and urban-rural cleavages, highlighted by the Winnipeg General Strike, have been important throughout the province's history. Lacking competition from other urban centres in the province, Winnipeg has frequently found itself at odds with the rural countryside and governments have had difficulty bridging the gap between city and farm. Kinnear maintains that "under both Roblin and Schreyer, the urbanized and comparatively innovative views of Winnipeg were imposed upon a recalcitrant and much more conservative countryside."[68] The urban-rural split in the electorate continued to play a modest role in the 1977 victory of the Conservatives who won only 45% of the Winnipeg seats compared to 70% of all other seats in the province. In Saskatchewan the tension between city and countryside has been of less importance. In part this is due to a smaller urban population; only in recent years has the rural population's dominance of legislative seats been even remotely challenged. In addition Saskatchewan lacks a single metropolitan centre with a position in the province comparable to that of Winnipeg in Manitoba. The urban population in Saskatchewan has been parceled out among a number of relatively small urban centres including Regina, Saskatoon, Prince Albert and Moose Jaw, a division that diminished the cultural, social and political distance between the cities and the rural countryside.

In some ways the situation in Alberta has been close to that of Manitoba although the longstanding rivalry between Calgary and Edmonton has no Manitoba counterpart. The urban electorates of Edmonton and Calgary were seldom fully in accord with the United Farmer and Social Credit governments. Although the Social Credit party was successful in winning urban seats it was less successful than in the countryside, the differential being only in part attributable to the proportionate representation systems prevailing in the cities. To the extent that the traditional parties were able to survive at all, and to the extent that the CCF was able to gain a toehold, it was within the urban electorates. In the 50s and 60s, as Alberta entered a period of rapid urbanization, electoral tension increased between farm and city as a disproportionate share of legislative seats remained in the countryside. However, with the redistribution of seats into the urban areas and with the coming to power of the Conservative party rural-urban electoral cleavages appear to have vanished. The Conservative party, like the Social Credit party before it, enjoys very substantial electoral success in both urban and rural ridings although the Conservatives, unlike their predecessors, are decidedly urban in social reference and in the background of party leaders. With reference to this last point, the Conservative victory in 1971 was in no small way due to Lougheed's ability to communicate with the new urban electorate and to Socred leader Harry Strom's failure or inability to do so.

In 1976 I conducted a detailed examination of the political orientations of urban and rural residents in Alberta. The issue areas under investigation included energy policy, gun control, social welfare programs, industrialization, resource development, environmental policy, wage and price controls, agricultural policy, and government spending priorities. On most of these issues there were no significant differences between urban and rural respondents and the few differences that did emerge were of a very modest nature. To take but one example, urban respondents were slightly *more* supportive of increased government aid to agriculture than were rural respondents. It appears, then, that the urban and rural electorates in the province are becoming increasingly homogeneous and it is difficult to conceive of an issue that would drive the two groups into opposing partisan camps. If these results can be generalized to other parts of the West it seems unlikely that urban-rural cleavages will long persist as an important ingredient in prairie provincial politics.

An issue area that is becoming increasingly important across the

Prairies is that of resource development. Not surprisingly resource development holds centre stage in Alberta and is likely to do so into the foreseeable future. Yet the same increasingly holds true of Saskatchewan; the development of the province's oil, potash and uranium resources has become the major issue in Saskatchewan provincial politics. In Manitoba the development of the mining and forestry industries is frequently in the political spotlight. Thus resource development forms an issue area that the three provincial systems increasingly share although the specifics of the issues vary considerably from province to province. Nevertheless while the importance of resource development is recognized by all parties, clearcut partisan differences on development strategies have been slow to emerge.

The discussion to this point demonstrates that the electoral similarities or commonalities across the three prairie provincial systems are limited. While points of convergence do exist they appear no more frequently than one might expect across a comparison of any three Canadian provinces. There is little evidence that the three provincial systems have been stamped from a common regional mold, that regional concerns and characteristics have orchestrated electoral politics within the three provinces. However, there is some additional evidence that can be examined concerning the insulary of provincial political behavior or, conversely, concerning the permeability of provincial political boundaries within the prairie region. Political regionalism should be associated with low insularity or high permeability. If political behavior is regionalized important political events within one province should produce detectable reverberations within the other two Prairie provinces; political change in one province should trigger similar change although perhaps to a diminished degree in the other two. Whereas the emergence of a new political party in Newfoundland would not be expected to significantly influence provincial politics in British Columbia, a regional perspective would predict that the emergence of a new political party in Saskatchewan would generate discernible effects within the provincial politics of Alberta and Manitoba. If, on the other hand, the provincial systems are relatively insular, if their containment within a common region has little bearing on provincial political behavior, then events within one province should not significantly affect the political course of other provinces within the prairie region.

The permeability or insularity of prairie provincial political systems can be examined with reference to three major events. The first is the 1935 victory of the Social Credit party in Alberta, the second is the 1944 victory of the CCF in Saskatchewan. The question in both cases is the extent to which electoral reverberations were felt outside the province immediately affected. The third event, the 1958 victory of the national Conservative party, is of a somewhat different nature than the first two in that the event, being national rather than provincial, was not initially localized in any single province. Our interest is in the degree to which the fortunes of the provincial Conservative parties on the Prairies were affected by the national win. Did a uniform surge in provincial Conservative support occur or was a regional pattern displaced by three quite distinct provincial reactions?

A) The 1935 Alberta Social Credit Victory

August 22, 1935 was the first time Social Credit candidates appeared on the ballot in Canada and on that day Alberta voters elected 56 of 63 Social Credit candidates with 54.2% of the popular vote—the first of nine consecutive Social Credit victories. The next provincial election on the Prairies was held in Manitoba on July 27, 1936. At that time twenty Social Credit candidates ran in the province's 55 ridings, doing so with little active support from the Alberta party. Five were elected with a total of 9.2% of the popular vote. Thus while the Social Credit victory in Alberta did not seriously disrupt provincial politics in Manitoba its effects were felt, although they proved to be short-lived. In 1941 only three Social Credit candidates were elected and in 1945 only two. Subsequently lone Social Credit candidates were elected in 1953, 1962, 1966 and 1969 while from 1941 to 1973 the Social Credit party averaged just over 3% of the provincial popular vote. While the impact of the Alberta Social Credit victory on Manitoba politics was at best modest, the Social Credit party did make more of a splash in Manitoba than in neighbouring Ontario where in 1937 the single Social Credit candidate received only 538 votes.

The first Saskatchewan provincial election following the Social Credit win in Alberta came nearly three years later on June 8, 1938. In Saskatchewan the influence of the Alberta Social Credit movement was much more strongly felt than it had been in Manitoba. Forty-one Social Credit candidates were nominated in the 52 provincial ridings, 10 more than were nominated by the CCF which failed to run candidates in Regina, Saskatoon, Moose Jaw or Prince Albert. Aberhart played a major role in the selection of Socred candidates, as he had done in Alberta.[69] Aberhart and his cabinet ministers also campaigned in Saskatchewan during the election with Ernest Manning serving as the campaign organizer for the Alberta effort. In addition to the active participation of Alberta politicians the Social Credit incursion into Saskatchewan was strengthened by the proximity of the two provinces, by the fact that a good portion of the Saskatchewan electorate fell within the range of Aberhart's radio broadcasts from Calgary, and by the myriad of family connections that crossed the Alberta-Saskatchewan border. Not surprisingly the threat posed by Social Credit was taken seriously by Saskatchewan politicians. The Liberals campaigned as the party to beat Social

Credit,[70] and the CCF sought out some form of electoral co-operation—some temporary reform coalition—with Social Credit such as that which had seen Tommy Douglas run with Social Credit endorsement in the 1935 federal election. The CCF overtures, however, were rebuffed by Aberhart. They were also resisted by William Irvine, leader of the Alberta CCF. Irvine, with a lack of insight that did not bode well for the future of the Alberta CCF, ". . . predicted an early end to the Social Credit experiment and did not want the CCF to be associated with such a failure."[71]

When the 1938 election was held only two Social Credit candidates were elected compared to 10 for the CCF. The Social Credit party received 16.3% of the popular vote, slightly less than the 21.5% received by the CCF. After the election the CCF lost any further interest in co-operation with Social Credit and by the time the next provincial election was held in 1944 the Social Credit party had almost vanished from Saskatchewan. Only one Socred candidate ran, picking up 249 votes. In 1948, 31 Social Credit candidates ran and received 8% of the popular vote. In 1956 the party reappeared in strength, electing three candidates and amassing 21.7% of the popular vote. Smith suggests that many of these votes came from disgruntled Liberals who, lacking a Conservative candidate to vote for, expressed their dissatisfaction by voting Socred.[72] Then in 1960 the party fielded 55 candidates, its largest number ever, but received only 12.6% of the popular vote and failed to elect a single member. In 1964 only two Social Credit candidates ran, in 1967 only seven, and none have appeared since. Thus the success of the Saskatchewan Social Credit party has been marginal and even episodic at that, and the party has left little mark upon the political evolution of the province, failing to significantly disrupt the electoral struggle between the Liberals and the CCF/NDP.

In summary, the overwhelming success of the Social Credit party in Alberta both in 1935 and in subsequent provincial elections had a noticeable but generally insignificant impact upon provincial politics in the other two Prairie provinces. Admittedly the impact in Saskatchewan and Manitoba was greater than that outside the prairie region. In British Columbia, for example, only 18 Social Credit candidates ran in the 1937 provincial election, none were elected, and the party received only 0.9% of the popular vote. Significant inroads into British Columbia were not made until the 1952 election when the Manning Social Credit organization entered the west coast contest in a manner analogous to Aberhart's entry into Saskatchewan in 1938. In both cases the actions of the Alberta party were unusual; it is not common for provincial party organizations in Canada to actively intervene in election campaigns in other provinces. True, the NDP and the CCF before it have utilized leaders and organizers from outside the province when such resources within were scarce but even this practice is in decline. The provincial political systems have become sufficiently autonomous that outside intervention is less likely to be tolerated and outside control, such as that exercised by Aberhart over the selection of Socred candidates in Saskatchewan, would now be totally unacceptable. Even within the prairie region it is unlikely that Peter Lougheed or Sterling Lyon would actively enter a Saskatchewan campaign on behalf of the Saskatchewan Conservative party. Thus a means of cross-provincial electoral orchestration used in the past with limited success by the Alberta Social Credit party is no longer tenable.

B) The Saskatchewan CCF

On June 15, 1944, the Co-operative Commonwealth Federation came to power in Saskatchewan winning 47 of the province's 52 seats and capturing 53.4% of the popular vote. To supporters of the political left in Canada it was a signal event demonstrating that electoral success was indeed possible for left-wing parties. Admittedly the conditions in rural Saskatchewan were very different from those in the industrial areas of Canada where a left-wing breakthrough might more reasonably have been expected, but the Saskatchewan victory was heartening nonetheless. It served as an inspiration and goad to other provincial CCF parties, particularly those in Alberta and Manitoba where conditions most closely paralleled Saskatchewan. Proof of potential victory was now in hand and the electorate could be solicited in a new spirit of zeal and optimism. It should also be noted, however, that the 1944 Saskatchewan election not only inspired the party faithful in other provinces—it also provided further demonstration to opponents of the political left that a serious threat was loose on the land. In future the electoral counterattacks were to be far more vehement than those faced by the CCF in the Depression era.

Voters in Alberta went to the polls less than two months after the 1944 Saskatchewan election. In the 1940 Alberta election the CCF had not fared well, winning only 11.1% of the vote and failing to elect a single member. On the heels of the party's Saskatchewan victory there was a marked improvement; the Alberta CCF captured 24.9% of the popular vote although electing only two members. This was the highest percentage of the popular vote ever to be won by either the CCF or the NDP in Alberta and never was the party to elect more than two members. Following the 1944 election the CCF's share of the popular vote fell steadily from 19.1% in 1948 to 4.3% in 1959. Thus it appears that the CCF victory in Saskatchewan did give the Alberta party a shot in the arm but that the effect was short-lived. Just as the Social Credit party was quick to leave the Saskatchewan electoral stage after its initial appearance following the 1935 Alberta Social Credit victory, so too did the

CCF cease to be a significant electoral factor in Alberta following the 1944 election. Although the CCF maintained an electoral presence in Alberta greater than that of the Social Credit in Saskatchewan it never again approached its 1944 peak of popularity.

Voters in Manitoba did not go to the polls until October, 1945. In the 1941 election the CCF had been a passive partner in an all-party wartime coalition government and had elected only three members, a fall from seven in 1936. The party did, however, pull in 17.3% of the popular vote. The CCF's participation in the coalition lasted less than two years and in the 1945 election the party was on its own. It was, moreover, very successful, winning 10 seats and 35.3% of the popular vote. Over the next four elections the party averaged only 21% of the popular vote and the 1945 highwater mark was not surpassed until 1969 when the New Democrats under Ed Schreyer captured 38.3% of the vote. If the Manitoba case is compared to Alberta it can be seen that the Manitoba CCF went into the post-Saskatchewan election with a stronger base of support than that enjoyed in Alberta and experienced a less-precipitous decline in popular support in the following elections. In both cases the post-Saskatchewan election produced a marked increase in support; the popular vote received by the CCF rose by 104% in Manitoba and by 124% in Alberta. In neither province was the CCF ever to enjoy a better election in terms of the popular vote. Thus initially there seems to be little question that the 1944 victory by the Saskatchewan CCF did produce regional electoral effects in the neighbouring Prairie provinces, no matter how modest they may have been in the long run.

Yet we cannot assume that the Alberta and Manitoba bulges in CCF support were entirely due to the success of the party in Saskatchewan. There may well have been more general factors at work across all three provinces, factors that would have produced an increase in CCF support even without the example of the Saskatchewan victory. Here we should note that the 1945 national election, which preceded the Manitoba provincial election held that year, also marked the electoral highwater point for the federal party. It would be erroneous to attribute the national increase from eight to 28 members solely to events in Saskatchewan although 18 of the 28 CCF MPs were elected in that province; while the national CCF vote increased from 393,230 in 1940 to 816,259 in 1945 only 14% of this increase came from Saskatchewan. Some light can be shed on this matter by looking at the success of the CCF in provincial elections outside the prairie region, particularly in British Columbia and Ontario where the party was a significant factor before the 1944 Saskatchewan election. In British Columbia the CCF captured 34.4% of the vote in 1941 and increased that to 39.1% in 1945. While the proportionate increase was less than in Alberta and Manitoba the initial vote was also much higher than in either of the Prairie provinces. In Ontario the CCF had elected 34 members with 31.6% of the popular vote in 1943.

Then in 1945 the fortunes of the party fell sharply; just eight members were elected and the party received only 22.4% of the popular vote. The 1943 Ontario election was more a forerunner of the following Saskatchewan election than was the 1944 Saskatchewan election a forerunner of later events in Ontario. The 1943 Ontario election also did more to galvanize the ideological opponents of the CCF into action; while a socialist win in the wilds of Saskatchewan was disturbing, the threat of a socialist victory in the Canadian heartland was vastly more alarming.

What can be concluded from this discussion of the provincial CCF? In the first place the victory of the Saskatchewan party in 1944 appeared to produce marked regional effects that were quite different in strength and character from those produced outside the prairie region. While the increase in the CCF vote in Alberta and Manitoba cannot be solely attributable to the influence of the Saskatchewan victory, the electoral patterns in the two provinces, with a peak in support immediately after the Saskatchewan election followed by a sharp decline in subsequent elections, do argue for a significant Saskatchewan impact. Secondly, the regional effects were short-lived; in neither Alberta nor Manitoba did the increase in CCF support last beyond the first election and in neither case did that first election propel the CCF into a position of permanent influence within the province. To extend this argument it appears that while the initial victory of the CCF in Saskatchewan affected voting patterns in the neighbouring Prairie provinces, the continued success of the Saskatchewan CCF over the next 20 years had little impact on electoral politics in Alberta or Manitoba. Apart from initial short-term effects the provincial political systems maintained a high degree of isolation and insularity. Although the provincial boundaries were breached briefly the figurative holes were quickly plugged.

C) The Diefenbaker Landslide

The Prairies had been barren ground for the Conservatives prior to Diefenbaker's leadership. Then in 1958 the Prairie provinces were swept into the Conservative camp; the Conservatives captured all but one prairie seat and won 56.7% of the vote in Manitoba, 51.4% in Saskatchewan, and 59.9% in Alberta. It was a remarkably impressive and uniform victory across the region. Here our concern lies with the impact of this regional sweep on *provincial* Conservative support on the Prairies. Was there a relatively uniform spillover of national party support at the provincial level, or did the three provinces react quite differently? Secondly, was the provincial impact on the Prairies similar to or different from the impact of the Diefenbaker sweep elsewhere in Canada?

Fortunately no provincial elections were held in Canada between the national elections of 1957 and 1958. It is therefore possible to compare levels of provincial Conservative strength prior to the 1957 and 1958 national elections to Conservative strength in provincial elections immediately following the 1958 landslide. This comparison has been made in Table 4:4 for all provinces except Quebec where the Conservative party was not provincially active at the time. The table presents the share of the provincial vote won by Conservative parties in provincial elections immediately prior to the 1957 national election, the share of the vote won in provincial elections immediately following the 1958 national election, and the percentage change in the level of provincial Conservative support. It also gives the post-1958 provincial share of the popular vote as a percentage of the pre-1957 provincial vote.

Table 4:4 has several interesting features, the first of which is the pre-1957 weakness of the provincial Conservative parties west of Ontario. Only in Manitoba did the provincial Conservatives enjoy a reasonable modicum of support and even that was well below the level of support held by provincial parties in the eastern provinces. In Saskatchewan and British Columbia the party was scarcely visible. Secondly, the 1958 national Conservative victory did little if anything to help the provincial Conservative parties in eastern Canada; in four of the five eastern provinces the Conservatives' share of the provincial vote fell after the 1958 national election. The situation west of Ontario was quite different. The provincial Conservatives made substantial percentage gains in all four provinces although in some cases, such as British Columbia, the initial share of the vote was so small that any improvement would be proportionately large. Nevertheless across the West and particularly across the three Prairie provinces the national Conservative victory seemed to rejuvenate the provincial wings of the party. In provincial elections following the 1958 national election the Conservative parties boosted their number of votes in the three Prairie provinces from 102,000 to 311,265, an increase of over 200%.

Only in Manitoba, however, where the Conservatives under Duff Roblin's leadership won 26 of 57 seats, was the party propelled into provincial office. In Saskatchewan and Alberta the parties started with such a small share of the popular vote that even a large percentage increase made little difference. The Saskatchewan party failed to elect a single candidate in 1960 and in 1959 only one Alberta Conservative was elected compared to three in 1955. Furthermore in neither province did the party fare very well over the next decade. A significant Conservative presence was not felt provincially in Alberta until 1967 and the Conservative party did not come to power until 1971. It can be argued that the eventual Conservative victory was in part due to the provincial party's successful mobilization of the national Conservative vote in the province, but that mobilization was a long time in coming. In Saskatchewan the provincial Conservatives remained more or less moribund until 1975. Thus while

TABLE 4:4

**Increase in Provincial Popular Vote Received by Conservative Party
From Provincial Election Preceding 1957 National Election to
Provincial Election Following 1958 National Election**

Province	Pre-1957 Per Cent of Provincial Vote	Post-1958 Per Cent of Provincial Vote	% Change In Vote	Post-1958 Vote As Per Cent of Pre-1957 Vote
Newfoundland	31.6	24.8	-6.8	78.5
Prince Edward Island	45.0	50.9	5.9	113.1
Nova Scotia	48.5	48.0	-0.5	99.0
New Brunswick	53.2	46.9	-6.3	88.2
Ontario	48.5	46.2	-2.3	95.3
Manitoba	21.0	40.5	19.5	192.9
Saskatchewan	1.8	13.5	11.7	750.0
Alberta	9.2	23.9	14.7	259.8
British Columbia	2.8	6.7	3.9	239.3

the Diefenbaker victories of 1957 and 1958 improved the short-term performance of the provincial Conservative parties on the Prairies the long-term impact is more questionable. The provincial political systems on the Prairies appear relatively although not totally immune to national electoral events just as they appear to be relatively immune to provincial electoral events outside their boundaries. To summarize more generally, provincial electoral behavior on the Prairies does not appear to be regionally orchestrated; the three provinces have been relatively insular in their political evolution and in their electoral behavior. If their co-existence within a common region suggests that provincial politics are cast within a regional mold, the suggestion is misleading.

There is one further investigative path to be pursued in this chapter and that is to determine whether there are features of provincial electoral politics on the Prairies that are unique to or distinctive of the region. Table 4:4 has presented a preview of the type of analysis to be pursued. While the prospects of regionally distinctive features emerging are not encouraging given that there seem to be few commonalities among the Prairie provinces to begin with, there is nonetheless a handful of interesting areas to be examined.

REGIONAL DISTINCTIVENESS OF PRAIRIE PROVINCIAL POLITICS

Historically, one of the regionally distinctive features of prairie electoral behavior was the rejection of the Liberal and Conservative parties in favour of a number of indigenous third parties including the Progressives, Social Credit and CCF. Although this rejection has not been characteristic of prairie politics during the last two decades it was the outstanding feature of the four decades following the end of the First World War. In many instances the national electoral strength of third parties on the Prairies was derivative from the provincial strength of these parties, particularly when they held provincial office. For example, the United Farmers of Alberta sustained national support for the Progressives in Alberta after that support had waned elsewhere on the Prairies, and the CCF government in Saskatchewan helped sustain the national CCF in that province. Perhaps the best example comes from the Social Credit party which from 1935 to 1957 won over two-thirds of the federal seats in Alberta. It was the provincial strength of Social Credit in Alberta that maintained national Social Credit representation from the province and which indeed maintained any semblance of a national party. The Social Credit MPs were little more than national offshoots from the provincial party, and weaker offshoots at that. While the provincial party received an average of 51% of the popular vote in elections from 1935 to 1957, the national party averaged only 39% of the vote in the province during the same period. The national party, moreover, was swept from the province in 1958 by the Diefenbaker Conservatives whereas the provincial party remained securely in office for another 13 years despite its decimated national wing. Unlike the national Social Credit organization the provincial party in Alberta could stand alone.

Given the relationship between third party support in national elections and that received in provincial elections, it is not surprising that third party governments stand out as one of the distinctive features of prairie provincial politics just as third party support stood out as a regionally-distinctive feature of national electoral behavior on the Prairies. This is particularly the case in Alberta where first the UFA and then Social Credit held office for 50 consecutive years. It was in Saskatchewan, furthermore, that the only CCF government in Canada was elected, a government that held office for 20 years. It has also been on the Prairies that the provincial NDP has enjoyed its greatest success, holding office in Manitoba from 1969 to 1977 and in Saskatchewan from 1971 until the time of writing. Finally, the long tenure of the Liberal-Progressive coalition government in Manitoba provides a further if somewhat qualified illustration of the weakness of the Liberal and Conservative parties in prairie provincial politics. Their historical weakness neatly parallels that of the national wings of the two parties, as the above discussion would lead us to expect. Prior to 1958 the provincial Liberal parties were far stronger than their Conservative counterparts just as the national Liberal party was far stronger on the Prairies than was the national Conservative party. During the last two decades, however, the national and provincial Liberal parties have been in full retreat across the region, replaced by a national Conservative hegemony and resurgent provincial Conservative parties now holding office in two provinces and forming the official opposition in the third.

Provincial third parties, then, have been relatively successful on the Prairies, relative at least to their success in Ontario or the Atlantic provinces. However, third parties have also enjoyed considerable success outside the Prairies in both Quebec and British Columbia. The Union Nationale held power in Quebec for a total of 23 years and the Parti Quebeçois is presently in office. The British Columbia electorate last elected a major-party government in 1937; since then the province has been governed by coalition, Social Credit and New Democratic governments. Thus while third party provincial strength is a regional characteristic of the Prairies it is not a characteristic that is unique to the prairie region.

While third parties have enjoyed provincial success in Canada the national government has yet to stray from the control of the Liberal and Conservative parties. This major party control of the national government coupled with the provincial strength of third parties on the Prairies suggests another regional feature of prairie provincial politics—the lack

TABLE 4:5

Percentage of Time (1945-1977)
That Party Forming Provincial Government
Also Held Office in Ottawa

Province	Per Cent of Time, 1945-1977
Prince Edward Island	84.3
Nova Scotia	74.9
Newfoundland[1]	58.0
New Brunswick	54.6
Manitoba[2]	51.8
Quebec	29.7
Saskatchewan	22.1
Ontario	17.9
Manitoba[3]	14.9
British Columbia	0.0
Alberta	0.0

[1] May 1949-December 1977
[2] Coalition government, 1945-1977, treated as a Liberal government
[3] Coalition government, 1945-1977, *not* treated as a Liberal government

of partisan correspondence between the national and provincial governments. Seldom have the provincial affiliates of the national government party simultaneously held office on the Prairies. One element of western alienation has been the belief that western interests have been hurt by the lack of partisan correspondence, that third party provincial governments have been unable to win a sympathetic ear with the Liberal and Conservative administrations in Ottawa. The underlying assumption here, one that is open to debate, is that a common party allegiance greases the wheels of federal-provincial diplomacy whereas third party governments throw sand in the gears.

Table 4:5 places the lack of partisan correspondence between prairie provincial governments and the national government into a comparative perspective. The table presents the proportion of time from 1945 to 1977 in which the same party was in power in both Ottawa and each of the 10 provinces. To take Prince Edward Island as an example, from 1945 to 1977 inclusive the party holding power in Ottawa also held power in Charlottetown for 84.3% of the period. At the other end of the scale it can be seen that at no time in the 1945-1977 period did the same party hold office in both Edmonton and Ottawa. There has never been a Social Credit national administration and when the Conservative party came to office in Alberta it did so during a time of Liberal dominance in Ottawa.

Manitoba, it should be pointed out, has been entered twice in Table 4:5, once with the Liberal-Progressive coalition government treated as a Liberal provincial government and once with it treated as a non-Liberal government. The Liberal-Conservative coalition in British Columbia, which was in office from 1941 to 1952, has not been equated with either of the contributing parties. Thus the coalition, Social Credit and NDP administrations in British Columbia never experienced a partisan counterpart in office in Ottawa.

In Table 4:5 the four Atlantic provinces display the greatest degree of partisan correspondence between national and provincial governments. The Prairie provinces in general display little correspondence, with Alberta sharing the bottom of the table with British Columbia. The placement of Manitoba depends upon how one assesses the partisan complexion of the Liberal-Progressive coalition. Interestingly, the provincial governments of both Quebec and Ontario also display little partisan correspondence with the national government. In Ontario, for example, the provincial government was of the same partisan stripe as the national government only during the Diefenbaker governments from 1957 to 1963. Apart from that period the Liberals have controlled the national government while the Conservatives have enjoyed an unbroken provincial tenure in Ontario that dates back to 1943. Thus while it is correct that provincial governments on the Prairies seldom correspond in party label to the national government, there is little about this lack of correspondence that is regionally distinctive. If any region stands apart it is that encompassed by the four Atlantic provinces. The existence of a traditional two-party system in the Atlantic provinces, one upon which third parties have made little impression, heightens the potential for correspondence between the provincial and national governments. Yet in Ontario the major parties have also been strong but without the resultant partisan correspondence that exists in the Atlantic region. This draws attention to an important aspect of the 1945-1977 period, that being the general dominance of the national Liberal party. The Liberals held office in Ottawa for over 80% of the period and thus Table 4:5 measures in large part the success of the provincial Liberal parties across Canada. Where the provincial Liberal party has been strong enough to capture provincial office the degree of partisan correspondence is high; where the Liberal party has been weak, as in Ontario, the correspondence is low.

It is another matter entirely whether a lack of correspondence between provincial and national governments works to the detriment of the provinces concerned—one would be hard pressed to argue that the interests of Ontario have been seriously short-changed by the electorate's steadfast choice of Conservative provincial governments during a period of Liberal dominance in Ottawa. Nor can it be assumed that the co-existence of Liberal (or Conservative) governments in both Ottawa and any particular province necessarily works to the advantage of the province. Ottawa-Ontario relationships were not unusually harmonious during the Diefenbaker years, nor did Ross Thatcher's Liberal administration in Saskatchewan work hand in glove with the national Liberal governments of the time. In fact Saskatchewan-Ottawa relations were frequently acrimonious. The lack of adequate provincial representation within the national government party, such as the absence of Alberta Liberal MPs during much of the 70s or the weakness of Quebec Conservative MPs during the Diefenbaker governments, is probably more harmful to provincial interests than is a partisan cleavage between the national and provincial government.

In summary, Table 4:5 supports the contention that in recent decades prairie provincial governments have seldom been in partisan correspondence with the national government; it was a rare circumstance when the same party held power in both Ottawa and one or more of the Prairie provinces. Yet this feature of prairie provincial politics is not particularly unique nor is its significance unambiguous. A characteristic that the Prairie provinces share with British Columbia, Ontario and Quebec does little to set the prairie region apart politically from the rest of the country.

Another electoral characteristic that has been associated with at least Alberta is one-party dominance of the electoral process and through it of the legislative assembly. Macpherson's above-noted description of Alberta's "quasi-party" system incorporates this characterization and more popular impressions of one-party dominance emerged from the 36 unbroken years of Social Credit government that stretched from 1935 to 1971. During that period the Social Credit party regularly won overwhelming legislative majorities; in 1959, for example, 62 of 65 seats and in 1963, 60 of 63 seats. The Conservative near-sweep of 69 of the 75 Alberta seats in 1975 and 74 of the 79 in 1979 only served to reinforce images of the Socred era with respect to one-party dominance. However, to advance the proposition that one-party dominance is a regional characteristic of prairie provincial politics two conditions must be met. First it must be demonstrated that one-party dominance is also a characteristic of electoral politics in Saskatchewan and Manitoba. Secondly it must be demonstrated that one-party dominance is a distinctive characteristic of prairie provincial politics rather than a general characteristic of Canadian provincial politics. To provide such demonstrations we must first generate some data on one-party dominance.

The measurement of one-party dominance can be approached in several ways. The least satisfactory is to measure the length or continuity of party tenure in office. Thus it could be noted that the Alberta Social Credit party was in office continually for 36 years and that at the time of writing the Ontario Conservative party is also in its 36th consecutive year of office. This approach, however, tells nothing about the strength of a party's grip on office; did a particular party hold on to office by the skin of its teeth or did the party enjoy such hefty legislative majorities that legislative opposition within the province was emasculated? While the latter case fits the notion of one-party dominance the former does not despite what may be a considerable tenure in office. A more satisfactory approach is to measure the percentage of the legislative seats received by the winning party in provincial elections. This gives a more accurate picture of legislative one-party dominance. Caution must be exercised though that situations of legislative dominance do not lead to assumptions about the homogeneity of the electorate as the division of legislative seats in Canada tends to understate the electoral diversity within provinces. The degree to which one-party legislative dominance will occur depends upon not only the percentage of votes received by the winning party but also upon the number of competing parties and thus the fragmentation of the opposition vote, the variance in popular vote among the opposition parties, the existence of malapportionment such that a rural-based party may do far better in terms of seats than its share of the total vote would appear to warrant, and the general quirkiness of the Canadian electoral system in translating votes into seats.[73] Therefore in the analysis that follows legislative one-party dominance is examined along with the percentage of the popular vote received by the winning party in provincial elections. This latter measure provides some index of the relative homogeneity or heterogeneity of the provincial electorate and, to the extent that party divisions represent divisions within the political culture, of the fragmentation of the provincial political culture.

Table 4:6 presents the percentage of the legislative seats and popular vote received by winning parties in Canadian provincial elections since 1905—the left-hand columns on the table incorporate all provincial elections from 1905 to 1976 whereas the right-hand columns incorporate only those elections held from 1945 to 1976 inclusive. From the table it is quite apparent that the Prairie provinces do not stand out as a regional block. While Alberta has been the least competitive province in terms of legislative majorities and in recent decades the second least competitive with respect to the popular vote, Manitoba has been the most competitive on both accounts. Saskatchewan occupies an intermediate position on both parts of the table; since 1945 Alberta has been closer to Newfoundland, Prince Edward Island, New Brunswick and Nova Scotia in the popular vote column than it has been to Saskatchewan. Thus one-party dominance is not a characteristic that Alberta shares with the other two Prairie provinces. It therefore cannot be considered a regional characteristic. In passing it should be pointed out that if one-party dominance is characteristic of any region it is the Atlantic provinces that stand apart. There the absence of provincially-active third parties has acted to increase the percentage of the popular vote and legislative seats received by the winning party. It should also be noted from Table 4:6 that there has been a slight but noticeable trend for the size of both the

TABLE 4:6

**Average Percentage of the Popular Vote
and Legislative Seats Received by the Winning Party
in Provincial Elections**

% Popular Vote

Province	1905-1976	Province	1945-1976
Nfld.	59.9	Nfld.	59.9
P.E.I.	52.9	Alberta	52.8
Quebec	52.2	P.E.I.	52.6
N.B.	51.9	N.B.	51.6
N.S.	51.1	N.S.	49.9
Alberta	50.8	Quebec	49.3
Sask.	48.1	Sask.	45.6
Ontario	46.6	Ontario	44.5
B.C.	44.8	B.C.	43.6
Manitoba	41.5	Manitoba	42.5

% Legislative Seats

Province	1905-1976	Province	1945-1976
Alberta	78.3	Alberta	83.5
Nfld.	78.1	Nfld.	78.1
P.E.I.	76.2	P.E.I.	75.7
Quebec	74.6	Quebec	70.8
N.S.	72.6	N.S.	68.3
Sask.	70.9	Ontario	67.8
Ontario	67.8	Sask.	66.0
N.B.	67.7	N.B.	64.9
B.C.	66.8	B.C.	64.1
Manitoba	56.0	Manitoba	55.4

legislative and popular vote margins of winning parties to diminish over time. Interestingly, however, this trend is reversed in Alberta where since the end of the Second World War the winning party's share of seats and of the popular vote has increased.

In drawing this chapter to a close two general conclusions can be advanced. The first is that the provincial electoral histories of the three Prairie provinces display few striking similarities. Although there are some points of commonality, as there would be among the electoral histories of any provinces in Canada, electoral politics in Manitoba, Saskatchewan and Alberta show few signs of having been stamped from the same regional mold. The second conclusion follows logically and empirically from the first—as there is little in common among the electoral histories of the three Prairie provinces there is little in those histories that is regionally distinctive, that sets the Prairie provinces apart from other provinces in the country. Yet it might be protested that to focus exclusively on electoral statistics is to adopt too narrow a stance, one that may miss the underlying essence of prairie politics, an essence that does indeed set the Prairies apart as a distinctive region. It is with this protest in mind that I would now like to turn from the electoral or behavioral dimension to a more attitudinal dimension of prairie politics, western alienation. It is within this attitudinal realm that the regionally distinctive features of prairie politics can be more readily detected, although even here many features of western alienation are not unique to the Prairies.

NOTES

1. The electoral data come from an invaluable standardized source, Loren M. Simerl, "A Survey of Canadian Provincial Election Results, 1905-1976," in Paul W. Fox, ed., *Politics: Canada,* fourth edition, Toronto, McGraw-Hill Ryerson, 1977, pp. 599-637.

2. M. S. Donnelly, *The Government of Manitoba,* Toronto, University of Toronto Press, 1963, p. 13.

3. Carl Berger, "William Morton: The Delicate Balance of Region and Nation," in Carl Berger and Ramsay Cook, eds., *The West and the Nation: Essays in Honour of W. L. Morton,* Toronto, McClelland & Stewart, 1976, pp. 20-21.

4. W. L. Morton, *Manitoba: A History,* 2nd Edition, Toronto, University of Toronto Press, 1963, pp. 232-33.

5. *Ibid.,* p. 245.

6. Donnelly, *The Government of Manitoba,* p. 58.

7. *Ibid.,* p. 51, and John Herd Thompson, *The Harvests of War: The Prairie West, 1914-1918,* Toronto, McClelland & Stewart, 1978, p. 90.

8. Thomas Peterson, "Manitoba: Ethnic and Class Politics," in Martin Robin, ed., *Canadian Provincial Politics,* Second Edition, Scarborough, Prentice-Hall, 1978, p. 85.

9. James A. Jackson, *The Centennial History of Manitoba,* Toronto, McClelland & Stewart, 1970, pp. 211-212.

10. W. L. Morton, "A Century of Plain and Parkland," in Richard Allen, ed., *A Region of the Mind,* Canadian Plains Studies Centre, University of Saskatchewan, Regina, 1973, p. 177.

11. Michael Kinnear, "The 1977 Manitoba Provincial Election," Paper presented to the 1978 Annual Meeting of the Canadian Political Science Association, London, Ontario, p. 46.

12. Peterson, "Manitoba," p. 104.

13. David E. Smith, *Prairie Liberalism: The Liberal Party in Saskatchewan, 1905-1971,* Toronto, University of Toronto Press, 1975, p. 19.

14. Evelyn Eager, "The Conservatism of the Saskatchewan Electorate," in Norman Ward and Duff Spafford, eds., *Politics in Saskatchewan,* Don Mills, Longmans, 1968, p. 9.

15. John C. Courtney and David E. Smith, "Saskatchewan: Parties in a Politically Competitive Province," in Robin, ed., *Canadian Provincial Politics,* p. 283.

16. Smith, *Prairie Liberalism,* pp. 84-5.

17. *Ibid.,* p. 176.

18. Courtney and Smith, "Saskatchewan," pp. 291-292.

19. Smith, *Prairie Liberalism,* p. 148.

20. *Ibid.,* p. 198.

21. *Ibid.,* p. 220.

22. Courtney and Smith, "Saskatchewan," p. 304.

23. Norman Ward, "The Contemporary Scene," in Ward and Spafford, *Politics in Saskatchewan,* p. 301.

24. Courtney and Smith, "Saskatchewan," p. 304.

25. Smith, *Prairie Liberalism,* p. 258.

26. Peter Sinclair, "The Saskatchewan CCF: Ascent to Power and the Decline of Socialism," in Samuel D. Clark, J. Paul Grayson, and Linda M. Grayson, eds., *Prophecy and Protest,* Toronto, Gage, 1975, p. 189.

27. John W. Bennett and Cynthia Krueger, "Agrarian Pragmatism and Radical Politics," in S. M. Lipset, *Agrarian Socialism,* Revised Edition, Berkeley, University of California Press, 1971, pp. 359-60.

28. Eager, "The Conservatism of the Saskatchewan Electorate," p. 16. A similar conclusion is reached in Lipset, *Agrarian Socialism,* pp. 151-52.

29. Smith, *Prairie Liberalism,* pp. 306-308.

30. *Calgary Herald,* October 19, 1978, p. D.19.

31. Smith, *Prairie Liberalism,* p. 3.

32. L. G. Thomas, *The Liberal Party in Alberta,* Toronto, University of Toronto Press, 1959, p. 206.

33. Thomas Flanagan, "Political Geography and the United Farmers of Alberta," in S. M. Trofimenkoff, ed., *The Twenties in Western Canada,* Ottawa, National Museum of Man, History Division, 1972, p. 149.

34. Thomas, *The Liberal Party,* p. 206.

35. *Ibid.,* p. 207.

36. Flanagan, "Political Geography," p. 147.

37. *Ibid.,* p. 153.

38. Quoted in James G. MacGregor, *A History of Alberta,* Edmonton, Hurtig, 1972, p. 265.

39. C. H. Douglas, *The Alberta Experiment,* London, Eyre & Spottiswoode, 1937, pp. 21-2.

40. *Ibid.,* pp. 22-3.

41. J. Anthony Long and F. Q. Quo, "Alberta: Politics of Consensus," in Robin, *Canadian Provincial Politics,* p. 5.

42. S. D. Clark, "Foreword," in William E. Mann, *Sect, Cult and Church in Alberta,* Toronto, University of Toronto Press, 1955, p. viii.

43. John J. Barr, *The Dynasty: The Rise and Fall of Social Credit in Alberta,* Toronto, McClelland and Stewart, 1974, p. 203.

44. MacGregor, *A History of Alberta,* p. 304.

45. W. L. Morton, "The Bias of Prairie Politics," in Donald Swainson, ed., *Historical Essays on the Prairie Provinces,* Toronto, McClelland and Stewart, 1970, p. 299.

46. Howard Palmer and Tamara Palmer, "The 1971 Election and the Fall of Social Credit in Alberta," *Prairie Forum,* Vol. 1, No. 2 (November 1976), pp. 123-4. Pratt also describes the 1971 election as the inevitable response to social change. L. R. Pratt, "The State and Province-Building: Alberta's Development Strategy, 1971-1976," University of Alberta Occasional Paper #5.

47. Barr, *The Dynasty,* p. 188.

48. Palmer and Palmer, "The 1971 Election," p. 124.

49. See E. C. Manning, *Political Realignment: A Challenge to Thoughtful Canadians,* 1967.

50. *Macleans,* October 17, 1976, p. 68.

51. *Macleans,* July 25, 1977, p. 19.

52. Robert J. Brym, "Explaining Regional Variations in Canadian Populist Movements," paper presented at the 1977 Annual Meeting of the Canadian Sociology and Anthropology Association, Fredericton, New Brunswick, pp. 24-5.

53. Myron Johnson, "The Failure of the CCF in Alberta: An Accident of History," Unpublished M.A. thesis, University of Alberta, 1974.

54. Long and Quo, "Alberta," pp. 6-7.

55. J. F. Conway, "On the Concept of Populism: Towards a Viable Political Sociology of the Prairie West," Paper delivered to a symposium on Society and Politics in Alberta, Edmonton, April 28, 1977, p. 28.

56. Peter R. Sinclair, "Class Structure and Populist Protest: The Case of Western Canada," *Canadian Journal of Sociology,* Vol. 1, No. 1 (Spring 1975), p. 11.

57. Lipset, *Agrarian Socialism,* p. 163.

58. *Ibid.,* p. 163.

59. Eager, "The Conservatism of the Saskatchewan Electorate," p. 15.

60. C. B. Macpherson, *Democracy in Alberta: Social Credit and the Party System,* Toronto, University of Toronto Press, 1953, pp. 215-16.

61. *Ibid.,* pp. 237-9.

62. Peterson, "Manitoba," p. 76.

63. Kinnear, "The 1977 Manitoba Provincial Election," p. 1.

64. Smith, *Prairie Liberalism,* p. 324.

65. For a discussion see Thomas F. Flanagan, "Ethnic Voting in Alberta Provincial Elections 1921-1971," *Canadian Ethnic Studies,* 3, pp. 156-161; and J. Paul Grayson and L. M. Grayson, "The Social Base of Interwar Political Unrest in Urban Alberta," *Canadian Journal of Political Science* (June 1974), pp. 289-313.

66. Peterson, "Manitoba," pp. 107-8; and Kinnear, "The 1977 Manitoba Provincial Election", pp. 18, 39.

67. F. C. Engelmann and M. A. Schwartz, *Canadian Political Parties: Origin, Character, Impact,* Scarborough, Prentice-Hall, 1975, p. 74.

68. Kinnear, "The 1977 Manitoba Provincial Election," p. 2.

69. Smith, *Prairie Liberalism,* p. 239.

70. *Ibid.,* pp. 238-9.

71. Sinclair, "The Saskatchewan CCF," p. 193.

72. Smith, *Prairie Liberalism,* p. 270.

73. For a discussion see Alan C. Cairns, "The Electoral System and the Party System in Canada, 1921-1965," *Canadian Journal of Political Science,* Vol. 1, No. 1 (March 1968), pp. 55-80.

CHAPTER FIVE

WESTERN ALIENATION

When the Prairie provinces are examined in terms of political organization and electoral behavior there appears to be little that knits the three into a regional entity. However, if we shift the analysis from behavior to political beliefs, values and perceptions a regional perspective comes more readily into focus. Western alienation constitutes a form of attitudinal regionalism that cuts across and integrates the rather disparate political histories of the Prairie provinces. Western alienation provides the distinguishing core of a prairie political culture within which the key elements are regional rather than provincial;[1] it engenders a western regional identification that transcends the narrower provincial arenas within which political behavior takes place. In this sense western Canada is a 'region of the mind'.[2]

CONCEPTUALIZATION

In coming to grips with the meaning of western alienation it is unfortunate that the term itself suggests an affinity with other forms of alienation. This is unfortunate because many of the principal characteristics of western alienation stand in direct contrast to characteristics commonly associated with more general forms of alienation.[3] Western alienation is not simply a specific form of a more generic phenomenon afflicting modern societies.

While western Canadians may be alienated from central Canada in general and from the national government in particular, a parallel sense of alienation is not evident towards prairie provincial governments. The latter, enthusiastically supported by their electorates, have provided little evidence of a generalized alienation that spills over from one level of the federal system to the other. If alienation reflects "estrangement between the self and the polity"[4] then western alienation embodies a more narrowly focused set of dispositions. Furthermore, even the character of western estrangement from the national government must be carefully qualified in that the major thrust of western sentiment has been for greater participation in and recognition by the national government. Western alienation has not been associated with the forms of political apathy, disengagement and withdrawal that more generally characterize political alienation.[5] To the contrary it has been a motive force behind the creation of the numerous movements of political protest. Western Canadians have not, as a consequence of western alienation, withdrawn from active political participation at either level of government.

Contemporary western alienation is not associated with the usual clientele of alienation—the dispossessed, the poor, the economically and socially marginal. While in the past the prairie region as a whole suffered from economic and social marginality, particularly during the Depression years, western alienation flourishes today in a prairie society that is prosperous and dynamic. Within that society, furthermore, there is little evidence that highly alienated individuals are found disproportionately among those suffering from economic or social deprivation. In a 1976 survey of western alienation within the Alberta electorate, discussed in detail below, no relationship was found between levels of alienation and the income, education or occupation of respondents.[6] The most prominent articulators of alienation in Alberta have tended to be individuals who have acquired wealth and success in oil, ranching, farming or construction. Christina Newman has neatly captured the creed of such individuals: "what Albertans want is to control their own destiny and to be recognized for what they are—not seen as imitators of Texans or enviers of Easterners, not as loud-mouths, rednecks, soreheads, or cowboys but as hard working, urban-dwelling, richly deserving, sweetly reasonable S.O.B.'s."[7] With respect to this last point it should be noted that western alienation has generally been linked with a strong sense of optimism and self-confidence. As Morton has explained ". . . the dominant note in the social philosophy of western people has been an unbounded confidence in themselves, a belief that their region was one with a great potential future if the hand of the outside exploiter could only be removed."[8] Western alienation is not the creed of the down-trodden.

The state of meaninglessness often attributed to alienation also seems inappropriate in the case of western alienation. In discussing alienation Finifter has written that meaninglessness exists to the extent that political decisions are perceived as unpredictable, that no pattern is perceptible to the individual.[9] On the Prairies, however, an almost conspiratorial view of national politics has existed, one in which political decisions by the national government are unfortunately seen as being all too predictable. In the eyes of the alienated Westerner systematic and predictable political patterns are clearly discernible; and West consistently gets shortchanged, exploited, and ripped-off. There is a parallel here to Lane's description of alienation as the feeling that "the rules of the game are unfair, loaded, illegitimate; the Constitution is, in some sense, fraudulent."[10]

Alienation is frequently viewed as a psychological disposition rooted within the personality needs of the individual. Yet the very pervasiveness of western alienation within the prairie population mitigates against characterizing it along such lines. In general, psychological or personality explanations are of little utility in trying to account for widely shared beliefs, beliefs that in this case are held by the majority of the western Canadian population. Unless one can support the position that the population at large shares some psychological trait or national character in the sense that "Germans are authoritarian" or "Canadians are cautious", little headway can be made. Psychological explanations are of far greater use in explaining the attraction to individuals of more deviant beliefs lacking social support in the surrounding community. The acquisition of beliefs such as western alienation is more readily accounted for by models of social learning and socialization than it is by psychological needs or traits.

In summary, western alienation is not appropriately conceptualized as a particular form of a more universal phenomenon, political alienation. Rather western alienation is best seen as a *political ideology of regional discontent.* By this I mean that western alienation embodies a socially shared set of interrelated beliefs with some degree of cultural embodiment and intellectual articulation, with a recognized history and constituency, and with recognized spokesmen and carriers of the creed. Western alienation encompasses a sense of political, economic and, to a lesser extent, cultural estrangement from the Canadian heartland. The ideological content of western alienation, of course, has not remained constant over time; the attitudinal baggage of beliefs, grievances and perceptions has changed as the conditions of the prairie society have changed. Yet at the same time there is great continuity with the past, continuity expressed through the interlocking themes that western Canada is always outgunned in national politics and that as a consequence has been subjected to varying degrees of economic exploitation by central Canada.

The conditions for a full-fledged political ideology are met to varying degrees by western alienation. Certainly it has a long and vigorous history, one that has been traced back to the Riel rebellions. Western alienation is a widely shared disposition, one that is explicitly linked to political activity. It has received organizational expression in a multitude of forms ranging from the Progressive Party in the past to the Independent Alberta Association today. It has received intellectual articulation through the editorial pages of the *Grain Growers' Guide,* the *Winnipeg Free Press,* and countless other prairie newspapers. However, the degree of formal articulation has been limited as the tools by which distinctively western Canadian cultural forms can be fashioned are in short supply. The difficulties here are similar to those facing the maintenance of an indigenous English-Canadian culture in the face of cultural exposure to the American society. English Canadians generally live within a culture that has been largely fabricated elsewhere. Western Canadians living within the same culture find that even its Canadian elements have been largely created outside the West. Western Canadians live within an eastern

Canadian cultural environment embedded within a larger American mass culture, and neither serve as a suitable vehicle for the cultural expression of the western society. It is for this and more political reasons that provincial governments have emerged as the principal articulators and orchestrators of western alienation.

THE MEASUREMENT OF WESTERN ALIENATION

A number of studies in Alberta have attempted to measure the components of western alienation and the degree to which western alienation characterizes the Alberta electorate.[11] The most recent data comes from a survey I conducted in the late spring of 1976. That survey, based on a random provincial sample of 502 respondents, utilized a 40 minute in-home personal interview, a substantial part of which was directed towards western alienation. Respondents were presented with a number of statements expressing sentiments commonly encountered in western Canada; these are provided in Table 5:1. In order to determine the extent to which the statements tapped respondent dispositions, respondents were asked to state their degree of agreement or disagreement with each.

As Table 5:1 makes abundantly clear western alienation was not a marginal disposition within the Alberta electorate. We find, for example, that close to three-quarters of the respondents agreed that Alberta politicians are not taken seriously in the East, and that Alberta usually gets ignored in national politics. Conversely less than one person in three agreed that Alberta benefits as much from the industries of the East as eastern Canada benefits from Alberta's natural resources such as oil. Less than one respondent in five disagreed with the statement that in many ways Alberta has more in common with the western United States than it does with eastern Canada.

The first eight statements in Table 5:1 can be used to construct an index of western alienation. This is accomplished by assigning for each statement a score of five for a strongly alienated response, a score of four for a moderately alienated response, and so forth through to a score of one for a strongly unalienated response. For example, a respondent who strongly agreed that "most Canadians seem to feel that Canada ends at the Great Lakes" would receive a score of five on that statement; a respondent who moderately disagreed would receive a score of two, and a respondent who neither agreed nor disagreed would receive an intermediate score of three. Then for each respondent scores on the eight statements are totalled to yield an index score that could potentially range from eight (minimal alienation) to 40 (maximum alienation). The resulting *Index of Western Alienation* meets conventional tests of internal consistency and unidimensionality.[12] Figure 5:1 presents the distribution of the 1976 Alberta sample on the index. Most of the

TABLE 5:1
Western Alienation in Alberta, 1976

Statement	Percent of Sample	
	Agreeing Strongly or Moderately	Disagreeing Strongly or Moderately
The economic policies of the federal government seem to help Quebec and Ontario at the expense of Alberta.	73.7	9.6
Because the political parties depend upon Quebec and Ontario for most of their votes, Alberta usually gets ignored in national politics.	77.1	13.9
During the past few years the federal government has made a genuine effort to overcome problems of economic discrimination against Alberta.	32.1	45.0
In many ways Alberta has more in common with the western United States than it does with eastern Canada.	62.5	18.9
Most eastern Canadians seem to feel that Canada ends at the Great Lakes.	64.5	16.3
Alberta benefits as much from the industries of the East as eastern Canada benefits from Alberta's natural resources such as oil.	23.9	62.7
It often seems that Alberta politicians are not taken seriously in the East.	71.3	13.5
If one part of Canada suffers we all suffer, and if one region prospers, we all share in the prosperity.	32.1	56.8
Albertans have to unite behind one party to get anything out of Ottawa.	63.9	18.3

Number of respondents = 502

FIGURE 5:1 **Distribution of 1976 Alberta Sample on an Index of Western Alienation**

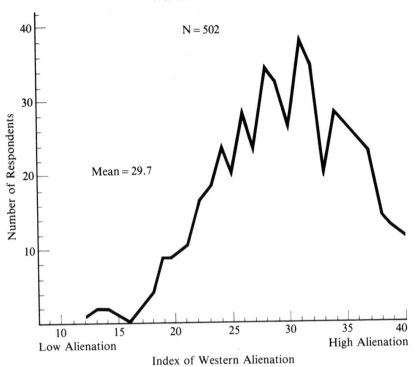

Index of Western Alienation

respondents (80.3%) fell above the mid-point of the scale, respondents being concentrated near although not at the alienated pole. Respondents, however, were not monolithic in their degree of western alienation, there being considerable variation in index scores. As our discussion of western alienation unfolds one of the factors accounting for much of this variation—political partisanship—will be examined.

Table 5:1 and Figure 5:1 provide a convenient introduction to western alienation as it was manifested in Alberta during the mid-70s. The extent to which the Alberta situation paralleled that in Saskatchewan and Manitoba unfortunately cannot be documented and is open to conjecture. To more fully grasp the nature of western alienation it is essential to turn to a detailed discussion of its major components. The development of western alienation has been analogous to that of a pearl in an oyster; at its core lies the abrasive grit of economic discontent reaching back into the early history of prairie settlement. Over time this grit has been covered with a regional amalgam of grievances, concerns, and political self-interest. Let us look, then, at the core of economic discontent, at the amalgam that has overlaid this core, and finally at the contemporary pearl of western alienation on the Canadian Prairies.

COMPONENTS OF WESTERN ALIENATION

A) Economic Discontent and Anti-Colonialism

The core of economic discontent lies in regionally-specific agrarian grievances including the National Policy, discriminatory freight rates, bottlenecks and monopolies in the transportation of grain, and treatment by eastern-based financial institutions that was insensitive at best to western circumstances. While some of these grievances may now have declined in importance, particularly within urban centres, others have demonstrated a remarkable continuity. As an example here, in a 1974 survey I conducted of over 200 Calgarians the most commonly mentioned grievance with the federal government was that of discriminatory freight rates. The continued centrality of this issue, I suspect, demonstrates its symbolic and communicative value rather than any firm grasp of the contemporary freight rate quagmire facing the West. As the western Canadian economy expanded and diversified many historical economic grievances persisted, albeit in an altered form. New grievances have also emerged as the resource base of the prairie economy spread from the soil itself to the oil, gas, potash and mineral wealth lying beneath it. Here conflicts between Alberta and Ottawa over the price and marketing of energy resources have become legion and Saskatchewan has run up against national institutions in its development of potash and petroleum industries.

Throughout the history of the West there has been a pervasive belief that the resource-rich Prairies were being exploited by the East, and the imagery evoked by former Alberta Premier Harry Strom still strikes a deep resonance within the region:

> We have always had a sense of economic exploitation. This notion has marked all political parties in the West. The cartoon that has captured these sentiments is one of a large cow standing on a map of Canada munching grass in Alberta and Saskatchewan with milk pouring from a bulging udder into the large buckets in Ontario.[13]

Saskatchewan Premier Allan Blakeney has argued that the western provinces get the short end of the stick from both discriminatory and non-discriminatory national policies. Speaking in 1977 to the Canadian Club (Toronto), Blakeney noted that oil, natural gas, uranium, and wheat are virtually the only natural resources regulated by the federal government. He then went on, in a speech worth quoting at length, to ennunciate a widely-held western perspective:

> . . . we in the West find it passing strange that the national interest emerges only when we are talking about Western *resources* or Eastern *benefits*. If oil, why not iron ore and steel products? If natural gas, why not copper? If

uranium—and we in Saskatchewan may well be Canada's biggest uranium producer in a few years—if uranium, why not nickle? And, to add insult to injury, we in the West are now being told by the Federal Minister of Transport that the national interest demands a rail transportation policy in which the user pays the full cost. What user will pay the most under that kind of system: land-locked Saskatchewan. Air transport is subsidized. The Seaway runs monumental deficits. Our ports are all subsidized. Truck transportation is subsidized by many provincial highway systems in Canada. But in rail transport—the one on which we depend, we are told that the user must pay.[14]

The August 1979 proposal by the Ontario government that the oil revenues of the western producing provinces be redistributed in some manner to the consuming provinces falls within the same tradition that Blakeney attacked.

Economic exploitation blends with another thread of western alienation, anti-colonialism. Colonial imagery provides an emotionally charged and politically potent rhetorical device. To give but one example, Premier Lougheed stated in an address to the Agricultural Promotion Association of Alberta that "we have too much of being a colony and we don't want to be a colony."[15] Given the international climate of the times it was perhaps inevitable that anti-colonialism be picked up in the West just as it has been by the Quebeçois and native groups. Yet it must be acknowledged that colonial imagery has some serious shortcomings, the most important being the fact that the colonizing power, the national government in Ottawa, is one in which the West—like Quebec—has full proportionate representation and to which the West—like Quebec—has contributed both prime ministers and many outstanding parliamentarians. Nevertheless if we consider a colonial situation to be one in which important decisions lie outside the hands of local residents and where the economic system locks a region into a state of dependency, then the colonial analogy has some merit.

There is no doubt that the prosperity of western Canada has rested in the hands of forces external to the region. Some of these such as the weather and foreign agricultural markets can only be borne with stoicism and a faith that "next year" things will be better. But the control by outsiders of public and economic policies vital to the West has been more difficult to tolerate. The fact that the levers of public policy rest outside the prairie region has been particularly aggravating for political leaders in the West as David Smith's discussion of Thatcher's problems leading up to the 1971 Saskatchewan provincial election illustrates: "Frustration was all the greater because the problems demonstrated what had always been true of Saskatchewan's economy but had frequently been ignored by advocates of private enterprise and individual initiative: that the economy responded to, indeed was determined by, external forces largely immune to the control of provincial leaders."[16] Unfortunately there is little likelihood that economic irritations between the West and the

feedstock

national government will ever be eliminated. Pessimism on this account springs from the fact that western Canada remains a relatively sparsely-populated economic hinterland within both the Canadian and North American market economies. As economist Kenneth Norrie has pointed out many of the economic grievances of western Canada rise from the region's peripheral location in these market economies. Thus they ". . . must be interpreted as dissatisfaction with a market economy rather than with discriminatory policies of the federal government", policies that Norrie feels have been exaggerated in their negative effects.[17] Norrie's very important thesis raises doubt whether even the most supportive national policies would be able to overcome market forces and encourage substantial expansion of manufacturing and secondary industry in western Canada. In the foreseeable future, then, economic peripherality will continue to generate regional grievances directed at a national government lacking the power even if it had the inclination to alter the existing economic state of affairs.

A major test of Norrie's argument looms on the horizon in the Alberta government's efforts to establish a large-scale petrochemical industry in the province. The government is determined that Alberta do more than supply natural gas feedstock to the industries of eastern Canada, that the production of petrochemical products along with the jobs that such production entails be brought back to the Alberta source of the feedstock supply. However the obstacles lying in the path of this objective are formidable. They include the distance that Alberta lies from concentrated consumer markets, rapidly escalating feedstock prices, the relative costs of transporting manufactured products as opposed to the pipeline transmission of feedstock, opposition from federally-controlled Petrosar Canada Ltd. in Sarnia, Ontario, which has a stranglehold on a saturated domestic petrochemical market, moderate opposition within the province to plans for extensive industrialization, and the reluctance of Americans to concede the tariff agreements that would make Alberta petrochemical products commercially competitive with those produced by American firms already enjoying comparative advantages in size, transportation, and labour costs. The next decade should decide whether the very considerable economic muscle of the Alberta government will be sufficient to overcome the market and governmental forces inhibiting this form of secondary industry in the West.

In discussing the economic grievances of the West care must be taken not to create the impression that western Canadians face a life of unmitigated hardship. In recent years the western economy has been booming despite the persistence of discriminatory freight rates *et al*. Also in some of the most contentious policy areas there have been some major accommodations between Ottawa and the western provinces. With reference to the proposed pipeline that will carry Alaskan gas southward through Alberta to American markets Premier Lougheed was able to say that he was "delighted" with the co-operation which Ottawa tendered his administration.[18] Further examples include the federal government's participation in the Syncrude tarsands development in northern Alberta, the federal tax breaks received by Syncrude, and the relatively amicable agreements between Edmonton and Ottawa on increases in the price of energy resources. These latter agreements have come in the face of strenuous opposition from the consuming provinces led by Ontario.

The chorus of economic discontent has been at least softened by the region's unprecedented economic prosperity. Ironically, though, economic prosperity itself has been a source of political discontent. Western Canadians, particularly those in Alberta, are searching for a degree of political power commensurate with their economic strength. That search was frustrated in the 70s by the region's Conservative partisan complexion in the face of the Liberals' hold on national office, and by the fact that western Canada remains a numerically small region within a country whose government is based on representation by population. Thus there has been a push to increase the region's political power by redistributing legislative responsibilities from a central government lying beyond the grasp of Westerners to provincial governments resting within their control.

B) Antipathy Towards Quebec

Antipathy toward Quebec and French Canadians is a long-standing pillar of western alienation, although the specific focus of western hostility has shifted over time across a number of distinct though interrelated targets. The taproot of hostility goes back to the problems western Canada faced in assimilating a large and polyglot immigrant population. Western Canadians were prone to treat the relatively small French Canadian population on the Prairies as, at best, just another minority; French Canadians were viewed rather myopically from the perspective of their western Canadian strength rather than from the more politically realistic perspective of the large Quebec population. Special rights or protections for French Canadians were irksome not so much in themselves but because they were obstacles in the assimilation of the much larger non-British, non-French immigrant population. Thus minority language and denominational rights in education, for example, rights lying at the heart of the Manitoba schools controversy, handicapped the public school system as a vehicle of assimilation.

As Denis Smith has observed, ". . . the prairie difficulty in accustoming itself to bilingualism and biculturalism is not simply bigotry: it is deeply entrenched policy that emerges from the prairie attempt to establish its own identity."[19] That identity was, and perhaps only could be, based on the assimilation of ethnic minorities into a composite Canadian nationality. Despite or because of the ethnic mosaic of prairie settlement, the nationalism that emerged in western Canada was close in spirit to the melting-pot nationalism of the United States, and it found itself in direct conflict with the desire of French Canadians to shelter their own ethnicity behind special legal and political rights. The one-Canada nationalism of John Diefenbaker faithfully reflects his prairie roots:

> We shall never build the nation which our potential resources make possible by dividing ourselves into Anglophones, Francophones, multiculturalphones, or whatever kind of phoneys you choose. I say: Canadians, first, last, and always![20]

Serious in its own right, the hostility arising from conflict over language and assimilation was exacerbated further by other factors. Quebec was wedded in western Canadian minds to "central Canada" and to the economic exploitation of the west thereby. Thus in the West French Canadians bore the cross of economic exploiters regardless of the rather questionable economic advantages that flowed to them from their central Canadian location. Perhaps more seriously the French language was closely associated with Catholicism in the predominantly Protestant environment of the West, and as a consequence religious and linguistic antagonisms became hopelessly entangled.

The conscription dispute during the First World War brought anti-French sentiment to a boil in western Canada. The refusal of French Canadians to match the generally enthusiastic support of the West for Canadian participation in the war and the vehement opposition in Quebec to conscription when western Canada seemed to be bearing a disproportionately large share of Canadian casualties greatly intensified western hostility. This hostility was deliberately used by the Union government in the 1917 election to repress class and regional cleavages within the English Canadian electorate.[21] To illustrate the character of the Unionist campaign J. H. Thompson cites Bob Edwards, widely known journalist and author of the *Calgary Eye Opener*. Discussing Liberal leader Sir Wilfred Laurier's opposition to conscription, Edwards asked readers if they were:

> . . . going to let this hoary four-flusher get away with this? Not on your tintype! Canada shall not desert her defenders to please any whited Sepulchre from Quebec . . . One would almost imagine that Wilfred as a child had been raised on sauerkraut instead of pea soup.[22]

In the Second World War, although anti-French sentiment was not fostered to the same degree, old wounds were nonetheless reopened and the fresh salt of the new conscription controversy rubbed in.

By the 60s and 70s the impact of conscription had subsided as had the religious base of hostility towards French Canadians, but new fuel was being added to the fire of western antipathy. Western Canadians felt that the national government had become too preoccupied with the problems of Quebec and that the equally legitimate concerns of the West were being neglected. Note a 1979 speech by Canada West President Stanley C. Roberts:

> The new fury of the Westerner demonstrates itself when it strikes home that Quebec's six million plus citizens have turned the country on its collective ear and created an enormous attention to their problems by the election of a pequiste government, while the West's six million plus citizens (still) can't be heard over the rush and scramble to accommodate Quebec. Sometimes the West's frustration and rage is misconstrued as antiQuebec in nature. It is not. It is, in most cases, envy of Quebec's political prowess combined with fury at the West's own impotence on the national scene.[23]

The Liberal government, led by a French Canadian Prime Minister with strong cabinet representation from Quebec and lacking adequate representation from the Prairie provinces, seemed at best insensitive to the concerns of western Canadians. When western Canada did catch the attention of the national government the result was not always beneficial, as David Smith notes: ". . . after a decade of singular devotion to Quebec's problem, the federal government is viewed from the Prairies, in the conflict over oil and natural gas, as once again turning its guns and not its ear to the West."[24]

The focal point of western Canadian hostility in the 70s was the bilingualism and biculturalism program of the federal government. The prairie electorate, firmly in the Conservative camp and generally distrustful of the Liberal government, needed a lot of convincing that bilingualism and biculturalism were either necessary or desirable. Unfortunately Liberal leaders made few attempts to explain the rationale of or the political necessity for programs such as the 1969 Official Languages Act. In the attempts that were made little sensitivity was displayed towards the multicultural character of the prairie population or towards the region's history of conflict with language legislation. Nor was an attempt made to combine the introduction of the controversial language policies with any serious compensatory effort to tackle some of the outstanding problems facing western Canada. As a result when bilingual signs began to appear in national parks and federal institutions in the West, when bilingual labelling appeared on consumer products, and when air controllers struck over the introduction of French as an aviational language, misunderstanding and anger grew like mushrooms in a heavy rain. Even metrification was seen as another aspect of bilingualism; Graham Smith, editor of Calgary's *North Hill News,* complained about the expense of implementing "the French metric system"[25]

The intensity of western reaction to bilingualism was recorded by Montreal Star reporter Claude Arpin in a 1976 special to *The Albertan.*[26]

On a tour through the West Arpin encountered little hostility directed towards him personally but the opposition he found to bilingualism was frequently venomous. Resentment towards public policy may nonetheless be used to mask a deeper, more personality oriented prejudice. Take for example the comments of an antique dealer from Brandon, Manitoba:

> It's hard to get used to bilingual labelling. When you go shopping, you gotta turn a package over and over to find some English. On the labels its French, French, French. And when you're watching a hockey game you say 'shut up with the French' you get so tired of hearing it. You feel like saying 'tell it in English, this is an English country.'

Or the words of a German-Canadian from Warburg, Alberta:

> I'm a religious man but I'm at the point now where I say let's take our guns and have it out with Quebec. If you win, we'll go back to the countries our parents came from but if you lose, you go back to France and we'll start over building a country that speaks only English.

In the summer of 1974 I surveyed 221 Calgarians in order to explore the relationship between western alienation and antipathy towards Quebec and French Canadians.[27] Western alienation was measured by a set of agree-disagree statements very similar to those in Table 5:1. Antipathy towards Quebec was also measured by a battery of agree-disagree statements such as "because the federal government is afraid of Quebec separating Quebec gets more than its fair share from Ottawa," and "French Canadians have made Canada a more interesting country by contributing a second language and culture." There was a strong positive relationship between scores on the indices of western alienation and antipathy towards Quebec. The greater the antipathy towards Quebec the more alienated respondents tended to be. Interestingly, however, orientations towards French Canadians and Quebec measured through the use of semantic differential scales had only the most modest correlations with the western alienation index. Whether Calgarians thought French Canadians were honest or dishonest, courteous or rude, or whether Calgarians thought Quebec was prosperous or poor, powerful or weak, bore little relationship to the degree of respondent alienation. It appears then that the orientations towards Quebec and French Canadians most tightly linked to western alienation are those that are explicitly political.

In concluding this discussion it must be kept in mind that although antipathy towards Quebec and policies such as the Official Languages Act is clearly a component of western alienation, this is not to say that such antipathy is unique to the West or that it is any more virulent in the West than elsewhere. It may be the case, however, that similar antipathies elsewhere in Canada are not so tightly interwoven with regional identifications as they are in the West. On the Prairies opposition to bilingualism and biculturalism, and to the strengthened French Canadian presence in Ottawa, fits neatly into and reinforces pre-existing antipathies towards the central government itself.

C) Political Elements

Western alienation is inextricably entangled with politics on the Prairies. It manifests itself in the repeated demand for increased provincial autonomy, it has become a conventional weapon in provincial election campaigns, and it is fed by and feeds upon partisan divisions within the prairie electorate. Let us look at each of these in turn.

The demand for increased provincial autonomy has been a rallying call throughout the history of the West. The national government's retention (until 1931) of the control of public lands in the West "for the purposes of the Dominion" led to continued provincial rights agitation. The issue dominated Manitoba provincial politics in the 1880s and 1890s. David Smith describes how in the early decades of Saskatchewan provincial politics the Liberal and Conservative parties, the latter running at times as the Provincial Rights Party, jockeyed continuously for the role of defender of provincial rights and powers.[28] A related issue, one that particularly affected Manitoba in the 1880s and Alberta in the 1930s, was the national government's disallowance of provincial legislation. Western Canadians felt with considerable justification that disallowance was used primarily against the weaker provinces in the West, not against Ontario or Quebec, and was used most frequently against provincial regimes that were neither Liberal nor Conservative.

There are some striking parallels between earlier provincial rights agitations and the contemporary political climate. The struggle for the provincial control of public lands finds expression today in the struggle for provincial control of the mineral wealth lying beneath those lands. Another example comes from a communique, issued from the 1978 Western Premiers' Conference in Yorkton, Saskatchewan, that listed 61 continuing and 11 new federal intrusions into provincial fields of jurisdiction.

While western alienation may have originated outside the arena of electoral politics its existence has been repeatedly exploited within that arena. Although it may seem overly cynical to state that party organizations on the Prairies have deliberately fostered western alienation, fanning the coals of western alienation has been a common and very effective electoral strategy. Western alienation has been useful to have around. It has been used frequently in conjunction with attacks on the national affiliations of provincial political opponents. In recent years the Alberta provincial Liberal party found its affiliation with the national Liberal party to be a crippling cross to bear and in 1977 all organizational links between the provincial and national parties were severed, a step taken by the Quebec Liberal organization a decade earlier for somewhat similar reasons. Such surgery within the minds of provincial voters will be more difficult to achieve. In discussing the success of early Manitoba Conservatives during a time of Liberal dominance in Ottawa Jackson notes that ". . . few provincial governments have ever suffered at the hands of their electorate for taking a strong stand against the aggression, real or imagined, of federal power."[29]

Smith's history of the Saskatchewan Liberal party has thoroughly documented the perils and pitfalls of provincial affiliations with national party organizations. For example, in the 1971 provincial campaign the New Democrats used an agricultural policy report by the national Liberal government as an effective club against the provincial Liberal government: "to the retort that the task force had nothing to do with Saskatchewan Liberals, the NDP replied that 'a Liberal was a Liberal' and that if the provincial voter wanted to protest about the task force and its recommendations, about the LIFT programme, and about the state of western agriculture generally, he should vote for the NDP."[30] Smith's history also points out, though, that in some circumstances the connection with the national Liberal party was an asset, as it had been when the first Liberal provincial government was formed in 1905. In the 1934 election campaign, when the Conservatives were in power in both Ottawa and Regina, the provincial Liberals used their connection with the national party to positive effect. The national connection then became a curse when the CCF came to power in Saskatchewan and the federal Liberals were in power in Ottawa. The CCF was so successful in attacking the provincial Liberals through the national government that the former contemplated breaking with the latter to ". . . deprive the CCF of one of its favourite pastimes—imputing blame to provincial Liberals for federal government actions."[31]

Shortly after its election in 1944 the CCF government passed the Farm Security Act which, during years of crop failure, suspended mortgage payments, wiped out interest payments on debt, and protected the home quarter section against foreclosure. When the national government threatened in 1945 to disallow this legislation Premier Douglas used a radio address to rally the people of Saskatchewan against the federal threat:

> We have just finished a war which was fought, we were told, for the preservation of democratic institutions. It would appear that the war is not finished. We have simply moved the battlefields from the banks of the Rhine to the prairies of Saskatchewan.[32]

It was a speech that, had circumstances allowed, Peter Lougheed might have been proud to make during the energy confrontations with Ottawa in the mid-70s.

Before leaving the Saskatchewan illustration it is interesting to note that Diefenbaker's victory in 1957 and his 1958 rout of the national Liberal party from Saskatchewan helped pave the way for the revival of the provincial Liberal party. As David Smith explains, the defeat of the federal party freed the Saskatchewan Liberals of the "albatross of responsibility" for federal government policies.[33] When the next provincial election came around the Liberals were able to force provincial issues on which the CCF government did not have a strong hand to the centre of the campaign. With the return to office of the federal Liberals entanglements with the national party returned to plague the provincial Liberal organization, then in power itself. The ideological disputes between Liberal Premier Ross Thatcher and the federal Liberals represented in part an effort by Thatcher to maintain some distance between himself and the federal party. By 1976 separation from the national party was being seriously considered as the Liberals wearied of fighting provincial campaigns on federal issues.[34]

Western alienation can be used by provincial governments to reduce opposition parties to a state of virtual irrelevance in provincial campaigns. The best contemporary example comes from the 1975 Alberta election. Premier Lougheed built the Conservative campaign around the call for a mandate from the voters that could be used to strengthen the provincial government's hand in energy pricing negotiations with the federal government. The Conservative strategy placed the opposition parties in an extremely uncomfortable position. When they tried to discuss purely provincial issues they were dismissed by Lougheed as "carping critics" who were ignoring the main issue of the day. When forced into a discussion of energy policy the opposition parties had no ground on which to stand. To endorse the position of the Alberta government was to declare themselves redundant and to support the position of the federal government was suicidal. The dilemma was demonstrated by a question in the 1976 Alberta survey discussed above. Only 13% of the respondents disagreed with the statement that "in disputes between Alberta and the federal government, the opposition parties should pull together with the provincial government." The alienated Alberta electorate enabled the Lougheed Conservatives to derail the opposition campaigns and turn the election into a two-party fight with the provincial Conservatives leading the Alberta electorate into battle against the federal Liberals.

While western alienation has been a valuable resource in the hands of prairie provincial politicians it should be emphasized that provincial politicians generally have regularly exploited the electoral opportunities inherent in federal-provincial conflict. It is not difficult to find examples outside the Prairies of provincial governments mobilizing their electorates against the federal government rather than against provincial opponents. The strategy has been frequently employed in British Columbia and it was honed to a fine edge by the Quebec Union Nationale governments led by Maurice Duplessis. In this respect Richard Simeon notes that at the elite level federalism tends to perpetuate regional differences ". . . by conferring leadership on a set of leaders in provincial governments who have vested interest in maintaining and strengthening the importance of the regional dimensions."[35] Simeon goes on to state that ". . . to maintain support, a provincial government is motivated to accentuate the degree of internal unity, and to exaggerate the extent of difference with Ottawa, and to divert political conflict onto an external enemy."[36] Although written prior to the 1975 Alberta election Simeon's argument describes that campaign to a tee.

The utilization of western alienation as an electoral resource, the employment of parallel electoral strategies in other provinces, and the argument of Richard Simeon all suggest that prairie provincial governments do more than respond to western alienation as a form of regional discontent. To some degree western alienation is deliberately sustained and manipulated by provincial politicians. Given that most provincial governments employ federal-provincial conflict as an electoral resource one might question the extent to which the phenomenon of western alienation rather than simply the label is unique to the West. While western alienation may be geographically delineated the political competition that helps sustain it and the electoral tactics that it fosters are clearly not. In this limited sense western alienation may be only a specific expression of a more general sense of regional alienation that characterizes the Canadian state.

The last political element of western alienation to be considered here is the relationship between western alienation and political partisanship. Since 1958 the national Conservative party has dominated electoral politics on the Prairies and the Conservative hegemony suggests that western Canadians, quite apart from freight rates, energy disputes, bilingualism, and so forth, may also have disliked the national government simply because it was usually in Liberal hands. The cutting edge of western alienation may have been a purely partisan dislike; western Canadians were alienated as much because they were Conservatives as because they were western Canadians. Of course the *relative* contribution of partisanship to the strength of western alienation, relative to regional economic grievances and so forth, is very difficult to gauge. Fortunately, however, the basic relationship between western alienation and political partisanship can be documented, at least for Alberta in the mid-70s. In the survey of the Alberta electorate discussed earlier respondents were asked the following: "As far as national politics are concerned, do you usually think of yourself as Conservative, Liberal, NDP, Social Credit, or what?" Respondents identifying with one of the four major parties were then asked: "How strongly Conservative [or whatever] do you generally feel—very strongly, fairly strongly or not very strongly?"

Together these two questions constitute a standard measure of political party identification. In this case they allow us to divide up the Alberta sample into Conservatives, Liberals, New Democrats, and so on. There were also enough Conservative and Liberal respondents for distinctions to be drawn among strong Liberals (or Conservatives), fairly strong Liberals, and not very strong Liberals. If we then compute the average score on the Western Alienation Index (Figure 5:1) for each partisan group in the sample the relationship between political partisanship and western alienation can be readily established. In Figure 5:2 this has been done using the national party identifications of the respondents.

Figure 5:2 shows a strong, even striking relationship between political partisanship and the strength of western alienation. Levels of alienation were lowest among two groups of respondents: those identifying with the Liberal party and those declaring themselves to be independents. Among respondents identifying with the Liberal party the strength of party identification was negatively related to levels of alienation; strong Liberals were significantly less alienated than were respondents with a weak identification with the Liberal party. Conversely, strong Conservatives were significantly more alienated than were weak Conservative identifiers. Weak Liberals and weak Conservatives had, on average, very similar alienation scores whereas strong Liberals and strong Conservatives were poles apart. When a similar analysis was performed using provincial party identifications the relationship portrayed in Figure 5:2 was essentially replicated.

It should not be surprising that Liberals and particularly strong Liberals were the least alienated. Liberals had an identification with the national government that other Westerners lacked, for in a partisan if not in a regional sense, it was *their government*. The relatively low levels of alienation among political independents may also be accounted for by the fact that independents, like western Liberals, did not carry a partisan grudge against the national government. Independents, identifying with no party, would not experience a sense of partisan exclusion from the national government. It should also be noted, however, that the close similarity in levels of alienation between Liberals and independents raises the suspicion that many of the independents in the sample may have been "closet-Liberals", individuals who although predisposed towards the party find the Liberal label too onerous a cross to bear in the overwhelmingly Conservative climate of Alberta.

The high level of alienation found among identifiers with opposition parties in general and the Conservative party in particular reinforces the possibility that western alienation reflects a partisan as well as a regional dislike of the national government. This is not to say that a general sense of regional discontent does not exist for even Liberals within the Alberta sample were less than enchanted with the national government. It does suggest that alienation is intensified by partisan considerations, that

FIGURE 5:2 **National Partisanship and Western Alienation Alberta, 1976**

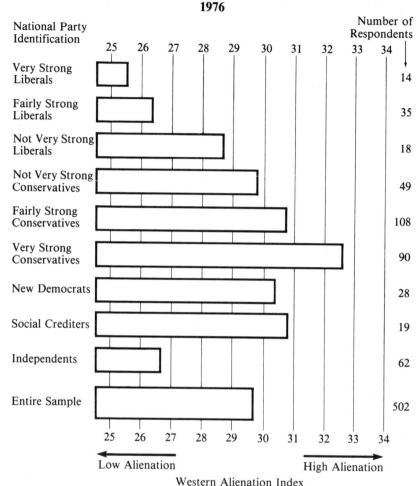

western Conservatives were alienated from the incumbent *Liberal* administration in Ottawa as well as from the national government per se. Admittedly, there is a chicken and egg problem with the entwinement of western alienation and support for the Conservative party. It may be the case that Conservatives were relatively alienated from the national government because their party had been excluded from that government for over 13 years. They did not see the national government as their government, they disliked the direction of its policies and programs, they disliked its leader, and they generalized their partisan dislike to a broader sense of regional disaffection. If this pattern holds then the election of a Conservative government in Ottawa should reduce existing levels of alienation in western Canada. However, it may also be the case that highly alienated individuals gravitated towards the Conservative party, seeing it as a means through which they could express dissatisfaction with the national government. In this manner alienation may foster support for the major national opposition party whatever its partisan complexion. If this is the case then the election of a Conservative national government will do little to reduce western alienation unless that government is able to overcome the longstanding economic grievances of the West. Failure of a new Conservative administration to do so would result in alienated Westerners searching for a new partisan vehicle through which to express their continued disaffection with the national government. Ironically, the Liberal party in opposition could well serve as such a vehicle.

While the linkage between political partisanship and western alienation has been empirically demonstrated only for Alberta it is likely that similar patterns existed within the Manitoba and Saskatchewan electorates. It would be surprising if during the mid-70s Conservatives in Manitoba or Saskatchewan turned out to be less alienated than their Liberal counterparts.

DISCUSSION

The concern in western Canada with federal government intrusions into provincial areas of jurisdiction is not unlike that expressed by Quebec premiers from Maurice Duplessis to René Levesque. Indeed the common push for greater provincial autonomy suggests some significant similarities between western alienation and contemporary Quebeçois nationalism, similarities captured in a remark by Canada West President Stanley Roberts—"just like Quebec, we want to be maitre chez nous—masters in our own house."[37] Premier Peter Lougheed, in a March 1977 speech to the Alberta Conservative party, also drew parallels between the positions of Alberta and Quebec on Canadian confederation:

> . . . just as Albertans want more control over their destiny—primarily for economic reasons—Quebecers, I sense, want also more control over their destiny, essentially for cultural and linguistic reasons. Hence, just as Albertans want more government decisions made in Edmonton than in Ottawa, I think Quebecers, for different reasons, but somewhat similar motives, want more government decisions made in Quebec City, and fewer in Ottawa.[38]

The parallels become superficial, however, when compared to the fundamental differences that exist. Despite the call for greater provincial autonomy western Canadians have persistently sought greater inclusion in the national political and social fabric. This point is of cardinal importance in coming to grips with western alienation. W. L. Morton has argued that:

the West has been defined as a colonial society seeking equality in Confederation. That equality was sought in order that the West should be like, not different from, the rest of Canada.[39]

The contrast with Quebec is sharp indeed. Denis Smith, commenting on the paradox that ". . . the achievement of national integration for the Prairie provinces over the last 50 years has not meant the disappearance of a distinctly Prairie viewpoint on national affairs,"[40] states that ". . . what distinguishes the prairie region from Quebec is that it *wants* to be a region like the others: that is, it wants, essentially, to occupy a place in the mainstream of Canadian life like that occupied by its ancestor Ontario, a province that has almost always been able to think of the federal government in a peculiar way not as something distant and foreign, but as its own government."[41]

Provincial politicians in the West have also made the case for greater regional inclusion within the national society and polity. In opening the 1969 Constitutional Conference, Alberta Premier Harry Strom said the central problem was how to make western Canadians feel more a part of the Canadian nation. The current Alberta premier, Peter Lougheed, placed great emphasis in the speech cited above on the statement "we are Canadian before we're Albertan," and argued that a strong Alberta is good for Canada. Lou Hyndman, then acting Alberta Minister for Intergovernmental Affairs, reacted to the 1978 federal government constitutional proposals by saying that what the national government has failed to understand is that the West has wanted an equal opportunity, has wanted to move into the mainstream of the Canadian society.[42] The contrast with Quebeçois nationalism is sharp.

Admittedly, there is a dimension to western alienation that is more exclusive than inclusive; certainly the bumper sticker "Let The Eastern Bastards Freeze in the Dark" is of this ilk. Yet as a counterpoint to such sentiments western Canadian political leaders have not been unwilling to promote the national interest. As an example, note a 1977 speech by Saskatchewan Premier Blakeney:

> Let me begin by saying I do not subscribe to the proposition that Easterners, whether born in or out of wedlock, should freeze in the dark. Most of us in western Canada would agree—and have agreed—that the national interest demands . . . that Canada should have first claim to our depleting energy resources. . . .[43]

While Premier Blakeney may be a more enthusiastic supporter of the national interest and the existing federal arrangements than are some of his western colleagues, the tone of his address nonetheless serves to underline the profound difference between western alienation and contemporary nationalism in Quebec. While the promotion of the "national interest" in the past frequently imposed heavy financial costs on the

West, western Canadians have not lost faith in national aspirations and goals that are transcendent to provincial or regional concerns. They simply demand that western Canada have a greater say in the establishment of such aspirations and goals, that the national interest be truly national rather than serving the economic self-interest of central Canada.

Other differences between western alienation and Quebeçois nationalism are not hard to find. Whereas the latter embodies the demand for some form of political independence, separatism has been at best a fringe element of western alienation. Public support for political independence has been miniscule even in Alberta, the relative hotbed of separatist sentiment in the West. A 1969 provincial survey in Alberta found only 5% of the respondents agreed that "Alberta would be better off if it were a separate country rather than a province of Canada."[44] Two years later 12% of another provincial survey agreed that "Western Canada should have its own separate government, independent of everyone else."[45] In a 1974 Calgary survey only eight of 221 respondents (3.6%) expressed even the most cautious support for separatism.[46] Finally, in early 1977 the *Calgary Herald* commissioned a poll of 300 Calgarians in which 2.7% said *Yes* and 93.7% *No* to the question "Would you like Alberta to separate?"[47]

The weakness of separatist sentiment in the general public is combined with the absence of significant organizational champions of the separatist cause. Nothing with even a glimmer of similarity to the Parti Quebeçois has existed nor has there been a prairie equivalent to the St. Jean Baptiste Society in Quebec. Although from time to time separatist parties have emerged they have attracted little more than a handful of active members. The parties have tended to emerge shortly after one election campaign and to disappear before the next; never has a separatist party made any dent whatsoever in prairie electoral politics. Nor have the major western Canadian protest movements—the Progressives, the United Farmers, the Social Credit, or the CCF—been tinged with separatist ideologies.

Among the separatist organizations that have emerged the most visible have largely restricted their activity to Alberta. There are a number of interrelated reasons for this, the first being the concentration of the oil industry in that province. Embattled oilmen, facing in their eyes overly restrictive government regulation and unreasonable levels of taxation from both levels of government, have formed a small pool of potential members and financial supporters of separatist organizations. Secondly, separatist organizations have been formed as much in reaction to a perceived left-wing drift of Canadian public policy as to regional grievances per se, even though regional grievances may be used to mask more fundamental disagreements with the social order. In this respect separatist organizations have found the political climate of Alberta to be more hospitable than that in the other two Prairie provinces. A third reason is that Alberta, because of its energy wealth, is in the best position of any of the three Prairie provinces to go it alone. Thus some adamant proponents of the free enterprise system have seen in the dream of an independent Alberta their last chance to fashion a society that is free of the socialistic and totalitarian influences that are seen to be at work in the national government.

The influence of all these factors can be illustrated by the Independent Alberta Association, a Calgary-based organization formed in 1974 as "a non-political fact-finding group with objectives of the re-negotiation of the terms of Confederation and the preservation and encouragement of the free-enterprise system."[48] Long-standing regional grievances did not provide the immediate impetus to the creation of the IAA; that came from the energy disputes which broke out in the early 70s among the oil industry, Ottawa and the Alberta government. This impetus was absent in Saskatchewan and Manitoba. The grievances of the IAA reached beyond energy issues to the general state of the Canadian society. As Calgary oilman and IAA president John Rudolph put it in a 1974 speech at High River, Alberta, "the gut issues are the high cost of Confederation, the incredible price we pay to be Albertans, and the rampant spread of socialist philosophy under the guise of every political label possible." The free-enterprise stance of the IAA pulled in the support of groups like the libertarian Association to Defend Property Rights, groups that were becoming increasingly anxious over the expansionist policies of the Lougheed government including the acquisition of Pacific Western Airlines and the creation of the Heritage Trust Fund.

Through the frequent public speaking of its president the IAA achieved considerable visibility in western Canada. It also commissioned a number of highly publicized reports including the *Cost of Confederation* study by University of Calgary economist Warren Blackman, a study estimating that confederation costs the people of Alberta between one and three billion dollars a year. Yet despite this cost the IAA shied away from advocating independence as a firm goal. Rather the threat of separatism was advanced as a bargaining tool to be used to secure better terms for Alberta and the West within confederation. Only if such terms could not be secured would independence be pursued. To members of the IAA this was a strategy that Quebec had been using effectively for years and one that other regions should be ready and willing to employ. In the 1975 Alberta provincial election the IAA kept its head down and stayed clear of electoral politics. However, the 1976 victory of the Parti Quebeçois spurred some members of the association into the electoral field. Following Rudolph's comment that the Parti Quebeçois win "can't do anything but help us—at this point the whole country is up for grabs," about 30 members of the IAA formed the Western National Association in February, 1977. The WNA paralleled the philosophy and objectives of the IAA, and its platform included the unusual constitutional proposal of "Freedom From Government of Evil Proportions". Two years later the WNA failed to field any candidates in the provincial election.

The future significance of the IAA cannot be predicted with any certainty. However, given that its impact on Alberta politics to date has been virtually undetectable, that its membership is small, and that its public image and public presentation rests in one individual who is tiring of the crusade, the prognosis is not good. As the IAA seemed to be slipping from public view in the late 70s, forecasts of its early demise would not be unreasonable. If this does happen then the best organized and best led of all the western Canadian independence movements will have vanished without having had any discernible impact on the unfolding of political events in western Canada.

In drawing this particular discussion to a close it is worth noting that separatist movements in Canada have by no means been restricted to Alberta and Quebec. In British Columbia the Western Canada Party and the Committee of Western Independence claimed a combined paid-up membership of 7,500 in 1977,[49] and separatist governments were elected in Nova Scotia in 1867 and 1886. Perhaps only Ontario has been wholly exempt from separatist organizations although even this would not be correct if we included sporadic demands for the political independence of the north and north-western parts of the province. Thus the existence of separatist movements in the Canadian west should not be given undue attention in evaluations of western alienation. Separatism has been at best a fringe element of western alienation, and an element that is not particularly unique to the Prairie provinces. The major thrust of western alienation is for greater, more equal participation in the Canadian polity, economy, and society.

As western Canadians have continually sought a better deal within Canada rather than without, the political beliefs embodied in western alienation are essentially federalist. The need for and advantages of a division of powers between a central and provincial governments are readily accepted.[50] The sources of conflict and tension are those endemic to federal states; the intrusion of the central power into the affairs of the provinces and the lack of adequate regional representation within the national government. In the future as in the past western Canadians will continue to seek some resolution on both these counts; the political drive will be for greater autonomy with respect to provincial areas of jurisdiction and greater power for western Canadians within the national government. The quest, however, will never be totally successful as long as a federal system and its inherent jurisdictional conflicts are maintained. Moreover the relatively small population of western Canada will mean inevitable weakness within the national government, and partisan advantage will still be gained by provincial politicians fanning the coals of western alienation. For these reasons and others to be discussed below it is unlikely that western alienation will depart the Canadian political stage in the foreseeable future.

Richard Simeon has pointed out that to be politically important regionalism must include ". . . some degree of self-consciousness, some widespread sense of the provincial community as the most relevant political unit or category, some sense that when people say *we* they are referring not to people of the same religion, or class, or educational groups, or occupation, nor to *we* in the sense of an undifferentiated whole national community, but rather to *we* the residents of this province."[51] While Simeon's limitation of regionalism to provincial boundaries may be unduly restrictive, his general argument is very important. In the case of regionalism on the Canadian prairies it is western alienation that serves as the subjective component or Simeon's "we-group" bond. In part this bond takes the form of a widely shared regional framework through which the Canadian political process is viewed. Western alienation constitutes a regionally-distinct political culture through and within which are expressed economic discontent, the rejection of a semi-colonial status within the Canadian state, antipathy towards Quebec and French Canadian influence within the national government, the irritation of the West's partisan weakness within a succession of Liberal national governments, and the demand from provincial political elites for greater jurisdiction autonomy.

There is also a second important aspect to the we-group bond of western alienation. Most western Canadians today do not experience a lifestyle that is substantially different from that experienced by English Canadians elsewhere in the country. Yet, like a pair of attitudinal cowboy boots, western alienation can be slipped on to distinguish oneself from other Canadians. In this sense western alienation might be considered an urban nostalgia for a rural past; it reflects the efforts of contemporary western Canadians to carve out and sustain a distinctive regional identity even though a regionally-distinctive lifestyle is clearly on the wane. In a country where the national identity of Canadians may be weak and where regional attachments have always been strong, and in a period of deep national malaise, the importance of this aspect of western alienation should not be underestimated.

Finally it should be noted that western alienation has been sustained by provincial governments which have been increasing in strength as the socio-economic foundations of prairie regionalism have been weakening. These provincial governments have been operating within relatively insular political systems. If we accept John Wilson's argument that the provinces are important crucibles and vehicles for political culture,[52] and if we acknowledge at the same time that the socio-economic foundations of political regionalism on the Prairies are crumbling, there is considerable tension concerning the *provincial* sustenance of *western* alienation. Given the near-absence of pan-provincial political organizations in the West, the relative insularity of provincial politics, and the frequently competing economic interests of the Prairie provinces, can western alienation continue to be sustained and fostered as a regional political culture, or must it too fragment into provincial political cultures lacking any regional cohesion and integration? Will the thrust of political evolution on the Prairies inevitably be away from regional forms and towards greater provincialism?

NOTES

1. For a discussion of western alienation as a form of political culture see David Elton and Gibbins, "Western Alienation and Political Culture," in Richard Schultz, Orest M. Kruhlak, and John C. Terry, Eds., *The Canadian Political Process,* Third Edition, Toronto, Holt, Rinehart and Winston, 1979, pp. 82-97.

2. The phrase comes from Richard Allen, ed., *A Region of the Mind,* Canadian Plains Study Centre, University of Saskatchewan, Regina, 1973.

3. For an elaboration of this point see Gibbins, "Western Alienation and the Alberta Political Culture," in Carlo Caldarola, ed., *Society and Politics in Alberta: Research Papers,* Toronto, Methuen, 1979, pp. 143-45.

4. D. C. Schwartz, *Political Alienation and Political Behavior,* Chicago, Aldine, 1973, pp. 7-8.

5. A. W. Finifter, "Dimensions of Political Alienation," *American Political Science Review* (June 1970), pp. 406-09; Robert S. Gilmour and Robert B. Lamb, *Political Alienation in Contemporary America,* New York, St. Martin's Press, 1975, Chapter 5; Schwartz, *Political Alienation.*

6. For some contrary evidence see R. R. Gilsdorf, "Western Alienation, Political Alienation, and the Federal System," in Caldarola, *Society and Politics,* pp. 168-189.

7. *Saturday Night,* September 1976, p. 18.

8. W. L. Morton, *The Progressive Party of Canada,* Toronto, University of Toronto Press, 1950, p. viii.

9. Finifter, "Dimensions of Political Alienation," p. 390.

10. Robert E. Lane, *Political Ideology,* New York, The Free Press, 1962, p. 162.

11. Gibbins, "Models of Nationalism: A Case Study of Political Ideologies in the Canadian West," *Canadian Journal of Political Science* (June 1977), pp. 341-373; Gibbins, "Western Alienation and the Alberta Political Culture"; Gilsdorf, "Western Alienation, Political Alienation, and the Federal System"; Thelma Oliver, "Aspects of Alienation in Alberta," paper presented at the 1975 Canadian Political Science Association Annual Meeting, Edmonton, Alberta.

12. A factor analysis of the eight items yielded only a single factor with an eigen value greater than one. The mean of the twenty-eight Pearsonian item—intercorrelations was .27, and the corrected split-half reliability coefficient was $r = .78$.

13. Harry E. Strom, "The Feasibility of One Prairie Province," in David K. Elton, ed., *One Prairie Province?*, Lethbridge Herald, 1970, p. 32.

14. Allan Blakeney, "Resources, the Constitution, and Canadian Federalism," in J. Peter Meekison, ed., *Canadian Federalism: Myth or Reality*, Third Edition, Toronto, Methuen, 1977, p. 181.

15. *The Albertan*, August 24, 1977, p. 5.

16. David E. Smith, *Prairie Liberalism: The Liberal Party in Saskatchewan, 1905-1971*, Toronto, University of Toronto Press, 1975, p. 314.

17. Kenneth H. Norrie, "Some Comments on Prairie Economic Alienation," in Meekison, *Canadian Federalism*, p. 325.

18. *Calgary Herald*, September 9, 1977, p. 1.

19. Denis Smith, "Liberals and Conservatives on the Prairies, 1917-1968," in David P. Gagan, ed., *Prairie Perspectives*, Toronto, Holt, Rinehart and Winston, 1970, p. 42.

20. Speech in the House of Commons, June 4, 1973. Cited in John G. Diefenbaker, *I Never Say Anything Provocative*, selected and edited by Margaret Wente, Toronto, Peter Martin Assoc., 1975, p. 113.

21. John Herd Thompson, *The Harvests of War: The Prairie West, 1914-1918*, Toronto, McClelland & Stewart, 1978, p. 137.

22. *Ibid.*, p. 137.

23. Stanley C. Roberts, "Canadian Federalism and the Constitution: What is at Stake in the West," Alan B. Plaunt Memorial Lecture, Carleton University, April 6 and 7, 1979, p. 2.

24. David E. Smith, "Western Politics and National Unity," in David Jay Bercuson, ed., *Canada and the Burden of Unity*, Toronto, Macmillan, 1977, p. 243.

25. *North Hill News*, September 3, 1975, p. 1.

26. *The Albertan*, October 6, 1976, p. 7.

27. For details see Gibbins, "Models of Nationalism."

28. Smith, *Prairie Liberalism*, p. 54.

29. James A. Jackson, *The Centennial History of Manitoba*, Toronto, McClelland & Stewart, 1970, p. 172.

30. Smith, *Prairie Liberalism*, p. 318.

31. *Ibid.*, p. 262.

32. Doris French Shackleton, *Tommy Douglas*, Toronto, McClelland & Stewart, 1975, p. 161.

33. Smith, *Prairie Liberalism*, p. 271.

34. Nicholas Hills, Southam News Service, *Calgary Herald*, September 17, 1976, p. 1.

35. Richard Simeon, "Regionalism and Canadian Political Institutions," in Meekison, *Canadian Federalism*, p. 301.

36. *Ibid.*, p. 302.

37. *Calgary Herald,* December 5, 1977, p. A1. For a discussion of further similarities see John J. Barr, "Beyond Bitterness," in John Barr and Owen Anderson, *The Unfinished Revolt,* Toronto, McClelland and Stewart, 1971, pp. 11-34.

38. *Calgary Herald,* April 12, 1977, p. 7.

39. W. L. Morton, "The Bias of Prairie Politics," *Transactions of the Royal Society of Canada,* Series III, Volume XLIX, June 1955, Section II, p. 66.

40. Smith, "Liberals and Conservatives," p. 42.

41. *Ibid.,* p. 39.

42. "The National," C.B.C. Television, June 12, 1978.

43. Blakeney, "Resources, The Constitution, and Canadian Federalism," p. 179.

44. Elton, *One Prairie Province?,* p. 144.

45. Oliver, "Aspects of Alienation," p. 22.

46. Gibbins, "Models of Nationalism," p. 358.

47. *Calgary Herald,* February 26, 1977, p. A1.

48. Independent Alberta Association News Release, November 13, 1974.

49. *Calgary Herald,* March 14, 1977, p. A8.

50. David Elton, "Public Opinion and Federal-Provincial Relations: A Case Study in Alberta," in Meekison, *Canadian Federalism,* pp. 49-63.

51. Simeon, "Regionalism and Canadian Political Institutions," p. 296.

52. John Wilson, "The Canadian Political Cultures: Towards a Redefinition of the Nature of the Canadian Political System," *CJPS,* September 1974, VII, no. 3, p. 440.

CHAPTER SIX

REGIONALISM RECONSIDERED

"Canada is many regionalisms."

—P. E. Trudeau[1]

"The tension between inherited traditions of the past and the constantly changing economic and social forces in the present is the central dynamic of western Canadian history—indeed of all history."

—A. W. Rasporich[2]

THE NEW PRAIRIE WEST

A new prairie society has emerged during the post-war period that more resembles the urban heartland of central Canada than it does its own rural, agrarian past. The western frontier is no more, apart from its yearly resurrection in events like the Calgary Stampede and Edmonton's Klondike Days. With its disappearance has passed the earlier youthfulness of the prairie society that had charged the West with the electricity of new ideas and which had been a critical ingredient in the eruption of radical politics. As Morton notes ". . . the West in its years of major settlement was subjected to influences such as Fabian Socialism, the Non-Partisan League, and Social Credit which the older communities of Canada had escaped, or were better equipped to resist."[3] But as Morton goes on to argue, these factors and that of simple distance from central Canada were modifiers, not determinants, of western history: "despite the lateness of settlement and the barrier of distance, the institutions and people of the West were, or became, Canadian."[4]

The distinctive values of the prairie society that grew out of agrarian conditions and the mix of ideological ideas that settlers brought with them found the soil of the new emergent prairie society increasingly less hospitable. Willmott, discussing mutual aid and co-operation on the early Prairies, concludes that ". . . it is plausible to believe that a significant ideological change away from communal values has been taking place, because many of the ecological and social conditions which underlay those values have disappeared.''[5] Willmott bases his conclusions on an examination of the contemporary rural prairie society; how much greater would be the change if the agrarian values of the past were compared to those prevalent today in the metropolitan centres of western Canada.

The changes that have transformed the face of the Canadian Prairies have eroded the earlier regional distinctiveness. Mildred Schwartz provides a theoretical handle on this erosion by treating regionalism as the emergent property of "special combinations of populations and resources . . . interacting in a given place."[6] In the past the combination of an ethnically-distinct immigrant population and a frontier agrarian economy, set in a unifying geographical locale remote from central Canada, yielded patterns of social and political behavior that were peculiar to and distinctive of the region. Today the 'special combinations' of the past are fading as the prairie society and economy become increasingly integrated into the social and economic patterns of the surrounding nation and continent, and as technological advancement diminishes the importance of geographical separation from the Canadian heartland.

In a study of political regionalism in western nations Rose and Urwin advance an argument similar to that of Schwartz:

> It could be argued that what appears on a map as a spatial difference is not caused by ecological effects but rather by social characteristics that are nationwide in their significance. In other words, apparently spatial differences may only be a reflection of different proportions of industrial workers or speakers of a minority language within a region.[7]

To apply this to the case of the Canadian Prairies, regional differentiation was brought about not by the forces of geography but by the fact that prairie residents were different from other Canadians, that they were engaged in different economic pursuits and as a consequence developed different and regionally distinct interests, concerns and political grievances. But, to put the argument into an evolutionary perspective, as differences in population, economic pursuits and social patterns diminished over time, as they clearly did, regional differentiation diminished also. What we are left with today is a spatial differentiation that is only weakly reinforced by the more immediate determinants of political behavior—the work people do, the languages they speak, the social patterns they pursue. David Bell has suggested that the conflict potential of regionalism depends upon how many cleavages in the social fabric reinforce the underlying territorial cleavage; with respect to the Prairies the number and potency of reinforcing cleavages have diminished over time.[8]

This line of argument suggests incidentally that regionally distinctive traits should be most evident among residents of the "old West"—farmers, individuals with strong ethnic ties, rural and small-town residents, individuals in general with deep roots in western Canada. Conversely regional traits should be less evident among the urban population, among those with a weakened ethnic self-identification, and among those who have recently moved into western Canada. Unfortunately, while impressionistic evidence would tend to confirm this suggestion it is difficult to find the empirical data that would permit a clear test. A further complication is provided by the fact that political elites within the West, while in many ways epitomizing the new urban, technocratic prairie society, find it useful to publicly reflect the values and styles of the older prairie society. The memory comes to mind here of a Calgary MP—a petroleum engineer and professor by training—riding a horse through a Conservative rally completely decked out in western regalia. Political elites walk a narrow line in trying to attract the new urban electorate through the incantation of the prairie past.

The general contention that western Canada is being increasingly integrated into the national society requires no further demonstration at this time. The homogenization of English Canadian patterns of economic, consumptive, cultural, and recreational behavior continues. It is part of a more global or at least continental trend in which regionally distinct elements are being submerged by the emergence of broader social and economic patterns many of which emanate from the United States. Nor need it be reiterated here that political behavior on the Prairies is shedding its regional cast. The more populist and radical features that in the past set the Prairies apart are in retreat.

Nevertheless, the area in which national integration has been the least evident in western Canada has been in the political system. Although considerable evidence has been introduced indicating that a distinctive regional style of prairie federal politics is on the wane, it has not yet disappeared and may temporarily have found a new host in the national Conservative party. Nor have the dissolving bonds of regionalism diminished the power of prairie provincial governments. The provincial political systems have been far more isolated from nationalizing effects than have been the region's economy, culture or lifestyle; increased nationalization elsewhere has not been accompanied by increased centralization of the Canadian federal system. The contemporary trend has been in quite the opposite direction. The federal system in Canada has given the provincial political systems a bulwark against the forces of integration, a bulwark that other aspects of the regional social order have lacked, and thus the provincial political systems have been far more successful in evading national regimentation.[9] However, the forces that have strengthened provincial governments in this context have also made *regional* political organization less likely.

POLITICAL ORGANIZATION AND
REGIONAL POLITICS

In his 1977 presidential address to the Canadian Political Science Association Alan Cairns challenged the notion that governments are simply the products of their social and economic environment: "the sociological perspective pays inadequate attention to the possibility that the support for powerful, independent provincial governments is a product of the political system itself, that it is fostered and created by provincial government elites employing the policy-making apparatus of their jurisdictions, and that such support need not take the form of a distinct culture, society, or nation as these are conventionally understood."[10] It is important, Cairns argued, that Canadian political scientists recognize the extent to which governments shape their environment:

> . . . it is no longer meaningful or appropriate to think of . . . economies and societies at the provincial and national levels as logically prior to governments. To an indeterminant, but undoubtedly significant extent they are the consequences of past government activity, and will increasingly be so in the future.[11]

The comments by Cairns are particularly germane to the analysis of this book which rests on the joint assumptions that political regionalism in the Canadian West springs from a regionally-distinct socio-economic environment, and that the progressive national integration of that environment is in turn destroying the underpinnings of political regionalism. Cairns suggests, on the other hand, that caution must be expressed in setting up political behavior as a dependent variable although the danger is less severe when, as in this case, the behavior under consideration is that of electorates rather than that of political elites. More importantly, the effort by Cairns to focus our attention on the environmental impact of governments provides a key element in the thesis that regional politics—that is patterns of political behavior that are shared across the three Prairie provinces and which distinguish the three from provinces elsewhere in Canada—are indeed on the wane in western Canada.

There is no doubt that governments in Canada exert a very considerable influence upon their environment. The survival of a vestigial independence north of the 49th parallel is a testament of sorts to the national government in its struggle with the environmental forces of continentalism. The ability of governments to influence their environment is dependent upon their size, budget and spirit of social activism, and in all these respects provincial governments in Canada have been expanding more rapidly than has the national government.[12] As Black and Cairns have pointed out, since 1867 Canadians have been involved not only in nation-building but in province-building. One of the reasons for the post-war decentralization of the Canadian federal system, they suggest, is "a relatively great increase in the competence and confidence of provincial administrations and a consequent growth in elites who identified their prospects with the fortunes and favours of the provincial governments."[13] The growth of provincial governments has enabled them to increasingly shape their provincial societies as the national government has tried to shape the national society. Across Canada provincial governments are becoming increasingly involved in the support of the arts and culture, in the mass media, and in industrial and resource development.

Given, then, the importance of government in Canadian life it is of great significance that there is no *regional* government in western Canada. Unlike Ontario, Quebec, or British Columbia the Prairies do not constitute a political unit. While the provincial governments are territorially-based there is no pan-provincial political organization to sustain, nurture or encourage a prairie regional culture, society or politics. There are only provincial governments which, although they operate within the prairie region, do so almost exclusively within their own limited territorial domains. In Canadian politics provinces and the national government, not regions, are the leading actors. Regions lack the infrastructure—the constitutional, institutional, and bureaucratic muscles—to act. If governments actively shape the fabric of society the absence of a prairie regional government has very serious implications as the provincial governments provide an inadequate vehicle for western Canadian regionalism.

The closest western Canada came to a regional government was the Territorial Council that controlled the local administration of the Northwest Territories prior to the formation of Saskatchewan and Alberta. In 1905 two provinces were carved out of the old Territories as Wilfred Laurier rejected the proposal for a single province largely on the grounds that such a province would threaten the political dominance of Quebec and Ontario.[14] The abolition of the very limited regional infrastructure provided by the Territorial Council and the creation of two provincial administrations (three if we include Manitoba) in its place encouraged the political fragmentation of the prairie region. As Black and Cairns note, "mechanisms set in motion by the creation of political institutions permit provinces such as Saskatchewan and Alberta which possessed little sociological legitimacy at their birth to acquire it with the passage of time and creation of a unique provincial history."[15] In the early part of the 20th century the prairie farm organizations provided some form of quasi-political regional infrastructure as they drew freely from a regional leadership pool, addressed concerns that were largely regional rather than provincial, and relied upon regional organs of communication such as the *Grain Growers' Guide*. Yet there was no corresponding move towards regional organization among the provincial governments. The Canadian federal system provided no precedent for a regional tier of government intermediate between that of the nation and those of the provinces, and the self-interest of provincial politicians and bureaucrats provided no incentives for the creation of regional structures. For those individuals who wanted to play upon a larger stage the national government provided the opportunity. For others the first priority was the protection and strengthening of the provincial bastion.

As the provincial governments grew in size and strength the fragmentation of the region along provincial lines continued. In the absence of an institutional arena for regional politics, one that could stand between the competing pressures of national integration and provincial fragmentation, provincial governments jockeyed for the position of regional spokesman. However they spoke with authority only for their provincial electorates, and as provincial interests began to diverge with the economic diversification of the West, increasingly competitive provincial governments exerted greater strain on the regional fabric. Admittedly to some observers the strain was not serious. Winnipeg's James Richardson, a former cabinet minister in the Trudeau government, has downplayed the significance of provincial fragmentation: "to the extent that the West is divided, it is divided more by artificial political boundaries, drawn by remote hands, in remote times, and by provincial administrations of differing political affiliation, than it is by any inherent regional difference."[16] Yet on this point I feel that Richardson is mistaken. If one accepts the importance of the 'governmental societies' discussed by Cairns then the division of the West into three provinces is of great importance. To suggest to the governments of Manitoba, Saskatchewan and Alberta that mere lines on a map separate their domains is to ignore entrenched and frequently competing provincial self-interests. The federal system, by creating self-interested provincial governments with no electoral entanglements beyond their own boundaries, has reinforced provincial particularities and peculiarities at the expense of broader regional traits and concerns. At the political level, then, western Canada is not one region but three, demarcated by provincial boundaries. There is no regional political unit towards which loyalty and affection can be directed and to which symbolic importance can be attached.

Given the absence of regional political organizations the provincial governments in the West have come to the fore as regional spokesmen. Thus as Engelmann and Schwartz explain, pressure may be ". . . exerted by the province—a legal, political, entity—on behalf of the region—a socio-economic entity."[17] As examples they mention the efforts of prairie provincial governments in the 1920s to assist the farm population at large. Governments may also cloak provincial self-interest in the garb of regionalism if only to mask the rawer edge of provincial ambition. In this sense just as the self-interest of Ontario tends to be equated with the national interest by Ontario politicians, so too have prairie politicians equated provincial and regional self-interests. In a speech given at Lac La

Biche, Alberta, Peter Lougheed asserted that a stronger Alberta will produce a stronger West and that a stronger West will mean a stronger Canada.[18] While this may indeed be the case its demonstration remains, and politicians in Saskatchewan and Manitoba may be excused for questioning the equation of Alberta's economic leverage with that of the region as a whole.

The role of provincial governments as regional spokesmen has been enhanced by the weakness of western Canadian representation in both the House of Commons and consecutive national governments. The combination of a small percentage of House of Commons' seats, the propensity of western Canadians to support either third parties or the major opposition party, and the existence of tight party discipline which prohibited regional bloc voting akin to that displayed by the "corn belt" or "cotton bloc" in the American Congress,[19] led to chronically-weakened national representation. Thus there was a natural tendency to turn to provincial governments for the assertion of regional demands. The position of Alberta at the end of the 60s, described by then Premier Harry Strom, has not been that atypical:

In the House of Commons, the majority of Alberta's MP's are backbenchers with little chance of making a meaningful contribution. Many are Opposition backbenchers—members of a party which recently repudiated western leadership, the influence of its western caucus, and which chose as a leader an individual who (well intentioned as he may be) knows little about western concerns and aspirations. What all this means is that the representation of the people of Alberta in Confederation and national affairs has increasingly become the responsibility of our provincial government.[20]

The replacement of Robert Stanfield, Diefenbaker's successor, by Joe Clark is unlikely to make the present Alberta premier any more likely than Strom to entrust the representation of Alberta's interests to the national Conservative party. Although Joe Clark is an Albertan Lougheed is unlikely to willingly relinquish his role as Alberta's spokesman in national affairs. The electoral advantages to be garnered from such a role are too great.

As provincial governments have moved to the fore as regional spokesmen the importance of the federal cabinet as an accommodative structure for regional interests has declined. In the past Westerners like Clifford Sifton, Jimmy Gardiner and T. A. Crerar acted as regional standard bearers in the federal cabinet. Today regional accommodation tends to take place outside the cabinet. The principal forum has become the First Ministers Conferences in which the regional spokesmen are provincial premiers rather than federal cabinet ministers, and where "federal-provincial disagreements are differences between governments as much if not more than between the regions the governments represent."[21] Furthermore, truly regional cabinet figures as opposed to provincial representatives are more difficult to find than in the past. When regional concerns could be more readily identified a cabinet minister could speak for the region by addressing those concerns; to speak for wheat was to speak for the West. Now, broad regional concerns and regional spokesmen are both harder to find. Cabinet posts which in the past were regional fixtures, such as the Minister of Agriculture, have become more functional and less regional in character. The appointment of Ontario's Eugene Whelan as Minister of Agriculture in the Trudeau government bears witness to this transformation as it does to changes that have been occurring within Canadian agriculture. The Minister of Agriculture must now speak for a more diversified range of agricultural concerns and for a more functionally and less regionally organized collection of agricultural interest groups.

As mentioned before, the contemporary prominence of provincial governments as regional spokesmen has also been accompanied by a weakening of organizational ties between national and provincial party organizations, although here we must be careful about any causal assumptions. There has also been a related letup, both inside and outside western Canada, in the reciprocal flow of politicians and party leaders between the two levels of the party system.[22] The weakening of party ties has helped free the hands of provincial governments in their bargaining with the national government, although provincial hands have never been terribly constrained by partisan allegiances in the past. Smith points out that a close relationship between provincial and national parties made sense in the past; ". . . an alliance with a national political party that formed the federal government offered even greater opportunity to influence policy; for during these years the principal issues of Canadian politics still were fought and settled within the majority party rather than through federal-provincial diplomacy."[23] Thus national parties, particularly when forming the federal government, provided an arena for regional politics. Now that arena has shifted to federal-provincial conferences where governments, not parties are the major actors. Hence the utility of a close rapport between national and provincial party organizations has diminished. We might also note here that the weakening of party ties reduces the potential significance of what appears to be an emergent federal-provincial Conservative hegemony in western Canada, an hegemony that may mean more in name than in practical political coordination and co-operation.

The fact that the provincial governments are the principal regional spokesmen does not necessarily mean that they are well-suited for the role. They are elected by provincial electorates and their concern with the region is limited by the extent to which regional and provincial interests coincide. At a time when problems centring upon the wheat economy were predominant the coincidence of provincial and regional interests was considerable. However with the economic diversification of the West the potential for conflicting provincial interests has been enhanced. Disagreement over the pricing of oil and natural gas on the Canadian market has acted as a solvent on the regional bond as has interprovincial competition over the location of regional head offices and industrial developments. Nevertheless, common regional problems do exist such as the perennial ones of rail transportation and adequate port facilities, and these problems provide a stage upon which the provincial governments can act in concert. Regional problems, together with the opportunities they provide for politicians to act upon a larger stage, to play for a larger audience, and to elevate provincial self-interest to the loftier heights of a regional grievance, have prompted more frequent and more formalized interaction among the governments of western Canada, including that of British Columbia.

In 1965 the Prairie Economic Council was formed consisting of the three prairie premiers. Established to address regional problems common to the three Prairie provinces its attention was primarily focussed on specific technical questions and intra-regional policy coordination; "no attempt was made to develop common policy positions nor to convey a 'western Canadian' viewpoint to the federal government."[24] The public profile of the Council was low and its impact on prairie governments limited. Then in 1973, following the loss of 20 western Canadian seats by the Liberals in the 1972 election, the federal government initiated plans for a Western Economic Opportunities Conference (WEOC) to be held in Calgary that summer. The federal government's intention was to provide a forum for the airing of western economic grievances and the bulk of the airing was to be done by the western premiers. In preparing for WEOC the prairie premiers met in March and expanded the Prairie Economic Council to include British Columbia when the new B.C. premier, Dave Barrett, proved more willing than his predecessor, W. A. C. Bennett, to meet with the prairie premiers.[25] The Council was renamed the Western Economic Council and the publication of background papers for WEOC ". . . marked the first occasion on which the federal government entered into discussions with a regional grouping of provinces that were united behind a common position on a broad range of issues."[26] Unfortunately WEOC was at best a limited success for the western provinces.[27] Following WEOC the Western Economic Council became the annual Western Premiers' Conference. The setting of the conference rotates among the four western provinces; in 1978 it was held at Yorkton, Saskatchewan and in 1979 at Prince George, B.C. The meetings are held in camera and provide an opportunity for a wide range of informal discussions covering constitutional developments, foreign trade, transportation, agriculture and national economic planning.

Saskatchewan Premier Allan Blakeney has written at some length about the Premiers' Conferences and the inter-provincial co-operation that they have induced. While admitting the diversity of western Canada,

Blakeney maintains that ". . . despite these differences, most of us regard the four western provinces as a distinct region, with shared perceptions, with mutual concerns, and, in many respects, with common objectives."[28] Blakeney states that the core of the western regional identity comes from the facts that all four provinces have economies built upon the exploitation of natural resources, that all depend heavily for their well-being on transportation, and particularly on rail transportation, and that "stemming from the first two—and perhaps most important of all—people in the four western provinces tend to have a common perception of Canada and what Confederation is all about."[29] Just what that common perception is and how it differs from the perceptions held by eastern Canadians is not clear. Blakeney notes that partisan differences among the provincial premiers have not been a source of disruption, as indeed they do not appear to be at federal-provincial conferences involving all eleven Canadian governments. The differences that did exist, Blakeney explains, ". . . tended to be geographically based, particularly between 'the Prairies', on the one hand, and British Columbia on the other."[30]

In his analysis of regional politics in the United States, Ira Sharkansky stressed the importance of regional organizations such as the Western Premiers' Conference. He points out that "the tendency of political leaders and government officials to acquire their cues from regional neighbors has several causes: the belief that neighbors have problems similar to one's own; the attitude among officials and interested citizens that it is 'legitimate' to adapt one's programs to those of nearby governments; and *the structure of officials' organizational affiliations, which put them into frequent contact with counterparts in neighboring governments.*"[31] In light of Sharkansky's comments on the American scene it is interesting to return to Blakeney's discussion of developments in western Canada:

> . . . as a result of our close collaboration in preparing for the [WEOC] Conference, personal rapport developed among the Premiers, Ministers and officials of the four western governments. Many of these personal relationships endure today, and a habit of close consultation and co-operation among the four western provinces has developed.[32]

It is important to note that co-operation and contact extends well beyond the premiers. There are now a large number of intergovernmental committees and task forces at the ministerial level or below. While the co-ordination in public policy that may result from this interaction has yet to be fully documented there have been some visible achievements including a jointly financed veterinary college and farm machinery testing institute.

Another regional development that has occurred is the creation of the Canada West Foundation. The Foundation, although lacking the direct political significance of the Premiers' Conferences, is an interesting attempt to provide an organizational setting within which the divergent interests of the West can be knit together. It was established in 1973 in response to the feeling that at WEOC the western Canadian representatives had been outgunned by the research capacity, computer models and general expertise of the federal officials. The Foundation was set up to pursue two objectives: 1) to initiate and conduct research programs regarding the economic and social characteristics and potentialities of Western Canada; and 2) to initiate and conduct informational and educational programs to encourage an appreciation of the Canadian heritage and to stimulate an awareness of the future throughout Western Canada.[33] The Foundation is committed to strengthening both Canada and the role of the West within Canada. It includes under its purview the three Prairie provinces, British Columbia, the Yukon and the Northwest Territories. It is supported by the governments of the above and by foundations, corporate donations and individual memberships. The affairs of the Foundation are managed by a 40 member council drawn from notables across the West including a liberal sprinkling of individuals with extensive political experience. The offices of the Foundation are located in Calgary.

At the present time the Canada West Foundation functions primarily as a research house. Several large projects have been launched including ones on water resources and the coal industry in western Canada. These studies, incidentally, have brought the Foundation up against the geological and meteorological diversity of western Canada. The water study will exclude British Columbia where more often than one would like ample water is available simply by stepping out into the rain. The coal study, on the other hand, will exclude Manitoba where coal reserves do not exist and where an abundance of hydro-electric power makes the prospect of significant coal consumption unlikely. Constitutional reform, however, is an interest likely to be shared throughout the West and it is here that the Foundation has pursued a much higher public profile. In March 1978 the Foundation sponsored a three-day Banff conference on constitutional review to which 300 delegates, half from western Canada, were invited.

Two aspects of the "Alternatives Canada" conference are of particular interest here. The first is that a majority of the delegates agreed that ". . . the appropriate size of a region for the purpose of negotiating regional concerns was a province—be it large or small."[34] There was no movement towards the endorsement of larger regional units such as one encompassing the Prairie provinces. The second is the reception given to the conference by the western premiers. Premiers Bennett of British Columbia and Lyons of Manitoba failed to make an appearance at the three-day event (the government of Manitoba was the only western provincial government that did not contribute financially). Saskatchewan's Allan Blakeney, on the other hand, was an active participant throughout. Peter

Lougheed of Alberta also attended and gave two major speeches including the opening address to the conference. In that address Lougheed unexpectedly and strongly defended the present federal system and indirectly poured cold water on the proposals for constitutional change.[35] He maintained that the present system of settling disputes between the federal and provincial governments has been working very well. Citing the annual First Ministers' meetings and the over 100 meetings held a year between federal officials and Alberta's Department of Intergovernmental Affairs, Lougheed appeared to go out of his way to challenge the need for constitutional reform. Lougheed urged strong caution against changes that might weaken provincial governments. In short, any proposal that would increase regional representation in Ottawa but which might in the process weaken provincial governments would not be supported by Alberta.

The Canada West Foundation has carved out a small but significant niche for itself in western Canada. The fate of an earlier regional initiative, however, was much less successful. In May 1970 the University of Lethbridge hosted a conference to examine the possibility of creating a single prairie province.[36] Behind the initiative lay the assumptions that the Prairie provinces formed a natural, economic, and social unit, that a single government would be more efficient and less expensive to the taxpayer, and that the formation of a single prairie province would increase the political muscle of the Prairies in dealings with the national government. While the proposal for a single prairie province received some although far from overwhelming endorsement at the Lethbridge conference, outside the conference it failed to generate any significant political or public support. This was not surprising as the obstacles faced by any initiative for prairie unification are immense. Unification proposals fail to recognize the political and institutional inertia of the existing political system. There are no incentives for provincial politicians or bureaucrats in the dismemberment of the existing provincial governments and their replacement by new regional institutions.

Given the opposition of the entrenched political structures unification could only come on the heels of vigorous and unrelenting public pressure. Yet public pressure for such a change is virtually non-existent and its creation would presuppose regional identifications within the western Canadian public that are stronger than provincial affiliations, a presupposition that cannot be seriously entertained. In September 1970 the Canadian Institute of Public Opinion explored the level of public support for prairie union. Nationally only 28% of the respondents questioned approved of prairie unity compared to 52% who disapproved and 20% who were undecided. Significantly the rate of disapproval was even higher among respondents from the four western provinces; 63% disapproved, 26% approved and 11% were undecided. In commenting on the higher rate of disapproval in the west Mildred Schwartz concluded that "the sense of separateness associated with provinces, even where there is also a broader regional identity, seems sufficient to block the likelihood of political union in the near future."[37] This is a conclusion that I would readily support.

Regional unification would require the knitting together of three very different provincial political systems. While provincial premiers of different partisan affiliations may be able to work together within the context of the annual Western Premiers' Conference, creating a single regional electorate from the very divergent prairie political systems would be altogether a different kettle of fish. Regional amalgamation with the Conservative electorates of Alberta and Manitoba would offer little appeal to the NDP government in Saskatchewan. More importantly, no provincial government would countenance a transfer of legislative and administrative control from provincial to regional institutions. No Alberta government regardless of the partisan complexion of Saskatchewan and Manitoba would place the province's energy resources under regional control. Where, as in the case of oil and natural gas, resources tend to be concentrated within one of the existing provincial units, the acceptance of regional control would be politically suicidal. One has only to imagine the public response within Alberta to any proposal to change the name and scope of the Alberta Heritage Trust Fund to the Western Canadian Heritage Trust Fund, the new venture to be controlled by a regional body within which Albertans would enjoy only proportional representation.

In summary, the amalgamation of the three Prairie provinces into a single regional unit would be disruptive in the extreme and would offer meagre off-setting returns. The proposal stood in 1970, and stands now, about as much chance as the proverbial snowball in hell. In 1905 the majority of residents in the Northwest Territories would have supported the creation of a single prairie province (excluding Manitoba) although even then "the division of the Territories into two provinces caused practically no comment in the North-West, apart from some dissatisfaction expressed by certain communities over the location of the dividing line."[38] Now after over 70 years of provincial autonomy the Prairie provinces cannot be put together into a regional Humpty Dumpty. Provincial governments and provincial identities overwhelm the region as an organizing vehicle for western Canadian politics.

One last form of regional political organization to be mentioned is that imposed by federal government programs, agencies, patterns of administration, and five-region formating of statistical reporting. In certain pieces of legislation such as the Prairie Farm Rehabilitation Act, and through the regional administration of other programs, the national government treats the Prairie provinces as a regional unit. However, the regional as opposed to provincial decentralization of federal administration poses some awkward problems for the national government. Not only must very tough political decisions be made as to what province will be singled out for the location of the regional administrative unit and which ones will be turned aside, but smooth working relationships with provincial bureaucracies are impeded by anything other than provincially-based decentralization. Thus the extent to which regional unity will be fostered on the Prairies through the imposition of regionally administered national programs is probably minimal.

To summarize the existing state of political regionalism in the Prairie provinces, it is safe to conclude that the major trend of political development has increased the strength and autonomy of provincial governments. Any counter-trend towards regional political integration has been weak and relatively insignificant in comparison. The region, lacking an institutional skeleton, bureaucratic muscles or a public will, remains an ephemeral political entity floating at the periphery of the political arena. The more general collapse of regionalism in western Canada has been accompanied by, and perhaps encouraged by, the steady onset of provincialism. In this sense the political system is approaching a classic model of federalism in which the constitutionally-defined political units—the national and provincial governments—are unentangled by formal or informal patterns of regional political organization.

The near-absence of regional political bodies in western Canada is reflected in the prairie society outside the political arena. The West has not developed and is unlikely to develop a regional infrastructure of associations, labour organizations, professional societies, newspapers, magazines, and cultural groups in any way akin to that which exists in Quebec and which serves to protect the French Canadian culture, language and society against the forces of national and continental assimilation. In western Canada there are both national and provincial economic and cultural organizations but virtually no regional ones. There are few regionally-structured dance troupes, theatrical companies, professional associations, trade unions, financial institutions, or interest groups. Prairie academics are not organized along regional lines although *Prairie Forum,* The Canadian Plains Research Centre at the University of Regina, and the annual Western Canadian Studies Conference at the University of Calgary all represent a step in that direction. Predominantly western organizations like the petroleum and cattlemen's associations do not represent the prairie region in the way in which farm organizations could do in the past. Even the wheat pools today speak for too narrowly-defined an economic interest and draw their memberships from too small a population base to serve as effective regional voices.

In bringing this discussion to a close I would like to return briefly to the thesis of this book—that the regional character of the Prairie provinces is in decline. What, however, if the more appropriate term is not decline but eclipse? What if the regional impulse is only lying dormant? Might not the next decade bring with it a vigorous Western Canada

Party, an attempt at secession, a new agrarian revolt? On balance, the prospects for a rejuvenation of regionalism or its accompanying political radicalism are not promising. The demographic trends that have undercut the regional distinctiveness of the Prairies are not susceptible to sudden swings or reversals. Nor is the pattern of economic development on the Prairies likely to change in any fundamental fashion. Economic diversification both within and among the three provinces will continue and will rule out the future emergence of a broadly based economic interest similar to the agrarian movement that spurred regional politics and political radicalism in the past. Nor is there any move towards political unification of the Prairie provinces, or any indications that regional identifications are supplanting provincial ones among political elites or the mass public. The eclipse analogy is misleading as it fails to appreciate the generally uni-directional nature of social and political change on the Prairies. The trend away from regionalism in whatever guise has been well established for decades and any major departure from the established route is not to be anticipated.

Yet there is one source of uncertainty with implications for prairie regionalism that are more difficult to forecast. Canada appears to be entering a process of fundamental constitutional change. Since the November 1976 election of the Parti Quebeçois a welter of proposed changes in the Canadian constitution have emerged from Quebec, from national unity groups across the country, from provincial governments and, most recently, from the federal government in the form of the Constitutional Amendment Bill introduced in the spring of 1978. If the constitutional structure of the Canadian state is altered in any major way there will undoubtedly be implications for political regionalism in the Canadian west. While at this time it would be foolish to predict the path of constitutional change, the alternatives that are open and their likely implications for political regionalism can be roughly sketched in.

PRAIRIE REGIONALISM AND CONSTITUTIONAL CHANGE

The future of regional politics will not depend solely upon developments within western Canada, developments upon which this book has focused. When we recall that the regional character of prairie politics was shaped in the past by the acrimonious interaction of western Canadian economic interests with the national political system, the importance of the latter to regional politics is clear. Moreover as the Prairie provinces constitute an important component of the national political system changes in the whole will reverberate through the constituent parts. And changes are indeed in the wind as Canadian politicians seek to rebuild the confederation agreement of 1867. The process of constitutional change upon which Canadians are now embarked provides an opportunity for western Canadians to renegotiate their position in confederation. It also opens up the prospect of constitutional change that may have a considerable impact on the nature of regional political activity.

While the specific direction of constitutional change cannot be forecast a number of hypothetical paths can be discarded. A revised federal constitution will not result in a diminution of provincial powers; this would be unacceptable either inside or outside Quebec. Nor will we see the creation of a new regional level of government between the existing national and provincial governments. Thus what is at stake is the distribution of powers among the existing political units and the representation of provincial and regional interests within the institutions and agencies of the national government. This suggests that the process of constitutional change is likely to follow one or both of two paths; one leading towards greater provincial and/or regional input into national policy making and administration, and the second towards a greater devolution of power to the provincial governments. While the two paths can be separated for the purposes of discussion they are not mutually exclusive alternatives. In all probability any constitutional settlement will be a hybrid of the two, a solution that hopefully will be well-tuned to the realities of the Canadian political environment no matter how ugly it may be in theory.

It has been a long-standing grievance of western Canadians that their interests are not given appropriate weight in the national government. Western Canadians have witnessed their representatives standing helpless before the legislative majorities of the major parties, majorities dominated by representatives from Ontario and Quebec. Given, then, the historical legacy of an insensitive national government one would imagine that constitutional proposals designed to strengthen regional input into the national government would be well received in the West. Difficulties arise, however, when the means of increased regional input are considered. The basic cause of western Canadian weakness comes from the democratic character of the national government, democratic in the sense that Canadians residing across the country are given roughly equal weight in national elections. The problem is that not many Canadians live in the Prairie provinces and thus in any electoral system based on the principle of one man/one vote the West will be outgunned. Ontario will receive greater attention from the national government because twice as many Canadians live in Ontario as live in the three Prairie provinces combined. Therefore if western Canadian interests are to be more adequately protected in the national government western Canadian representatives must be given more power than they would be entitled to by any calculation based on the premise of one man/one vote. Equality of representation will not protect western Canadian interests if those interests again come into conflict with those of central Canadians.

Western Canadians are thus placed in a rather difficult theoretical position. They must argue that representation based on the premise of one man/one vote is unfair because it is innately prejudicial to western Canadian interests. The catch is in coming up with some alternative principle of representation. One cannot simply say that western Canadians should have two votes, or three votes, for every one in central Canada; such a stance would be untenable theoretically and certainly could not be sold to the central Canadian electorate. Potentially the most viable approach is to argue that territorial units should receive equal representation as they do in the American Senate. While territorial representation would not be the principle to be followed in the House of Commons it could be adopted in other national government institutions such as the Canadian Senate, provided that the latter possessed the power to check the House of Commons when regional interests were at stake.

There are several interesting ramifications to the notion of territorial representation. The first, and one that cannot be pursued in detail here, is that the principle itself is suspect; it is not clear why within a democratic society territory rather than people should be the basis of representation. The second is that equal territorial representation in Canada could not be based on provincial units. The disparities in size, population and political power among the Canadian provinces are too great to make equal provincial representation possible. To state the obvious, residents of Ontario would not tolerate a significant national institution in which Ontario had the same representation as Prince Edward Island, Saskatchewan or Alberta. Therefore territorial representation would have to be based on regional rather than provincial equality. The central Canadian electorate might well accept a Canadian upper house in which the regions would be equally represented, much as they are at this moment in the existing Senate. Admittedly Ontario would still contain more people than would any other region but the discrepancy between the population of Ontario and that of the Prairies or the Atlantic provinces combined would be far less than that between Ontario and individual provinces. If ultimate legislative power resided in the House of Commons the interests of the heavily-populated regions would be twice-protected.

The delineation of senatorial regions would for the most part cause little controversy. The Atlantic provinces would constitute one region for although Newfoundlanders would argue against lumping Newfoundland in with the other three Atlantic provinces, neither Newfoundland nor any Atlantic province could stand alone as a separate region. Ontario and Quebec would each be regions unto themselves. The only potential disagreement would come from the four western provinces which at present constitute a single senatorial region. A single western Canadian region would have a population greater than that of Quebec and close to that of Ontario. It would thus help rationalize the principle of equal regional representation. Yet it is very unlikely that British Columbia politicians would consent to a single western Canadian region. Both former Premier W. A. C. Bennett and the present Premier Bill Bennett have insisted that Canada is composed of five regions and that British Columbia constitutes a region unto itself. It is therefore unlikely that a single western Canadian region could be formed and hence the three Prairie provinces would be set off as one of five regions. The consequence of this path of constitutional development would be to tie the Prairie provinces together in a single and distinct regional unit. The long-term significance of this constitutional union would depend upon the political importance of the reformed Upper House, the degree to which regional demands were vocalized in this as opposed to alternative political arenas, whether Upper House members were elected or appointed, and, if appointed, by whom. It would also be of considerable importance whether Upper House members came from and thus represented the region at large or provincial constituencies.

A related constitutional matter is the representation of regional interests in the administrative boards and agencies of the national government. As Black and Cairns point out, "appointments to the Supreme Court, the Board of Broadcast Governors [now the Canadian Radio-Television and Telecommunications Commission], the Board of Transport Commissioners, and numerous other central government institutions reflect to a greater or lesser extent the division of Canada into a number of regional societies and interests whose explicit recognition is essential to the legitimization of central government activities."[39] There is a problem, however, in deciding upon the appropriate form of regional representation. In the ongoing discussions on constitutional change some provincial governments have been arguing that they themselves should appoint representatives to national boards and agencies. Premier Lougheed, for example, suggests that 40% of the appointments to the Canadian Wheat Board, the National Energy Board and the Canadian Transportation Commission should come from the provincial governments. Yet provincially-appointed representatives raise a number of problems; the awkwardness of having at least 10 provincial representatives on most boards or agencies, the related problem as to whether all provincial representatives should carry the same decision-making clout, and whether such representatives are responsible to the provincial governments that appointed them or to some broader conception of the regional interest. It would seem that regional rather than provincial representation within the federal bureaucracy would be less cumbersome but this approach is unlikely to win acceptance from the provincial governments. This introduces in turn the second path of constitutional change, that of a substantial devolution of powers from the national to the provincial governments.

Steps to provide greater regional representation in the national government go only part way in protecting provincial rights and powers from federal government intrusions. In fact some of the proposals for constitutional change have been interpreted as a threat to provincial governments. Lou Hyndman, Alberta's Minister for Inter-governmental Affairs, described the 1978 constitution proposals of the national government as an attempt to weaken provincial governments by undermining their status as defenders of provincial interests.[40] To many provincial politicians the only sure way of protecting the constitutional powers of the provinces and thereby protecting provincial interests is through a further devolution of powers to the provincial governments. To outsiders what appears to be taking place is a classic power struggle between provincial politicians and bureaucrats on one side and their national counterparts on the other. Whether the ultimate goal is the protection of provincial interests or the simple maximization of political and bureaucratic power is difficult to determine.

The case for devolution has been most forcefully put forward by the province of Alberta. Speaking before the 1977 annual convention of the Alberta Progressive Conservative party, Premier Lougheed laid out the basic philosophy of his government:

> It's well accepted over the past years that Alberta has been the new leader in Canada for provincial rights. We intend to continue to be. First, because we believe it's necessary to reach our goals here. Secondly, because we believe it will strengthen Canada economically in strengthening the West. And thirdly, because we sense that it is in tune with the desires of many citizens of Quebec who wish to see their future resolved more within their own province. Hence, we believe, as leading spokesmen for strong provinces, that our position is good for Alberta, good for Canada, and that it could well be a very constructive and positive force to sustain unity in this country.[41]

The theme that a stronger Alberta will benefit both the West and Canada is a recurrent one with the Lougheed Conservatives, one that not only shows a very decentralized philosophical stance towards the federal system but which blunts what might be seen as the raw edge of provincial ambition. In a manner reminiscent of Henry Ford Canadians outside Alberta are being told that what is good for Alberta is good for them.

Devolution alone cannot provide the solutions to many long-standing western Canadian grievances. It does not address the problems of discriminatory national policies, including those related to tariffs and transportation. Presuming that even a weakened national government will retain control of tariffs and have a major say in inter-provincial transportation, only strengthened regional input into the national government can provide any hope of remedy. Thus the two paths of constitutional change may both have to be travelled at once.

In concluding this brief discussion of devolution it should be noted again that the socio-economic changes that have undermined regionalism in western Canada have not undermined the strength of western provincial governments. Rather provincial governments have grown in strength over time and have emerged as the principal spokesmen for regional interests. To the extent that devolution occurs provincial governments in the West will be strengthened still more, and if this occurs the incentives for regional political action will be reduced. As power passes to the provinces the need to organize against the national government decreases. In this sense devolution may further fragment the prairie region by removing the incentive for inter-provincial political orchestration. The provincial governments, in retreating behind the heightened walls of provincial autonomy, will further carve up a region with a rich political past but an uncertain political future.

NOTES

1. "News Magazine," CBC Television, March 27, 1977.

2. Anthony W. Rasporich, *Western Canada Past and Present,* Calgary, McClelland and Stewart West, 1975, p. 13.

3. W. L. Morton, "The Bias of Prairie Politics," in Donald Swainson, ed., *Historical Essays on the Prairie Provinces,* Toronto, McClelland & Stewart, 1970, p. 290.

4. *Ibid.,* p. 290.

5. Donald E. Willmott, "The Formal Organizations of Saskatchewan Farmers, 1900-65," in Rasporich, *Western Canada,* p. 40.

6. Mildred A. Schwartz, *Politics and Territory: The Sociology of Regional Persistence in Canada,* Montreal, McGill-Queen's University Press, 1974, p. xi.

7. Richard Rose and Derek W. Urwin, *Regional Differentiation and Political Unity in Western Nations,* London, Sage Publications, 1975, p. 11.

8. David V. J. Bell, "Regionalism in the Canadian Economy," in Paul W. Fox, ed., *Politics: Canada,* 4th edition, Toronto, McGraw-Hill Ryerson, 1977, p. 80.

9. Richard Simeon, "Regionalism and Canadian Political Institutions," in J. Peter Meekison, ed., *Canadian Federalism: Myth or Reality,* Third Edition, Toronto, Methuen, 1977, p. 303.

10. Alan C. Cairns, "The Governments and Societies of Canadian Federalism," *Canadian Journal of Political Science,* X:4 (December 1977), p. 699.

11. *Ibid.,* p. 723.

12. For evidence on this account see J. E. Hodgetts and O. P. Dwivedi, *Provincial Governments as Employers,* Montreal, McGill-Queen's University Press, 1974.

13. Edwin R. Black and Alan C. Cairns, "A Different Perspective on Canadian Federalism" *Canadian Public Administration,* IX:1 (March 1966), p. 35.

14. See Norman Ward, "One Prairie Province: Historical and Political Perspectives," in David K. Elton, ed., *One Prairie Province?,* Lethbridge Herald, 1970, pp. 183-4, and C. Cecil Lingard, *Territorial Government in Canada: The Autonomy Question in the Old North-West Territories,* Toronto, University of Toronto Press, 1946, pp. 199-206.

15. Black and Cairns, "A Different Perspective," p. 40.

16. James A. Richardson, "Federalism—and the Western Canadians," in Elton, *One Prairie Province?,* p. 24.

17. F. C. Engelmann and M. A. Schwartz, *Canadian Political Parties: Origin, Character, Impact,* Scarborough, Prentice-Hall, 1975, p. 67.

18. *Calgary Herald,* May 30, 1978, p. A3.

19. J. E. Hodgetts, "Regional Interests and Policy in a Federal Structure," *Canadian Journal of Economics and Political Science,* XXXII:1 (February 1966), p. 9.

20. Harry E. Strom, "The Feasibility of One Prairie Province," in Elton, *One Prairie Province?,* p. 34.

21. Richard Simeon, *Federal-Provincial Diplomacy: The Making of Recent Policy in Canada,* Toronto, University of Toronto Press, 1972, p. 29.

22. David E. Smith, *Prairie Liberalism: The Liberal Party in Saskatchewan, 1905-1971,* Toronto, University of Toronto Press, 1975, p. 330.

23. *Ibid.,* pp. 325-6.

24. M. Westmacott and P. Dore, "Intergovernmental Co-operation in Western Canada: The Western Economic Opportunities Conference," in Meekison, *Canadian Federalism,* p. 343.

25. *Ibid.,* p. 346.

26. *Ibid.,* p. 347.

27. For an analysis see *Follow-up on the Western Economic Opportunities Conference,* Canada West Foundation, May 1974.

28. Allan Blakeney, "Western Provincial Co-operation," in Meekison, *Canadian Federalism,* p. 239.

29. *Ibid.,* p. 239.

30. *Ibid.,* p. 242.

31. Ira Sharkansky, *Regionalism in American Politics,* Indianapolis, Bobbs-Merrill, 1970, pp. 12-13.

32. Blakeney, "Western Provincial Co-operation," p. 242.

33. Preface to *Alternatives: Towards the Development of an Effective Federal System for Canada,* a revision of a discussion paper prepared for the Canada West Foundation by David Elton, F. C. Engelmann and Peter McCormick, 1978.

34. Stanley C. Roberts, *A Summary Report on the Proceedings of "Alternatives Canada," A Canada West Conference on Confederation,* The Canada West Foundation, May 1978, p. 6.

35. *Calgary Herald,* March 28, 1978, pp. A1-A2.

36. See Elton, *One Prairie Province?*

37. *Schwartz, Politics and Territory,* p. 325.

38. Lingard, *Territorial Government in Canada,* p. 203.

39. Black and Cairns, "A Different Perspective," p. 38.

40. *Calgary Herald,* June 17, 1978, p. A3.

41. *Calgary Herald,* April 12, 1977, p. 7.

POSTSCRIPT ON THE 1980 ELECTION

The 1980 winter election was a paradoxical one on the Prairies. On the one hand, little changed. Across the region the Conservative share of the popular vote dropped only slightly, from 53% in 1979 to just under 51% in 1980 (unofficial figures). The Liberal share of the popular vote edged upwards from 22.4% to 24.4% while the NDP regional vote increased only fractionally from 23.0% in May 1979. The Liberal increase yielded no new seats—Alberta and Saskatchewan remained barren of Liberal MPs—and the Conservative stranglehold in Alberta was untouched; the Conservatives rolled up 65% of the popular vote and all 21 seats. On the other hand, significant change did occur. The regional Conservative hegemony was eroded. The 1979 Conservative lead of six seats over the NDP in Saskatchewan was reduced to a seven-seven split, and in Manitoba the Conservatives fell from 7 seats to 5 while the NDP increased its representation from 5 seats in 1979 to 7 in 1980. Yet the most dramatic change occurred outside the prairie region. In a recurrent pattern, the election was over before the polls closed in the four western provinces. The Liberal party ran up gains in Ontario (20 seats), Quebec (6 seats) and the Atlantic provinces (7 seats); after less than a year in office the Joe Clark Conservative government was turfed out of office and replaced by a majority Liberal government virtually devoid of western Canadian representation.

In the West the election outcome was widely seen as an eastern Canadian repudiation of a western-based national government. Although Joe Clark lacked the regional statute and support of John Diefenbaker, his defeat was seen by many as yet another prairie leader being pilloried on the economic and political self-interest of central Canada. The election was greeted by cries of alarm over the future of confederation, and by more reasoned concern over the representation of western Canadian interests within the new national government. Champions of western separatism, prowling the fringes and margins of prairie politics, were given a new media platform by the election results and roasted temporarily in their glow. In some cases separatist or quasi-separatist sentiment spread beyond open-line programs and the born-again separatist organizations to endorsation by the press. Albertans were particularly quick to see the election in its most threatening light; an editorial by the publisher of the *Alberta Report* (February 29, 1980) provides a vitriolic example:

> The people of central Canada have now served notice upon the West that if it does not sell what's left of its most valuable asset at something close to half

price, then they will elect a government that is committed to move in and seize it. That is the meaning to Albertans of last week's general election . . . do we want to be Canadians at any price? My answer is no. The day the Central Canada Party, what was once called the Liberal Party, gains passage of a bill to seize the West's oil resources is the day that I cease to consider myself Canadian.

Writing only days after the election, it is difficult to predict with any certainty the election's impact on the evolution of prairie politics. Nonetheless, the election results can be linked in a very tentative manner to the themes and arguments of this book. The first point to note is that the general process of socio-economic change—change in the direction of reduced regional distinctiveness and reduced regional homogeneity—will not be touched by the election results. The momentum of post-war socio-economic change will not be significantly slowed or deflected by the electoral events of February. The second point has been touched on above; the Conservative electoral hegemony on the Prairies—the most distinctive regional characteristic of the last two decades—was eroded somewhat by a New Democratic surge in seats, although not in the popular vote. Thus in the years ahead the Conservative party, as a regional spokesman for western Canada, will experience intensified competition from the NDP. The renewed western strength of the NDP, incidently, suggests that the nationalization of the NDP described in Chapter Three has been checked; with 27 of its 32 MPs coming from the West the NDP has more of a regional cast than it has experienced since the party's founding.

The third point is that the election will further strengthen and legitimate the prairie provincial governments as regional spokesmen. Thus the provincial dismemberment of the prairie region described in Chapter Six should continue unabated. There is a caveat here, however. The 1980 election results did spur a great deal of interest in electoral reform. In particular, proposals have been made to introduce a limited form of proportional representation in order to ensure that all regions will enjoy at least minimal representation in future governments. If these proposals are acted upon, then the representation of regional interests *within* the national government could be revitalized. In this case the role of provincial governments in representing regional and provincial interests within the national political system could be significantly reduced.

In the short run, the 1980 election will unquestionably strengthen western alienation. At this time, however, the proponents of western separatism are not to be taken seriously. While the weakness of western representation in the national government is a matter for serious concern, it does not pose an immediate threat to national unity. Provincial governments in the West, by far the most critical actors in any proposed restructuring of confederation, are not unhappy with the election outcome; their role within the Canadian federal system has been enhanced by the shortage of western Liberals. The Conservative party, the only national party with MPs from every province and territory in Canada, will moderate its articulation of western discontent as it moves once again to rebuild in Ontario and the East. In the long run, the strength of western alienation will depend more on what the national government does than upon its regional balance or composition. Moreover, the standards used by westerners to rate the performance of the government may have more to do with *national* issues—inflation, government spending, energy supply, etc.—than regional ones. That the national government faces a serious challenge in western Canada is not to be disputed, but it is a challenge with the capability of leaders with vision, courage, or even simply a strong partisan sense of political survival.

Index

—